Concord
ED

POWER BASICS ®

Biology

Robert Taggart

D0735371

WALCH PUBLISHING

POWER BASICS ®

Senior Author	Robert Taggart
Editorial Director	Susan Blair
Project Editor	Holly Moirs
Director of Marketing	Jeff Taplin
Senior Production Editor	Maggie Jones
Interior Design	Mark Sayer
Cover Design	Roman Laszok
Typesetting	Sheila Russell
	Mark Sayer
	Ian Weidner
Editorial Staff	Elizabeth Lynch
	Richard Lynch
	Kate O'Halloran
	Mary Rich
	Erica Varney

3   4   5   6   7   8   9   10

ISBN 0-8251-5616-5

Copyright © 1998, 2001, 2005

J. Weston Walch, Publisher

P. O. Box 658 • Portland, Maine 04104-0658

walch.com

Printed in the United States of America

WALCH PUBLISHING

Table of Contents

Table of Contents, *continued*

To the Student

Welcome to *Power Basics® Biology.* Biology is the study of living things. In this book, you will learn about the features that all living things share and the features that make them unique.

In **Unit 1: Building Blocks of Living Things,** you will learn what it means to be alive. You will learn about the structure of all living things and how they grow, develop, and change over time. You will also learn how scientists organize living things.

In **Unit 2: Simple Organisms,** you will learn about Earth's simplest life-forms. They include bacteria, protists, and fungi.

In **Unit 3: The Plant Kingdom,** you will learn how plant life first developed and about the structure of most plants. You will learn how plants make other life on Earth possible by adding oxygen to the atmosphere. You will also learn about the diversity of plant life and the different ways that plants reproduce.

In **Unit 4: The Animal Kingdom,** you will learn about the many different types of animals on Earth, from worms and insects to fish, frogs, birds, and mammals.

In **Unit 5: The Human Body,** you will learn how the human body works. You will learn about the structure of the body and the many complex processes that go into keeping it strong and healthy.

In **Unit 6: Ecology,** you will learn how all living things on Earth interact with one another. You will learn about the energy cycle, in which some organisms produce energy and others consume it. You will learn about different regions on Earth and the life-forms that live in them.

Power Basics Biology has many special features that make learning easier. "Tips" give you hints on ways to master the ideas and facts in the text. "In Real Life" sections show you how the skills you are learning are used in the world outside the classroom. "Think About It" questions ask you to look at biology in new ways. The "Words to

To the Student, *continued*

Know" section at the start of most lessons includes important new terms introduced in the lesson. The first time each word is used, it is defined for you. In the first use, the term appears in **bold type.** All the terms in the "Words to Know" section are also defined in the glossary at the end of the book. If you cannot remember what a term means, you can look it up in the glossary. Finally, the appendixes at the back of the book include a summary of important information introduced in the book.

As you move through *Power Basics Biology*, you will learn about the study of living things. We hope that you enjoy this material as you learn.

UNIT 1

Building Blocks of Living Things

LESSON 1: Characteristics of Living Things

 GOAL: To learn about the basic organic molecules that form the basis of life

WORDS TO KNOW

amino acids	molecules
atoms	offspring
carbohydrates	organic molecules
element	organism
energy	reproduction
enzymes	solvent
glucose	spontaneous generation
lipids	

It's Alive!

Most people have little trouble figuring out whether something is alive or not. A living thing is an **organism.** Living things move and grow. They respond to the environment.

But what about a seed that lies in the soil for hundreds of years? It does not move. There are no chemical reactions taking place inside it. In fact, it looks dead. But, under the correct conditions, the seed will sprout and grow into a vibrant plant.

As you can see, defining what constitutes life is not that simple. Life is not the result of some magic force. Nor is life just a collection of chemicals responding to the laws of physics. You cannot just throw the correct chemicals together and expect life to begin. Scientists have, however, come up with a list of characteristics that all organisms share. They include acquiring nutrition, movement, respiration, excretion of wastes, transport of nutrients and water through the body, responding to the environment, growth, and reproduction.

Complexity: Living things contain chemicals of amazing complexity. These chemicals in turn are intricately arranged into complex structures that interact with one another. Nothing in the nonliving world is as complex as the structures that make up living organisms.

Energy: Energy is the ability to do work and cause change. All organisms use energy to grow, carry out life processes, and maintain themselves. Without energy, an organism will break down. Organisms differ in how they get energy. Plants, algae, and some bacteria get their energy directly from the sun. Animals, fungi, some protists, and some bacteria get their energy from other organisms.

Growth and Development: All living things grow bigger and become more complex. Different organisms grow at different rates and reach different sizes. But all organisms, from a tiny ant to a huge redwood, grow and develop.

Reproduction: All living things produce **offspring,** or new organisms. Single-celled organisms, such as bacteria, form new cells by dividing. Fungi produce spores. Flowering plants produce seeds. Mammals give birth. These are all forms of **reproduction,** or producing offspring.

Responsiveness: All organisms respond to the environment in which they live. The response may be short-term. As the sun moves across the sky each day, some plants turn to catch the light. When it is warm, humans sweat to cool themselves. The response may be long-term. A thick layer of fat has developed in seals to help them survive in cold water. The ability to run quickly has developed in cheetahs. This ability helps them hunt other animals.

We have discussed some of the characteristics that living things share, but how did life begin in the first place? Think about the following observations. Maggots appear on a piece of rotting meat. Moths flutter from the sweaters in your closet. Mold sprouts from an old loaf of bread. How do you explain these events? For many years, scientists held the theory of **spontaneous generation.** This theory said that, through a combination of the correct physical conditions and a kind of mystical force, life could suddenly appear from nonliving matter.

A *theory* is an idea, not a fact. Scientists develop theories to explain things that they observe. Then they set up experiments to see if their theory makes sense. If many careful experiments all support a theory, it is usually accepted as true. Many of the scientific ideas held today started out as one person's theory.

It was difficult to prove that spontaneous generation did not exist. It required well-designed experiments. The first serious challenge to the theory came from a fifteenth-century Italian scientist named Francesco Redi. Redi showed that maggots do not miraculously appear on rotting meat. For his experiment, Redi put pieces of meat in three sets of flasks. He left the first set of flasks uncovered, covered the second set with screen mesh, and tightly sealed the third set. Flies laid their eggs directly on the meat in the first set of uncovered flasks. The eggs hatched, and maggots emerged to feed on the meat. Flies could not reach the meat in the second set of flasks. They laid their eggs on the screen, and the maggots hatched there. Since the third set of flasks were tightly sealed, the flies could not lay eggs at all, so no maggots developed.

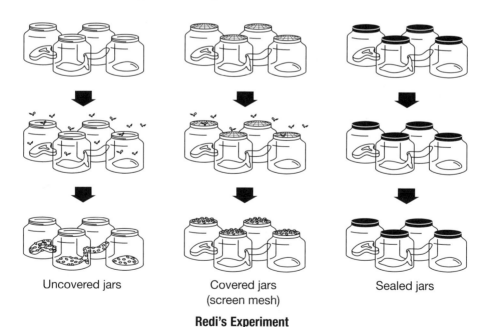

| Uncovered jars | Covered jars (screen mesh) | Sealed jars |

Redi's Experiment

Why did Redi include open flasks in his experiment? Write your answer on a separate sheet of paper.

Redi's results could not be disproved. Still, they did not put an end to the belief in spontaneous generation. Scientists had just started to use microscopes to study tiny single-celled organisms such as bacteria. Many scientists argued that these organisms appeared through spontaneous generation. Two centuries later, after a couple of tries, a French scientist named Louis Pasteur finally put the idea of spontaneous generation to rest.

Pasteur performed two sets of experiments. In his first experiment, Pasteur boiled broth inside sterilized flasks, killing any bacteria inside. Then he sealed half of the flasks and left the other half open. Bacteria reappeared in the open flasks within a couple of days. The closed flasks remained bacteria-free for up to 18 months. Pasteur concluded that dust particles floating in the air were the source of the bacteria. Pasteur's conclusions were still not enough to convince some critics that spontaneous generation did not exist. Some people argued that by sealing the flasks, Pasteur was shutting out some life-giving essence.

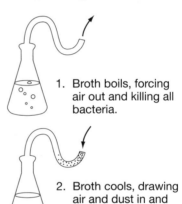

1. Broth boils, forcing air out and killing all bacteria.

2. Broth cools, drawing air and dust in and trapping dust in the S-shaped neck.

For his second experiment, Pasteur designed a special flask with an S-shaped neck. Again, broth was boiled and sterilized inside the flask. Air could still pass through the neck, but dust loaded with bacteria was trapped in the curve of the S and did not reach the broth. If Pasteur tipped the flask so the broth touched the dust in the neck, bacteria quickly appeared in the broth.

3. With the flask tipped, the dust mixes with the broth.

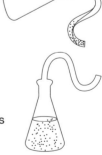

4. Bacteria appears in the broth.

Pasteur's Experiment

This experiment finally silenced Pasteur's critics and disproved the theory of spontaneous generation.

Today, scientists agree that all life comes from other life. However, that still leaves the difficult puzzle of how life started in the first place. Scientists think that life began between 3.5 and 4 billion years ago. Earth was a lot different then. There was no oxygen in the air. Ultraviolet radiation—the radiation that gives you a sunburn—scorched Earth. (Today, a protective layer of ozone prevents much of the ultraviolet radiation from reaching Earth.) The chemicals needed for life, however, were present. Energy from the sun and heat from Earth caused these chemicals to react and combine. Other complex chemicals may have arrived on meteors or comets that bombarded Earth. These complex chemicals eventually became the building blocks of simple cells. In the next sections, you will look closely at these chemicals that remain the building blocks of life.

■ PRACTICE 1: It's Alive!

Decide if each statement that follows is true (**T**) or false (**F**). Write the correct letter on each line.

_____ **1.** All organisms need energy to survive.

_____ **2.** No life can start because of spontaneous generation.

_____ **3.** The results from Pasteur's experiments with broth did not support the results of Redi's experiments with meat.

_____ **4.** In Pasteur's broth experiment, bacteria grew in the open flasks with straight necks but did not grow in the flasks with S-shaped necks.

Basic Chemistry

Before you begin to learn about the chemical building blocks of life, you must learn about some basic chemistry.

Atoms

Everything in the universe—from the stars in the sky to the air you breathe, to the water you drink, to the paper in this book—is made of tiny particles called **atoms.** Atoms are so small that they cannot be seen even with the most advanced microscopes. If you lined up 3 million atoms side by side, they would only reach across the period at the end of this sentence.

Chemists have identified over 100 different types of atoms. Each type of atom is called an **element.** The elements that are most common in living things are oxygen, carbon, hydrogen, nitrogen, phosphorus, and sulfur.

Scientists use one- or two-letter abbreviations to symbolize each element. The first (or only) letter is always capitalized. The second letter (if there is one) is always lowercase. Here are the abbreviations for some of the more common elements.

Element	Symbol
Hydrogen	H
Carbon	C
Nitrogen	N
Oxygen	O
Sodium	Na
Phosphorus	P

Element	Symbol
Sulfur	S
Chlorine	Cl
Potassium	K
Calcium	Ca
Iron	Fe

Molecules

Most of the substances you see are not made of only one type of atom. Instead, atoms bind together to form larger particles called **molecules.** Some molecules have only a few atoms. The oxygen molecules that you breathe, for example, are each made out of two oxygen atoms. Water molecules are made from one oxygen atom and two hydrogen atoms. However, some of the chemicals you will study in this lesson contain many thousands of atoms.

Scientists use abbreviations and numbers to symbolize molecules. For example, water is written as H_2O. The small 2 written below the line after the H means that water has two hydrogen atoms. The fact that there is no number after the O means that water has only one oxygen atom. **Glucose,** a sugar that is the major source of energy in plants and animals, is written as $C_6H_{12}O_6$. That means that glucose has six carbon atoms, twelve hydrogen atoms, and six oxygen atoms. If scientists are dealing with more than one of the same kind of molecule, they write the number of molecules before the symbol of the molecule. For example, a quantity of six oxygen molecules (O_2) is written as 6 O_2.

Water

Water is one of the most important molecules in living things. Your body is 70 percent water. Water helps prevent your body from overheating. It helps transport substances through your body. It is one substance in which essential chemical reactions take place.

To understand why water is such a special molecule, look at its structure. As you can see in the diagram below, water is made up of two hydrogen atoms attached to one oxygen atom. The atoms in a water molecule do not form a straight line. Instead, they form a triangle.

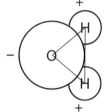

Water Molecule

Water molecules act like tiny magnets. The hydrogen atoms of one water molecule form weak bonds with the oxygen atoms of other molecules. These bonds cause water molecules to stick to one another. This explains why water remains a liquid at room temperature and why it beads up into drops. Water serves as a **solvent** (a dissolver) for many other molecules. Salt and sugars dissolve easily in water. Other molecules, such as oil, do not dissolve in water.

■ PRACTICE 2: Basic Chemistry

Decide if each statement that follows is true (**T**) or false (**F**). Write the correct letter on each line.

_____ **1.** Carbon is one of the most common elements in living things.

_____ **2.** The molecule H_2O has one hydrogen atom and two oxygen atoms.

_____ **3.** Atoms are made up of molecules.

_____ **4.** Scientists use abbreviations to symbolize elements.

_____ **5.** Oil dissolves in water.

The Molecules of Life

Living things are made up of many types of chemicals. However, there are four groups of molecules that are unique to living things and make life possible. These molecules are very large. Carbon atoms form the backbone of all four. These molecules are referred to as **organic molecules.** This section discusses three of the four groups of molecules—carbohydrates, lipids, and proteins. We will discuss the fourth group of molecules, nucleic acids—the blueprints of life—in Lesson 3.

Carbohydrates

Carbohydrates include sugars, starches, and cellulose. Organisms use carbohydrates to store energy. Cells break down glucose (a type of sugar) to get energy. Complex carbohydrates are the major structural component of plants.

Lipids

Lipids are the molecules that make up fats and oils. They serve as important energy reserves in plants and animals. Layers of fat insulate animals from the cold. Lipids are also major components of nerve cells, hormones, and cell membranes. Lipids do not dissolve in water.

Proteins

Proteins are fascinating, complex molecules that serve a huge number of functions in your body. Proteins hold your skin together and help give your bones their strength. Proteins in your red blood cells bind to oxygen so your blood can transport oxygen throughout your body. Proteins help you fight diseases. Proteins can be used as a source of energy. Most importantly, proteins control the chemical reactions in your body.

Marcus was concerned about maintaining a healthy diet but found much of the available information confusing. He was especially confused by the different types of fat. He had heard people talk about "good" fat and "bad" fat. He decided he had better ask his doctor for more information. Marcus learned that "good" fats include polyunsaturated fats. They are liquid at room temperature and are found in fish and vegetables. Saturated fats ("bad" fats), on the other hand, may increase the risk of heart disease. They are solid at room temperature and are found in meats and dairy products.

Proteins are composed of long strings of units called **amino acids.** There are 20 types of amino acids. Each amino acid has a central carbon atom. There are three groups of atoms bound to this carbon.

Your body has many different proteins, each with a specific function. Each protein contains a specific sequence of amino acids, linked together in a chain. If even one of thousands of amino acids in the chain is out of order, the entire structure of the protein may change. As a result, the protein may not be able to perform the function it was designed to perform. Here is why.

The chains of amino acids are not straight. Instead, each chain folds in on itself many times so that it resembles a wadded up piece of string. These folds, however, are not random. Amino acids in the chain form weak bonds with amino acids farther down the chain and with amino acids in other chains. The sequence of amino acids determines how the chain folds and how it binds to other chains. If the sequence of amino acids changes, the chain may not fold in the same way, and the shape of the protein will change.

TIP

Think of amino acids as letters and proteins as words. If you change the order of the letters, you change the meaning of the words.

There are other ways to change the shape, and therefore the function, of proteins. Heat and chemicals, such as acids, can disrupt the weak bonds between the amino acids. As a result, the protein may partially unravel. Once it unravels, it can never regain its original shape. You can see this process when you fry an egg. The egg white, which is made of protein, turns from a clear liquid to a white solid. No matter how much you cool the egg, the egg white will never go back to its original form.

Enzymes

Enzymes are some of the most important proteins in all living things. They are involved in almost every chemical reaction in your body, from breaking down food to repairing tissue to manufacturing chemicals. Without enzymes, all chemical activity in your body would stop.

All chemical reactions need energy to get going. A teaspoon of sugar will eventually break down into carbon dioxide and water, but it would take millions of years at room temperature. Your cells cannot wait that long to break down sugars for energy. Nor can cells provide enough energy to break down the sugars. Instead, they use enzymes. **Enzymes** are proteins that speed up reactions by reducing the amount of energy needed for these reactions to take place.

Enzymes can bind only to specific molecules. Because of this, each enzyme triggers only one type of reaction. Scientists compare the way molecules bind to enzymes with the way keys and locks work. Just as only one key can fit into one lock, only one type of molecule can bind to one type of enzyme.

■ PRACTICE 3: The Molecules of Life

Decide if each statement that follows is true (**T**) or false (**F**). Write the correct letter on each line.

_____ **1.** Carbohydrates are made up of proteins.

_____ **2.** Lipids dissolve easily in water.

_____ **3.** The order of amino acids determines the structure of a protein.

_____ **4.** Enzymes change the rate at which reactions take place.

LESSON 2: Cells

GOAL: To learn about the structure of cells and the biological processes that go on inside cells

WORDS TO KNOW

active transport	mitochondria
ATP (adenosine triphosphate)	nuclear envelope
cell wall	nucleoli (singular *nucleolus*)
cells	nucleus
cellulose	organelles
chlorophyll	osmosis
chloroplasts	passive transport
cytoplasm	permeable
dark phase	phosphate
diffusion	photosynthesis
endoplasmic reticulum (ER)	respiration
Golgi complex	ribosomes
impermeable	semipermeable
light phase	transport
lysosomes	vacuoles
membrane	

What Is a Cell?

Just as atoms are the basic units of all matter, cells are the basic units of all living things. Atoms are composed of protons, neutrons, and electrons. Cells are composed of molecules such as carbohydrates, lipids, and proteins.

All living things are made up of cells. Some organisms, such as bacteria and certain types of algae, are composed of just a single cell. Humans are made up of trillions of cells working together. Like all living things, individual cells require energy to grow, reproduce, and adapt to their environments.

Cell Membranes

In 1665, a scientist named Robert Hooke looked through a primitive microscope at a sliver of cork. He saw a series of tiny boxlike structures aligned side by side. He called them cells because they reminded him of small rooms, such as prison cells. In some ways, a living cell is similar to a room or a prison cell. Rooms have walls that form boundaries between the inside and the outside. Cells also have a boundary that separates the inside and the outside. This boundary is called a **membrane.** Cell membranes are thin and flexible, not rigid like the walls of a room. But they carry out a critical function. Cell membranes control which molecules enter and leave the cell.

Diffusion

Before discussing cell membranes, it is important to understand a process called diffusion. **Diffusion** is the movement of molecules from an area of higher concentration to an area of lower concentration. You can see diffusion in action by putting a drop of food coloring in a glass of water. The food coloring spreads through the water until it is evenly distributed. When the drop hits the water, the molecules are tightly concentrated. They quickly spread to areas where the concentration is lower. Once the concentration is the same in the whole glass, the process stops.

Now you will learn how diffusion applies to cell membranes. Imagine that you are in a large, closed room filled with 100 bumper cars. The bumper cars do not have steering wheels, so the drivers move around helplessly, bumping into one another and bumping off the walls. Now imagine that there are doors in the walls that lead into another room of the same size. As the bumper cars move around, some go through the doors into the next room. These cars randomly bounce around the second room. Some reenter the first room.

As time goes by, more and more cars randomly enter the second room, until half the cars are in the first room and half the cars are in the second room. At this point, the number of cars moving from the first room to the second room equals the number of cars moving from the second room to the first room. Therefore, each room will always contain approximately 50 bumper cars.

This scene occurs in a similar way on a cellular level. Instead of a wall between two rooms, you have a cell membrane. Instead of bumper cars, you have molecules moving around. These molecules could be gases, liquids, or solids. At first, all the molecules are on one side of the membrane. Then some of these molecules randomly move across the membrane to the other side. As a result, the number of molecules on the first side decreases, and the number on the second side increases. Eventually, there are equal numbers of molecules on both sides of the membrane.

IN REAL LIFE

Miko met her friend at the movie theater, and they took their usual seats in the front row. Before the movie started, Miko opened a bottle of perfume she had bought the day before to let her friend have a sniff. When Miko started to hand it over, she accidentally spilled the entire contents of the bottle on the seat.

Diffusion began. The perfume molecules first reached the people two rows back. Miko heard them commenting on the powerful fragrance. Halfway through the movie, her friend went to get popcorn. She told Miko that the perfume molecules had now spread throughout the whole theater and had even reached the lobby!

Now suppose there are two sizes of bumper cars. Only the small cars can fit through the doors and enter the second room. The large bumper cars must stay in the first room forever. In biological terms, you would say that the wall is **permeable** to small bumper cars. They can pass through the wall. The wall is **impermeable** to the large bumper cars. They cannot pass through the wall. Because the wall lets some cars across but not others, it is said to be **semipermeable.**

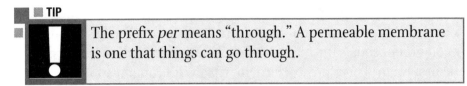

■ TIP

! The prefix *per* means "through." A permeable membrane is one that things can go through.

Cell membranes are also semipermeable. They allow some types of molecules to pass through and keep others from passing through. In this way, cell membranes control what enters and leaves the cells.

Osmosis

Now look at a special case of diffusion. The diffusion of water across a semipermeable membrane from a high concentration to a low concentration is called **osmosis.** How do you determine the concentration of water? You cannot simply compare the number of water molecules on either side of the membrane. Instead, you have to look at the concentration of molecules dissolved in the water.

Say you add a teaspoon of sugar to a glass of water. You are increasing the concentration of sugar in the water. You started with a glass of water that was 0 percent sugar and ended with a glass of water that was 10 percent sugar. At the same time, you are decreasing the concentration of water in the glass. You started with a glass containing pure water and ended up with a glass that was only 90 percent water.

Now you take a container of water and stretch a semipermeable membrane through the middle (shown in the diagram on the next page). Water can pass through this membrane, but sugar cannot. Adding a teaspoon of sugar to the water on one side of the membrane will decrease the water concentration. Because molecules move from an area of higher concentration to an area of lower concentration, the water will flow across the membrane to the side with the sugar. You would actually see the water level rising on the side with the sugar.

Osmosis is important because cells must control the amount of water they take in. If cells lose too much water, they dry out and shrink. If cells take in too much water, they burst. Cells are filled with many dissolved particles. If the concentration of dissolved particles inside the cells is greater than the concentration outside, the cells take in water. If the concentration of dissolved particles is greater outside the cells, the cells lose water.

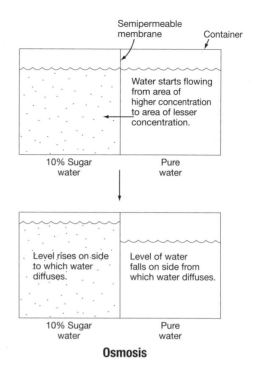

Semipermeable membrane

Container

Water starts flowing from area of higher concentration to area of lesser concentration.

10% Sugar water

Pure water

Level rises on side to which water diffuses.

Level of water falls on side from which water diffuses.

10% Sugar water

Pure water

Osmosis

THINK ABOUT IT

Often people who are hospitalized are unable to eat. Therefore, doctors hook them to intravenous (IV) lines that drip fluids filled with nutrients into their veins. Why is it critical that these fluids contain exactly the correct concentration of dissolved particles? Write your answer on a separate sheet of paper.

Cell Membrane Structure

Now take a look at the structure of the cell membrane. Surprisingly, this barrier that separates the inside of the cell from the outside is not thick, nor is it particularly sturdy. It is composed mostly of layers of lipids.

Cell membranes also contain various proteins. Some proteins are attached to the surface of the membrane. Others extend completely through the membrane.

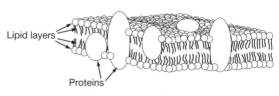

Lipid layers

Proteins

Cell Membrane Structure

Transport

Other proteins in the membrane act as gatekeepers. They **transport,** or carry, molecules back and forth across the membrane. Cell membranes are permeable to water and gases such as oxygen and carbon dioxide. These molecules are free to diffuse back and forth depending on the level of concentration. Other molecules need help from proteins in the membrane. These proteins bind to the molecules on one side of the membrane and release them on the other side. Like enzymes, transport proteins are specialized; each type can transport only one type of molecule.

There are two kinds of transport.

PASSIVE TRANSPORT

In **passive transport,** the protein moves molecules from an area of high concentration to an area of low concentration. Passive transport does not require the cell to expend, or use, energy.

ACTIVE TRANSPORT

Active transport moves molecules against the level of concentration. In other words, it moves molecules from an area of low concentration to an area of high concentration. Active transport is equivalent to pushing a rock uphill. The cell must expend energy.

■ PRACTICE 4: Cell Membranes

Decide if each statement that follows is true (**T**) or false (**F**). Write the correct letter on each line.

_____ **1.** Cell membranes are composed entirely of lipids.

_____ **2.** In diffusion, molecules move from an area of low concentration to an area of high concentration.

_____ **3.** Osmosis is the movement of water across a semipermeable membrane.

_____ **4.** Adding sugar to water decreases the concentration of the water.

_____ **5.** Active transport of molecules requires energy.

Inside a Cell

Inside most cells, you will find a jellylike substance called **cytoplasm.** Within the cytoplasm are a series of structures called **organelles.** Each type of organelle carries out a special task for the cell. Like the cell itself, organelles are surrounded by membranes that control what enters and leaves them.

Nucleus

The **nucleus** is the largest, most visible structure in most cells. (The plural form of *nucleus* is *nuclei.*) The nucleus is often referred to as the control center of the cell. It starts and controls cell division. It contains molecules called genes that serve as blueprints, or plans, for the organism's characteristics. You will examine these remarkable molecules in detail later on.

The nucleus is surrounded by another membrane called the **nuclear envelope.** The nuclear envelope contains large pores through which giant molecules can pass. Proteins within these pores serve as gatekeepers, controlling which molecules can pass through the nuclear envelope.

Inside each nucleus are one or two dark structures called **nucleoli.** (The singular is *nucleolus.*) The nucleoli manufacture tiny structures called **ribosomes.** As you will learn in the next lesson, ribosomes are the site of protein synthesis (the building or making of large molecules from smaller ones).

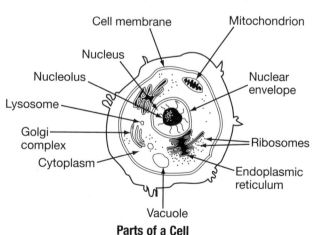

Parts of a Cell

Manufacturing and Transport

One of the chief activities of cells is making and exporting molecules, especially proteins. Although you will study this process in detail in the next lesson, you will now look at the cellular structures involved in this process.

Endoplasmic Reticulum: The **endoplasmic reticulum,** or **ER,** is a network of folded membranes within the cell. This network manufactures and stores many chemicals. It also acts as a passageway to move these chemicals to other parts of the cell.

Golgi Complex: The **Golgi complex** is a series of flattened sacs where new proteins are sorted and modified for transport.

Lysosomes: **Lysosomes** are the cell's waste-disposal sites. They contain powerful enzymes that help digest food taken in by the cells. Lysosomes also break down defective parts of the cell.

THINK ABOUT IT

Why is it important that digestion takes place inside the lysosomes? Write your answer on a separate sheet of paper.

Energy Production

The next two organelles you will look at are responsible for capturing energy and converting it into a form that the cells can use.

Chloroplasts: **Chloroplasts** are found only in plant cells. They are not found in the cells of animals or fungi. Chloroplasts help plants make food.

Mitochondria: **Mitochondria** (singular *mitochondrion*) are organelles that are found in both plant and animal cells. Mitochondria break down glucose to make energy. The cell then uses this energy to power biological processes.

Plant Cells

Animal cells and plant cells share many common features. Both have cell membranes, a nucleus, mitochondria, and structures to manufacture and export protein. There are, however, some fundamental differences between them. You have already learned one difference—plant cells have chloroplasts.

The most important difference between animal and plant cells is that the cells of plants, algae, and fungi are surrounded by a rigid barrier called the **cell wall.** In plants, this cell wall is made of **cellulose.** Cellulose is made up of carbohydrates woven together into tough fibers. Cell walls protect the cells from damage and provide structural support. The cell walls in tree trunks are especially thick and give the wood its strength. Cell walls help plant cells keep their shape.

TIP

A plant cell is similar to a bicycle tire. The outer tire is the cell wall, and the inner tube is the membrane. The cell wall protects the cell just as the tire shields the inner tube from sharp objects. The cell wall prevents the cell from bursting when water rushes in through osmosis, just as the tire prevents an inflated inner tube from bursting. But like a tire without air, a plant without water will wilt.

Plant cells also have membrane-bound sacs called **vacuoles.** Vacuoles take up 90 percent of the volume of some cells. They serve as storage sites for salts, proteins, and carbohydrates, which are dissolved in a watery solution. Some vacuoles serve the same function as lysosomes. They contain enzymes that break down waste and recycle worn-out parts of the cell.

■ PRACTICE 5: Inside a Cell

Look at the list of terms below. Fill in each line with the letter of the term that correctly completes each of the following statements.

a. proteins   e. vacuoles
b. nucleus   f. energy
c. nucleoli   g. chloroplasts
d. mitochondria   h. glucose

1. The _____, _____, and _____ are surrounded by membranes.

2. Ribosomes are manufactured in the _____ .

3. The Golgi complex modifies _____ for export.

4. Plant cells contain large, membrane-bound storage sacs called _____ .

5. Mitochondria break down _____ to create _____ .

Making and Using Energy

Cells need energy to survive and function. They need energy to synthesize large molecules such as proteins. They also need energy to break down other molecules. They need energy for active transport. They need energy to move around. Muscle cells need energy to contract. Nerve cells need energy to fire electrical signals.

Cells get their energy by breaking down glucose into carbon dioxide. But what form does this energy take? If you were to try this reaction at home—for example, by setting fire to a log in the fireplace—you would get energy in the form of heat. Heat is useless to your cells (although chemical reactions in your cells produce enough heat to keep your body warm). In fact, if your cells were to break down glucose in the same way that you break down the log in your fireplace, you would burst into flames. Instead, your cells break down glucose through a long, complex series of controlled reactions that release a little bit of energy at a time. Some of this energy is in the form of heat. But a lot of it is in a form that your cells can use.

Instead of producing heat, your cells put the energy from the breakdown of glucose into a molecule called **adenosine triphosphate,** or **ATP.** ATP is a fairly complex molecule. The most important part of ATP is the string of three phosphate molecules. A **phosphate** consists of a phosphorus atom surrounded by three oxygen atoms. The bonds between these phosphates, especially the second and third ones, are unstable. When they break, they yield a lot of energy.

Adenosine Triphosphate (ATP)

TIP

Think of the bond between the two phosphates as a coiled spring. By triggering the spring, you release a lot of energy.

Think of ATP molecules as dollar bills. Whenever your cells need energy to drive a reaction, they grab some of the billions of ATP molecules floating around the cytoplasm and spend them. With the help of a special enzyme, one of the phosphates gets lopped off and energy is released. Some of the energy is lost as heat, but the rest goes directly into fueling the reaction.

Respiration

If ATP molecules are dollar bills, then mitochondria are the banks. When a cell gets low on ATP, the mitochondria create more by breaking down glucose in a process called **respiration.** Respiration is a complex process.

There are many intermediate reactions, each of which is assisted by different types of enzymes.

Photosynthesis

Earlier, the mitochondria were compared to banks that store energy in the form of glucose. The ATP molecules are like dollar bills that the cell spends when it needs energy to power reactions. But where does the energy originally come from? Animals and fungi get their energy by devouring other organisms. Plants, however, get their energy directly from the sun through a process called **photosynthesis.**

Like respiration, photosynthesis involves many complex steps. Enzymes are involved in most of these steps. Here is a look at the highlights of the process.

There are two phases of photosynthesis: the light phase and the dark phase. The **light phase** is driven by energy from the sun. **Chlorophyll—** green pigment in the chloroplasts—absorbs the sunlight. The energy from the sun is then used to split water into hydrogen, oxygen, and electrons. In fact, the splitting of water during the light phase is the source of all the oxygen in the atmosphere.

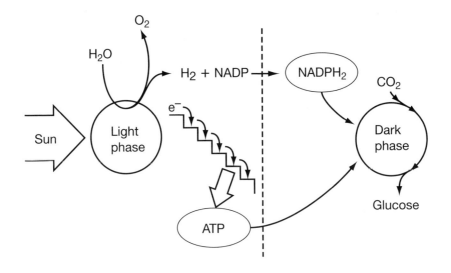

Photosynthesis

The next reactions in the light phase closely resemble the electron transport chain in respiration. The electrons from the water are propelled to a higher energy level. Think of the light energy as throwing the electrons to the top of a flight of protein stairs. As the electrons bounce down these stairs, they trigger the formation of ATP and another high-energy molecule called NADPH.

The next phase is called the **dark phase.** (Actually, although this phase does not depend on light, it does not have to take place in the dark.) During the dark phase, ATP and NADPH from the light phase are broken down to fuel the synthesis of glucose from carbon dioxide. ATP is a high energy molecule. It is broken down to run the active transport of molecules across a cell membrane. Here, it joins with NADPH to run this complex set of chemical reactions.

■ PRACTICE 6: Making and Using Energy

Look at the list of terms below. Fill in each line with the letter of the term that correctly completes each of the following statements.

a. light phase
b. NADPH
c. mitochondria
d. ATP
e. carbon dioxide
f. chlorophyll

1. During respiration, the _____ break down glucose to make energy.

2. _____ and _____ are energy-rich molecules created during the light phase of photosynthesis.

3. Green pigment in chloroplasts called _____ absorbs sunlight.

4. Oxygen is produced during the _____ of photosynthesis.

5. During the dark phase, _____ is converted into glucose.

LESSON 3: Nucleotides and Protein Synthesis

 GOAL: To understand the structure of DNA and RNA; to understand how these molecules direct the construction of proteins

WORDS TO KNOW

adenine	nucleotides
anticodons	ribonucleic acid (RNA)
chromosomes	ribose
codons	ribosomal RNA (rRNA)
cytosine	RNA polymerase
deoxyribonucleic acid (DNA)	start codon
deoxyribose	stop codon
double helix	thymine
guanine	transcription
messenger RNA (mRNA)	transfer RNA (tRNA)
nitrogen-containing base	translation
nucleic acids	uracil

Structure of DNA and RNA

So far, you have learned three of the four major organic molecules that make up living things—carbohydrates, lipids, and proteins. In this lesson, you will examine the nucleic acids and the two major types of **nucleic acids**—**deoxyribonucleic acid,** or DNA, and **ribonucleic acid,** or RNA.

These molecules of nucleic acid are said to contain the code of life because they contain instructions for the manufacturing of proteins. Remember, proteins not only serve as important structural components in your body, but they also form enzymes that direct almost every chemical reaction in your body. Therefore, the proteins your cells produce shape every detail of your body—from the color of your eyes to how many fingers and toes you have.

Remember also that the function of proteins depends on the precise order of amino acids. It is the nucleic acids that provide the instructions for assembling the amino acids into proteins.

DNA and RNA are found in the cells of all living things, from bacteria to elephants. Mitochondria and chloroplasts contain DNA, but the DNA examined here is found in the nucleus. RNA is found both in the nucleus and in the cytoplasm.

Just as proteins are made of long chains of amino acids, DNA and RNA are made of long chains of units called **nucleotides.** You will first learn about the structure of DNA.

DNA

The nucleotides of DNA have three parts—a phosphate group (like the phosphate groups in ATP), a five-carbon sugar called **deoxyribose,** and a **nitrogen-containing base.** Nitrogen bases are composed of one or two rings of nitrogen and carbon.

There are four types of nucleotides in DNA, each of which has a different type of nitrogen base. These four bases are called **thymine,**

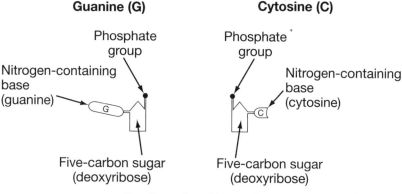

Two Examples of Nucleotides

adenine, guanine, and cytosine.
For the rest of this unit, these
bases will be called T, A, G, and C.

Each DNA molecule is
composed of two long chains
containing millions of nucleotides.
The DNA code is determined by
the order of T, A, G, and C in the
chain. The two DNA strands wrap
around each other to form a
double helix. This is a structure
that looks a bit like a twisted
ladder.

In this double helix, the
nitrogen bases in the first strand
pair up and form weak bonds with
the nitrogen bases in the second
strand. These bonds hold together
the two strands. This pairing of
nitrogen bases is very orderly. The
nitrogen base A always pairs up
with T, and C always pairs up with
G. These precise pairings are
critical both to the replication of
DNA and to the process leading to
the synthesis of proteins.

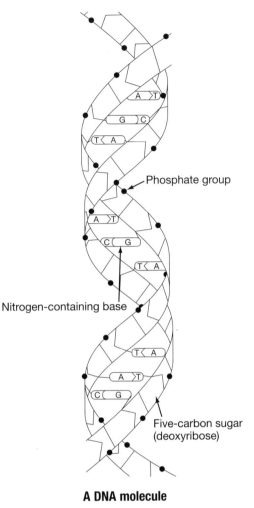

A DNA molecule

Inside the nucleus, the DNA is coiled into bundles called **chromosomes.**
Proteins in the chromosomes bind the DNA together. Each type of
organism has a different number of chromosomes in each cell. Human
cells have 23 pairs of chromosomes.

TIP

Think of the two DNA strands in a double helix as the two
banisters on a spiral staircase.

RNA

Like DNA, RNA molecules are made up of long strings of nucleotides. The nucleotides in RNA, however, are different from the nucleotides in DNA. RNA nucleotides contain a five-carbon sugar called **ribose** instead of the five-carbon sugar deoxyribose found in DNA. Three of the nitrogen bases, A, G, and C, are the same as in DNA, but instead of T, RNA nucleotides have a nitrogen base called **uracil** (U). Unlike DNA, the RNA molecules are composed of only a single strand of nucleotides. As you will learn, the nitrogen bases in RNA can pair up with the nitrogen bases in DNA. The U in RNA pairs with the A in DNA.

There are three types of RNA. **Ribosomal RNA (rRNA)** is found in the nucleolus and the ribosomes. This type of RNA is involved in the construction of ribosomes. **Messenger RNA (mRNA)** and **transfer RNA (tRNA)** are involved in protein synthesis.

THINK ABOUT IT

A scientist claimed that he had sequenced (determined the order of) a section of a DNA double helix. He said he found 10,685 A's, 15,996 T's, 11,658 G's, and 9851 C's. Why should you be skeptical? Write your answer on a separate sheet of paper.

■ PRACTICE 7: Structure of DNA and RNA

Decide if each statement that follows is true (**T**) or false (**F**). Write the correct letter on each line.

_____ **1.** DNA is double-stranded, and RNA is single-stranded.

_____ **2.** In DNA, A always pairs with T, and C always pairs with G.

_____ **3.** DNA and RNA have the same type of five-carbon sugar.

_____ **4.** Nucleic acids are found only in cytoplasm.

Protein Synthesis

In this section, you will go step-by-step through the process by which DNA directs the construction of proteins. As you will see, it is a complex process that takes place both inside and outside the nucleus. It involves DNA, mRNA, tRNA, and ribosomes.

Transcription

Transcription is the process by which mRNA is manufactured.

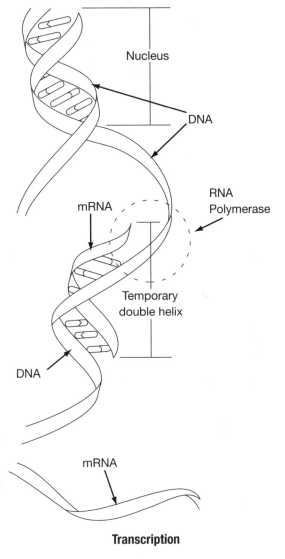

Transcription

1. An enzyme called **RNA polymerase** binds to a strand of DNA inside the nucleus. This enzyme causes the weak bonds between the nitrogen base pairs to break. As a result, part of the DNA molecules unwinds and exposes the nitrogen bases.

2. With the help of RNA polymerase, individual mRNA nucleotides floating around in the nucleus couple with the nucleotides along one of the unraveled DNA strands. RNA U's, A's, C's, and G's pair up with DNA A's, T's, G's, and C's. The result is a temporary double helix containing one strand of DNA and one strand of mRNA.

3. Once the complete mRNA chain has formed, it falls off. The DNA re-forms into its original double helix. The mRNA, however, is not in its final form. A series of enzymes modify the mRNA by adding special sequences of nucleotides to both ends and splicing out other nucleotide sequences. The mRNA then leaves the nucleus through the large pores in the nuclear membrane.

Translation

The DNA has now transcribed ("written") its code onto the mRNA. Now take a look at the **translation** of this code.

Think of the mRNA molecule as a very long sentence. There are four letters in the RNA "alphabet"—A, U, C, and G. These letters are combined in various three-letter sequences to stand for special amino acids. These three-letter sequences are called **codons.** There are 64 possible codons. Each codon stands for a specific amino acid. Remember that there are 20 different amino acids. So, for example, the codons CCU, CCC, CCA, and CCG translate into the amino acid called proline. The codons CUU, CUC, CUA, and CUG translate into the amino acid leucine. All codons together will describe the amino acid sequence of the protein that is being made.

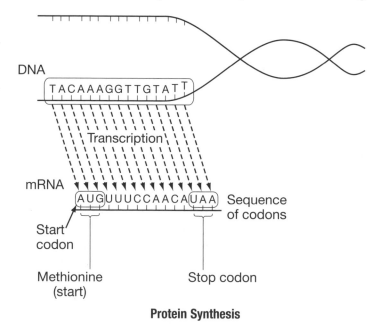

Protein Synthesis

Second letter in the codon

		U	C	A	G	
First letter in the codon	U	Phenylalanine Phenylalanine Leucine Leucine	Serine Serine Serine Serine	Tyrosine Tyrosine Stop Codon Stop Codon	Cysteine Cysteine Stop Codon Tryptophan	U C A G
	C	Leucine Leucine Leucine Leucine	Proline Proline Proline Proline	Histidine Histidine Glutamine Glutamine	Arginine Arginine Arginine Arginine	U C A G
	A	Isoleucine Isoleucine Isoleucine Methionine	Threonine Threonine Threonine Threonine	Asparagine Asparagine Lysine Lysine	Serine Serine Arginine Arginine	U C A G
	G	Valine Valine Valine Valine	Alanine Alanine Alanine Alanine	Aspartic acid Aspartic acid Glutamic acid Glutamic acid	Glycine Glycine Glycine Glycine	U C A G

(Third letter in the codon shown in rightmost column)

AUG = methionine, the start codon

How to use this chart:

To determine which amino acid a codon codes for, find each letter of the codon in the chart. Where these letters intersect is the amino acid they code for.

For example: UGG

Find the "U" in the part of the chart labeled "first letter in the codon." Then find the "G" in the column labeled "second letter in the codon." Finally, in that section (the "G" section), find the third letter of the codon, which is also a "G." The amino acid is tryptophan.

Note that some amino acids have as many as 6 different codons. Therefore, the column labeled "third letter in codon" has all 4 bases listed to provide the possibilities for multiple codons. For example: Proline has the codons CCU, CCC, CCA, and CCG.

There are also two special types of codons. (They are shown in the diagram on page 31.) The first codon in the sequence is called the **start codon.** The sequence of the start codon is always AUG. The final codon in the sequence is called the **stop codon.** There are three different stop codons. The three elements involved in translation from mRNA to protein are the ribosomes, mRNA, and tRNA.

As you recall, ribosomes are small units that are attached to the endoplasmic reticulum. There are also ribosomes that float freely in the cytoplasm. Each ribosome contains two pieces—a large subunit and a small subunit.

Transfer RNA (tRNA) is a relatively short molecule (only about 90 nucleotides) that curls in on itself and forms a series of loops. On one side, there are three exposed nucleotides called **anticodons.** These anticodons bind to the codons on the mRNA. The other end of the tRNA is bound to an amino acid. The type of amino acid corresponds to the codon or mRNA sequence.

Now look at what happens during translation. Once again, enzymes are involved in every step. You will want to study the illustration on page 34 as you read the steps 1 through 6. The art on page 34 is also labeled 1 through 6.

1. The mRNA binds to the small unit of a ribosome. The ribosome always binds to the part of the mRNA that contains the start codon. Remember that the start codon is always the first AUG in the sequence. An anticodon "matches" the mRNA codon. Its purpose is to hold the tRNA in place long enough so the amino acid it is carrying can bond to the growing protein chain.

2. The tRNA with the anticodon UAC binds to the start codon. This tRNA is carrying the amino acid methionine. At this point, the large unit of the ribosome binds to the small unit and locks the mRNA in place. Protein synthesis has begun.

3. A second tRNA, with an anticodon corresponding to the next codon in the mRNA sequence, binds to the next codon and brings its amino acid with it. Now there are two tRNA molecules bound side by side on the mRNA.

4. The amino acids attached to the tRNA's bind together, creating a protein with two amino acids. The first tRNA (the one with the starter anticodon) breaks away from the mRNA and from the amino acid it was carrying. It returns to the cytoplasm where it picks up another amino acid.

5. The ribosome slides up the mRNA to the next codon. A third tRNA with the corresponding anticodon binds to the mRNA and brings its amino acid with it. The third amino acid binds to the second amino acid. The second tRNA drops off and returns to the cytoplasm. Now there is a three-amino-acid chain.

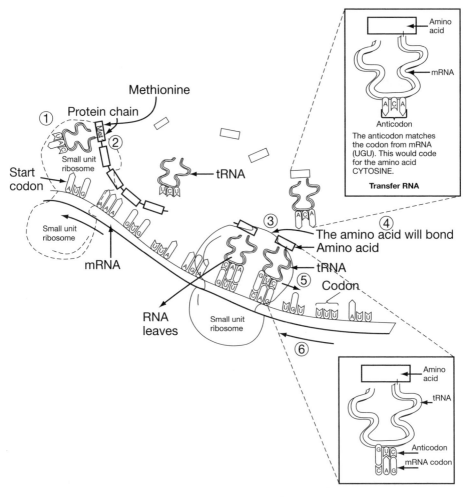

Translation in Detail

6. The ribosome slides up the mRNA to the next codon, and the preceding steps are repeated until the stop codon is reached. The result is a long sequence of amino acids—in other words, a protein.

The discovery in the 1950s of the structure of nucleic acids, and their role as the chemical basis of heredity, revolutionized the entire field of biology.

■ PRACTICE 8: Protein Synthesis

Decide if each statement that follows is true (T) or false (F). Write the correct letter on each line.

_____ 1. mRNA is manufactured in a process called transcription.

_____ 2. mRNA is divided into three-nucleotide sequences called anticodons.

_____ 3. The anticodon corresponding to the codon CGC is GCG.

_____ 4. The nucleotide sequence AUG is called the start codon.

_____ 5. There are 64 possible stop codons.

_____ 6. Enzymes are involved in every step of translation.

_____ 7. The amino acid that the tRNA with the anticodon UUU carries is called lysine. (Use the codon chart of amino acids on page 32 to answer this question.)

LESSON 4: The Cell Cycle

GOAL: To understand how cells replicate; to understand how new copies of chromosomes are made

WORDS TO KNOW

anaphase	gene	nondisjunction
autosome	haploid cells	prophase
centriole	histones	sex cells
chromatid	homologous	sister chromatids
chromatin	interphase	sperm
crossing over	M phase	spindle
daughter cells	meiosis	substitution
diploid cells	meiotic interphase	telophase
DNA polymerase	metaphase	translocation
egg	mitosis	tumor
fertilization	mutagens	
gametes	mutation	

The Life Cycle of a Cell

The cells in your body are not independent living organisms. But, like all living things, they grow, reproduce, and die. In fact, it has been estimated that every hour almost 200 billion cells in your body die and are replaced. Cells die from a variety of causes. Cells in your skin—especially in areas like the palms of your hands—and in your small intestine are constantly being worn away. These cells must be replaced. Cells in your liver typically live for about 500 days. Liver cells are so good at replacing themselves that if you were to lose a section of (or a piece from) your liver, it would eventually grow back. Other cells have very long life spans. Nerve cells, for example, live as long as you do. Unfortunately, if your nerve cells get damaged, they can rarely replace themselves.

Cells reproduce by dividing. Like all living things, the cells produce exact replicas of themselves. This is a tricky, complex process. The new cells, known as **daughter cells,** must contain not only the same cytoplasm and organelles as the parent cell, but they also must contain exact copies of the parent cell's DNA.

In this lesson, you will study the life cycle of the cell, especially cell division and the replication of DNA.

Chromosomes

Remember that a cell's nucleus contains molecules called nucleic acids. The most prominent of these molecules is DNA. DNA is composed of two long strands of units called nucleotides. There are four different types of nucleotides. Each nucleotide has a different nitrogen-containing base— A (adenine), T (thymine), C (cytosine), and G (guanine). Each DNA molecule contains instructions for assembling amino acids into proteins. The language of these instructions is contained in the sequence of nucleotides in the DNA.

A single DNA molecule contains millions of nucleotides. It also contains the instructions for many different proteins. In fact, a single strand of DNA is almost 13 centimeters long. Each DNA molecule is divided into regions called genes. In technical terms, a **gene** is a sequence of nucleotides that codes for a single protein or group of proteins. But usually genes are described as regions of DNA that determine specific traits such as eye color or height. In Lesson 5, we will look at how genes interact to determine who you are.

So how does such a large molecule fit inside a structure as small as the nucleus of a cell? How does the cell keep all that DNA organized? The answer is that the DNA is wrapped into tight bundles called chromosomes. In fact, this tight wrapping produces a chromosome that is only $\frac{1}{10,000}$ the length of the DNA. These bundles are well organized. If you were to unwrap a chromosome, you would see what looks like beads on a string.

The beads are globular proteins called **histones.** The DNA string wraps $2\frac{1}{2}$ times around each histone. Other histones cause the DNA to coil farther in on itself. The combination of histones and DNA is called **chromatin.**

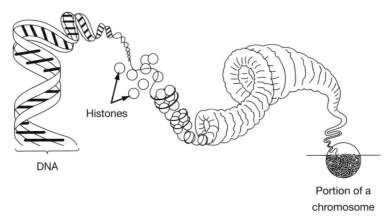

Histones

DNA

Portion of a
chromosome

The Makeup of a Typical DNA

 TIP

To get an idea of how DNA bundles up into chromosomes, take a rubber band and twist it many times. Note how the rubber band shortens as you twist it.

Most of the cells in your body contain 23 pairs of chromosomes, or a total of 46 chromosomes. The cells that contain 23 pairs (46 total chromosomes) are called **diploid cells.** In the word *diploid*, the prefix *di-* means "two" and the suffix *-ploid* refers to the number of chromosome "pairs." Your red blood cells have no chromosomes.

 **TIP**

If you multiply 2 times the number of pairs, you get the total number of chromosomes for the cells in a particular organism. For humans, $2 \times 23 = 46$ total chromosomes. The number of total chromosomes is called the diploid chromosome number.

Of the 23 pairs of chromosomes in the cells, 22 pairs are called autosomes. An **autosome** is a chromosome that determines all of your body features. These features include hair and eye color, the shape of your ears and nose, and how your liver, heart, or lungs will form. Both of the chromosomes in each pair of autosomes are the same size and shape. They have information for the same characteristics or traits. But these chromosomes are not identical. They are said to be **homologous.** This means that they are similar in structure but may function differently. For example, both chromosomes in a single pair might have information for eye color. But one chromosome of the pair may carry the information for blue eyes while the other in the pair carries information for brown eyes. The reason these autosomes are homologous instead of identical is because one of each pair was inherited from the mother, and one of each pair was inherited from the father. You will see how this happens at the end of this lesson.

Each chromosome contains many units of information for traits. These units or sections on the chromosomes for a trait are called genes. The chromosomes and nucleotide sequences within each chromosome are identical in every diploid cell of your body. This means that the chromosomes in your brain cells are exact copies of the chromosomes in the skin cells of your big toe.

TIP

Think of homologous chromosomes as a pair of mismatched shoes. They both serve the same function—protecting your feet—but one is a sneaker and one is a dress shoe.

Now look at the chromosome pair number 23. These chromosomes, called sex chromosomes, determine whether you are male or female. There are two types of sex chromosomes. There is an X chromosome and a Y chromosome. Females contain two homologous X chromosomes. Males contain one X chromosome and one Y chromosome. The X and the Y chromosomes are not homologous. They contain different genes. The Y chromosome looks similar to the X chromosome, but it is much smaller than the X chromosome.

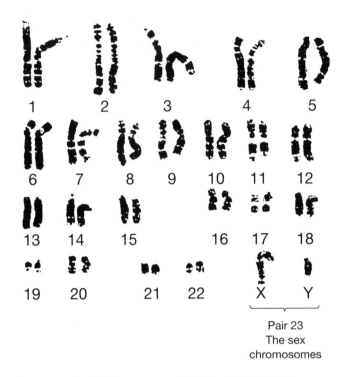

The 23 Chromosome Pairs in a Diploid Cell

■ **PRACTICE 9: Chromosomes**

Look at the list of terms below. Fill in each line with the letter of the term that correctly completes each statement.

a. homologous
b. histones
c. females

d. males
e. autosomes
f. sex chromosomes

1. Chromatin is a combination of DNA and proteins called _____.

2. Human cells contain 22 pairs of _____ and 1 pair of _____.

3. The chromosomes within each pair are said to be _____ instead of identical.

4. _____ have two X chromosomes. _____ have one X and one Y chromosome.

Mitosis

For a brief amount of time, you were just a single cell. This cell divided and created two cells. These two cells divided, their cells divided, and so on. At one stage of your development, cells started differentiating into skin cells, muscle cells, brain cells, liver cells, and many other types of cells. All of these cells have one trait in common. They all contain exact copies of the chromosomes found in that first cell. In this section, you will learn about mitosis. **Mitosis** is the replication of DNA and the division of the nucleus.

Interphase

It takes about 30 minutes for one cell to divide. **Interphase** is the period between divisions. Interphase is an active time for cells.

The stage of interphase immediately following mitosis is called G_1 (for gap 1). During this stage, cells carry out all of their normal life functions. They grow, manufacture new organelles, synthesize proteins, and import and export molecules. Remember that in order to code for proteins, the chromosomes must unravel. Therefore, the DNA in cells during G_1 look like a tangled mass of yarn.

The length of the G_1 phase depends on how rapidly the cell divides. Nerve cells enter a permanent G_1 phase. Other cells remain in the G_1 phase 8 hours or more.

The second stage of interphase is called the S stage (for *synthesis*, or "combining"). During this stage, which takes about 6–10 hours, all of the DNA in the cell replicates itself. This process is similar to the synthesis of mRNA. You learned about mRNA in Lesson 3. An enzyme called **DNA polymerase** inserts itself into thousands of points along the DNA molecule. Then the DNA

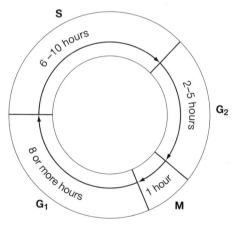

The Cell Life Cycle

polymerase unwinds the entire double helix. Complementary DNA nucleotides bind to the exposed nucleotides of each strand (A to T, C to G). The result is two identical DNA double helixes. At the same time, the cell starts producing histones. These histones combine with the DNA to form chromatin.

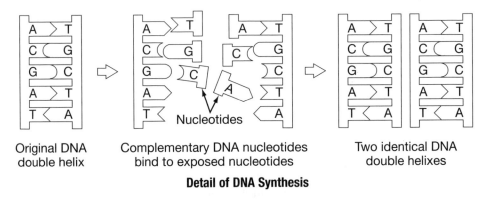

| Original DNA double helix | Complementary DNA nucleotides bind to exposed nucleotides | Two identical DNA double helixes |

Detail of DNA Synthesis

The Second Stage of Interphase

The second stage of interphase is called G_2 (for gap 2). In this stage, the cell makes final preparations before it divides. In particular, the cell manufactures a protein that plays a critical role during mitosis.

Following the G_2 phase is the **M phase.** The M stands for mitosis. In cell division, the nucleus divides first. Mitosis includes four stages: prophase, metaphase, anaphase, and telophase.

Prophase

Prophase is the first stage of mitosis. Enormous changes start to take place inside the nucleus. First, the DNA condenses into chromosomes. Remember, there are now two copies of DNA. Therefore, there are two copies of each chromosome. Each copy of the chromosome is called a **chromatid.**

Duplicated chromosome

These two chromatids, known as **sister chromatids,** bind with each other. As a result, the chromatid pairs appear to take on an "x" shape. (*Note:* The "x" shape of the chromatid pairs is not the same as the X chromosome.)

Sister Chromatids

At the same time, a complex structure called a **spindle** starts to form. The spindle is essentially a set of fibers made of protein. These protein fibers, called spindle fibers, will eventually control the movement of the chromosomes during mitosis. Finally, the nucleoli and the nuclear membrane disintegrate.

Metaphase

The second stage of mitosis is called **metaphase.** In metaphase, the spindle takes on its final shape. Think of the cell as a globe with a north pole and a south pole. At each pole, there is a structure called a **centriole.** Spindle fibers radiate out from these centrioles. The other end of each spindle fiber latches on to a chromatid pair. Each chromatid pair is suspended between two spindle fibers. One originates from the centriole at the north pole. Another spindle fiber originates from the centriole at the south pole. These spindle fibers guide the chromatid pairs to the middle of the cell, or the "equator," where the chromatid pairs line up.

Anaphase

Anaphase—the third stage of mitosis—is when the real action takes place. Each duplicated chromosome splits, and the sister chromatids separate. The spindle fibers then pull the chromosomes in opposite directions toward the poles. At the end of anaphase, each pole contains a copy of each chromosome.

Telophase

Telophase is the fourth and final stage of mitosis. The spindle disintegrates, and the chromosomes start to unravel. This happens so the DNA can get back into the business of synthesizing proteins. A new nuclear envelope begins to form at either pole, indicating the reforming of the nucleus and nucleoli.

At the same time, the other part of the cell begins to divide. This process differs in animal cells and plant cells. In animal cells, a furrow, or groove, develops at the equator of the cell. It is as if somebody tied a loop around the middle of the cell and tightened it, splitting the cell in half. This loop is actually made out of protein fibers. These fibers contract until only a thin thread of cytoplasm connects the two new cells that are forming. These new cells are called daughter cells. Each daughter cell has a diploid chromosome number of 46. That is, each daughter cell has 23 pairs of homologous chromosomes. Each chromosome has been formed from a single chromatid. Finally, this thread of cytoplasm disappears, and the two cells separate.

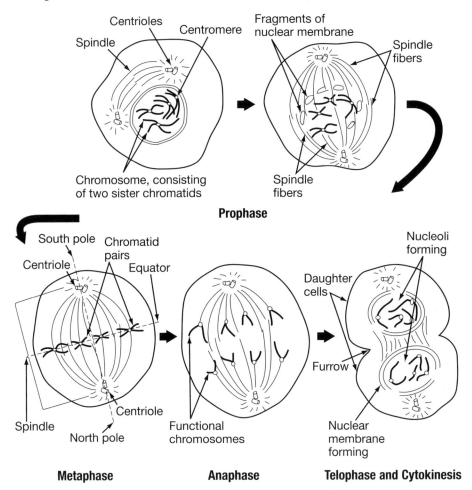

Prophase

Metaphase   **Anaphase**   **Telophase and Cytokinesis**

In plant cells, the cell wall prevents a furrow from forming. Instead, a new cell wall, called a cell plate, forms in the middle. This plate cuts the cell in half and forms two new cells.

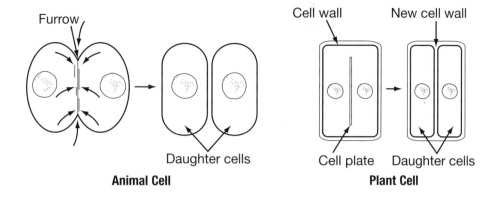

Furrow

Daughter cells

Animal Cell

Cell wall   New cell wall

Cell plate   Daughter cells

Plant Cell

◼ PRACTICE 10: Mitosis

Look at the list of stages below. Write the letter of the correct stage on the line before each statement.

a. S stage of interphase   **d.** anaphase
b. prophase   **e.** telophase
c. metaphase

_____ **1.** The spindle fibers pull chromosomes to opposite poles.

_____ **2.** The DNA in the cell replicates itself.

_____ **3.** The spindle disappears, and the chromosomes start to unravel.

_____ **4.** The DNA condenses into chromosomes, and the spindle begins to form.

_____ **5.** The spindle takes on its final shape, and the chromatid pairs line up in the middle of the cell.

Meiosis

During mitosis, a diploid cell (a cell with pairs of homologous chromosomes) divides and produces two identical diploid cells. The vast majority of cells in your body are produced through mitosis. A few cells, however, are produced through a different process. These cells divide twice to form four cells with half the diploid number of chromosomes. Since these cells have only half the diploid chromosome number, they are called **haploid cells.** The prefix *hap-* means "half." Haploid cells contain only one of each type of chromosome. So instead of having 23 homologous pairs of chromosomes, these new cells contain 23 single chromosomes. This type of cell division is called **meiosis.** The haploid cells that are produced during meiosis are called **gametes,** or **sex cells.** Every multicelled organism, whether it is a plant, an animal, or a fungi, produces these cells. In humans, these cells are the **sperm** and the **egg.**

During meiosis, the cells divide twice. The first division, called meiosis I, produces two cells. Each cell contains one of each type of chromosome in its duplicated or sister chromatid form. These two cells divide again during meiosis II. In meiosis II, sister chromatids are separated. The result is four separate cells, each with a haploid number of chromosomes. Follow the diagram on page 48 as you read about the stages of meiosis.

Prophase I

Prophase I in meiosis starts out the same way as prophase in mitosis. The DNA has already bundled up into chromosomes and duplicated itself during the S phase of interphase. Since they are duplicated, the chromosomes are described as two sister chromatids. The nuclear membrane and nucleoli come apart. A spindle starts to form, made up of spindle fibers and centriole.

Chromatids

One duplicated chromosome is also called a sister chromatid pair.

Remember that you have two sets of chromosomes, one from each parent. Each type of chromosome from your mother matches with each type of chromosome from your father to form a homologous pair. They are homologous because each pair carries the same kind of genetic information. The homologous pairs come together.

Homologous pair of duplicated chromosomes

What happens next is quite amazing. The chromatids are zipped together and swap segments of DNA. In other words, genes from one chromatid become incorporated into the other chromatid. This DNA exchange is called **crossing over.**

Once crossing over is completed, the bonds holding together the two chromatids dissolves. The homologous pairs stay together.

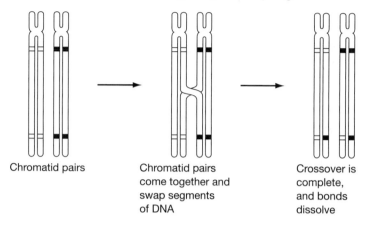

| Chromatid pairs | Chromatid pairs come together and swap segments of DNA | Crossover is complete, and bonds dissolve |

Crossing Over

Metaphase I and Anaphase I

In metaphase I, spindle fibers guide the chromatid pairs to the equator. The homologous sister chromatids remain paired as they line up. Each chromatid pair is attached to a single spindle.

During anaphase I, the sister chromatids do not separate as they do in mitosis. Instead, the chromatids remain intact. The spindle fibers pull each set of sister chromatids in the homologous pair in opposite directions.

Telophase I and Meiotic Interphase

Telophase I in meiosis is just like telophase in mitosis. The spindle breaks down, the nuclei reform, and the cell divides. The daughter cells produced in meiosis I, however, are different from the daughter cells produced in mitosis. Rather than having 23 pairs of homologous chromosomes, each daughter cell has one of each type of the 23 chromosomes attached to its identical duplicate. At the end of meiosis I, there are two remaining daughter cells.

Meiotic interphase is the period between meiosis I and meiosis II. Unlike normal interphase, there is no S stage. The DNA does not replicate.

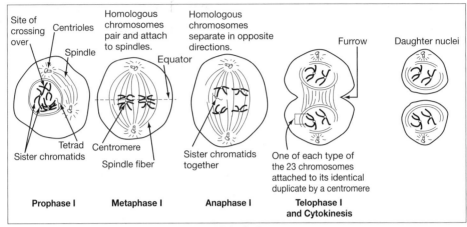

Meiosis I

↓ **Meiotic Interphase** ↓

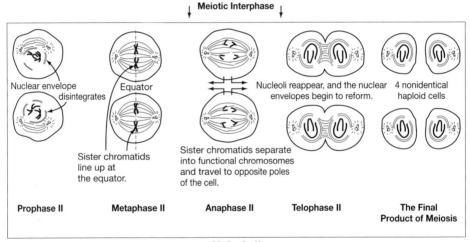

Meiosis II

Meiosis II

The cells produced in meiosis I divide again. This second stage of meiosis, meiosis II, is similar to mitosis. But there are half as many chromosomes involved. Each cell undergoes a second prophase, metaphase, anaphase, and telophase. These stages are called prophase II, metaphase II, anaphase II, and telophase II. During prophase II, the nuclear membrane and the nucleoli disintegrate. In metaphase II, the chromatids line up at the equator. During anaphase II, the sister chromatids separate into functional chromosomes, and each type of chromosome travels to an opposite pole of the cell. Finally, during telophase II, the nuclear envelopes begin to reform and the nucleoli reappear. The final result of meiosis is four nonidentical cells containing 23 individual chromosomes. Crossover during prophase I causes these cells to be different from one another. These haploid cells will now develop into eggs or sperm depending on whether the cells were produced in a female or a male.

What happens to these haploid gametes? A male gamete, or sperm, can fuse with a female gamete, or egg. The result is a single diploid cell with 23 pairs of homologous chromosomes. Half the chromosomes come from the father and half from the mother. This process is called **fertilization.**

■ PRACTICE 11: Meiosis

Look at the list of stages below. Write the letter of the correct stage on the line before each statement.

    a. prophase I   **d.** telophase I
    b. metaphase II   **e.** meiotic interphase
    c. anaphase II

_____ **1.** Sister chromatids separate and travel to opposite poles of the cell.

_____ **2.** Sister chromatids line up at the equator.

_____ **3.** Crossing over takes place.

_____ **4.** This is the period of time between meiosis I and meiosis II.

_____ **5.** Cytokinesis takes place.

Mutations

As you have seen, cell division is a complex process. Chromosomes containing millions of nucleotides make identical copies of each other.

Then they must line up exactly and travel where they are supposed to. Not surprisingly, mistakes happen. Sometimes, the order of the nucleotides gets changed. Sometimes entire genes get deleted or left out. Sometimes the daughter cells end up with too many or too few chromosomes. This kind of mistake is called a **mutation.**

Mutations can happen in any cell in the body. If a mutation occurs and the cell survives and divides, the cell will pass the mutation on to its daughter cells. These daughter cells will then pass the mutation to their daughter cells. As a result, there may be a group of cells that contains the mutation. No other cells in the body are affected.

But what happens if a mutation occurs in a cell that develops into a sperm or an egg? If that sperm or egg becomes fertilized, and the fertilized cell starts dividing, every cell in the developing individual, including the sperm or egg cells, will contain that mutation. If that individual reproduces, the mutation may get passed on to the next generation.

Most mutations involve changes in the nucleotide sequence. This can alter the proteins that the cell produces. Some of these changes, however, are more serious than others. Most mutations have little effect. Often the mutation does not significantly alter the protein or change its function. Or the mutation occurs in a gene that is not particularly important.

Some mutations, however, are harmful or even deadly. For example, a mutation may occur in the gene that controls how often a cell divides. The mutated cell and its daughter cells divide uncontrollably. This can create a mass of cells called a **tumor.** The result can be cancer.

Mutations to sperm or egg cells can be especially problematic. Usually, harmful mutations prevent the embryo from forming. This will end the pregnancy. Offspring born with mutations are often seriously disabled. Conditions caused by mutations are called genetic disorders. Examples include sickle-cell anemia, cystic fibrosis, and hemophilia.

Every once in a while, a mutation will occur that actually benefits the organism. It gives the organism an advantage over other organisms in the species. As you will learn, these mutations help drive evolution.

Causes of Mutations

Energy and chemicals constantly bombard the cells in your body. Some of these agents can break up DNA. They can also interfere with replication, transcription, or translation. Agents that cause mutations are called **mutagens.** Energy mutagens include ultraviolet radiation from the sun, X rays, and radiation released from the decay of radioactive material. Chemical mutagens include many human-made pollutants, such as dioxin. Even some chemical preservatives such as nitrates can be mutagens. Other chemical mutagens occur naturally in the environment.

Mutations are relatively rare, despite the presence of all these mutagens. One reason that mutations are relatively rare is that DNA is a tough and resilient molecule. Consider the structure of the double helix. The sugar-phosphate backbone on the outside of the double helix shields the nitrogen bases on the inside from mutagens. Another reason mutations are rare is the fact that the DNA is tightly wound around the histone proteins, which further protects them. DNA can also repair itself. If only one strand of the double helix gets damaged, it can reassemble itself. This can be done based on the order of nucleotides in the intact strand. It is as if you had a photograph and a negative. If the photograph gets damaged, you can reproduce it using the negative. There are also enzymes that "inspect" the DNA for irregularities. If the enzyme encounters any irregularities, it cuts them out and repairs them. Still, some mutations do get through. Here are some types of mutations.

Substitutions

A **substitution** occurs when a nucleotide in the sequence is replaced by a different nucleotide. The following is an example.

A gene sequence and the protein it codes for:

> AGA TAC GTG CTG CAT (gene sequence)
>
> ser–met–his–asp–val (protein)

A gene sequence with substitution and the protein it codes for:

> AGA TAC G**G**G CTG CAT (gene sequence)
>
> ser–met–**pro**–asp–val (protein)

As you can see, the change from a T in the third codon to a G resulted in a different amino acid in the protein. Often, a change of a single amino acid does not affect the protein. Sometimes the effects are severe. Sickle-cell anemia results from such a substitution. Sickle-cell anemia is a genetic disorder that reduces the blood's ability to carry oxygen.

THINK ABOUT IT

Explain why some substitutions have absolutely no effect on the amino acid sequence of a protein. Write your answer on a separate sheet of paper.

Additions and Deletions

Sometimes a nucleotide will be added to or deleted from a sequence. As you will see, the effects are drastic. Here is an example.

AGA TAC GTG CTG CAT

ser–met–his–asp–val

Now see what happens when the C in the second codon is deleted.

AGA TAG TGC TGC AT . . .

ser–ser–thr–thr–

Note how the removal of a single nucleotide changes every codon down the line. As a result, the DNA codes for a completely different protein.

Chromosomal Mutations

Sometimes, entire sections of chromosomes break off. Usually, enzymes can splice the chromosomes back together. Sometimes during meiosis, the chromosome is not repaired in time. This is when one of the gametes ends up with an incomplete chromosome. The results are often fatal. Sometimes a piece that breaks off one chromosome becomes fused to a different chromosome. This mutation is called a translocation. Again, these types of mutations are often fatal.

Problems During Meiosis

Occasionally, during anaphase I or anaphase II of meiosis, the homologous chromosomes or sister chromatids do not separate. They travel to the same pole instead. As a result, one cell has an extra chromosome, and one cell has one too few chromosomes. This failure of chromosomes to separate properly is called **nondisjunction.** Compare the normal anaphase I and anaphase II of meiosis in the diagram on page 48 with the diagrams below.

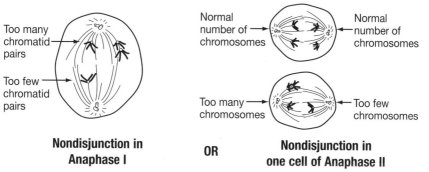

Too many chromatid pairs

Too few chromatid pairs

Normal number of → chromosomes

Normal number of ← chromosomes

Too many → chromosomes

Too few ← chromosomes

Nondisjunction in Anaphase I

OR

Nondisjunction in one cell of Anaphase II

Nondisjunction almost always results in the death of the unborn baby. Those individuals who do survive are almost always severely disabled, both mentally and physically. One of the least severe forms of nondisjunction is called Down's syndrome. People with Down's syndrome have three copies of chromosome 21 rather than two. Despite the physical and mental differences associated with this disorder, many people with Down's syndrome reach adulthood and lead happy, productive lives.

■ PRACTICE 12: Mutations

Look at the list of terms below. Fill in each line with the letter of the term that correctly completes each statement.

  a. translocation   **b.** mutagens   **c.** nondisjunction

1. Agents that cause mutations are called _____.

2. The failure of homologous chromosomes to separate during meiosis is called _____.

3. If a piece of one chromosome breaks off and fuses to another chromosome, it is called a _____.

LESSON 5: Genetics and Heredity

GOAL: To understand how traits get passed from generation to generation

WORDS TO KNOW

allele	heterozygous	Punnett square
codominance	homozygous	recessive
dominant	phenotype	sex-linked
genotype	polygenic traits	zygote

What Is Heredity?

So far, you have learned about the molecular basis of genetics. Most of your cells contain chromosomes. Each chromosome is made up of sequences of DNA called genes. Each gene contains instructions for the manufacture of specific proteins. These proteins determine specific traits. You have genes that determine your height, the texture of your hair, the digestive enzymes you produce, the number of fingers you have, and so on.

You have also learned how these genes are passed on from generation to generation. Certain cells undergo meiosis and form haploid gametes. The male gamete (sperm) and the female gamete (egg) fuse and create a diploid cell in a process called fertilization. This diploid cell contains chromosomes from the father and the mother. This cell, called a **zygote,** divides. All the subsequent cells contain exact copies of the chromosomes, and, therefore, exact copies of the genes.

It was not until the 1950s that scientists realized that DNA was the key molecule in genetics. However, interest in how traits got passed from generation to generation dates back much further. In fact, the first major breakthrough occurred 90 years earlier. The setting of this breakthrough was not what you would normally consider a scientific laboratory. Instead, it was the greenhouse of a monastery in what is now the Czech Republic.

Mendel's Experiments

Theories about inheritance date back to around 400 B.C.E. Hippocrates (a Greek physician who is considered the father of medicine) proposed then that different parts of the body (arms, legs, liver) somehow passed hereditary information in the form of a fluid to the reproductive organs. The fluids of the mother and the father combined to form the offspring. For over 2000 years, variations of this theory persisted. Then, in the 1880s, a German biologist named August Weismann conducted a series of experiments. He cut off the tails of mice and then bred them. If the theory of the time was accurate, the offspring of Weismann's mice would be born without tails. But the offspring did have tails. So Weismann proposed that hereditary information was contained in the "germ plasm" of gametes (sperm and egg). According to his blending theory of inheritance, the "germ plasm" from the parents blended together when the two gametes fused.

Weismann was correct about the gametes. But it is now known that he was incorrect about the blending. Look at Labrador retrievers as an example. There are Labrador retrievers with dark coats and Labrador retrievers with light coats. According to the blending theory, if a dark dog mates with a light dog, the puppies would all be a medium shade. Instead, a typical litter of Labrador retrievers consists of some dark puppies and some light puppies. In fact, it is possible to breed two dark dogs and get light puppies. Clearly, something else is going on.

The first person to decipher the true patterns of inheritance was an Augustinian abbot with a university education named Gregor Mendel (1822–1884). Mendel was a dedicated botanist and gardener. He also was a brilliant mathematician, statistician, and scientist. While living at a monastery in what is now the Czech Republic, Mendel undertook a series of intricate experiments. He crossbred several varieties of garden peas and examined how traits are passed from generation to generation.

Mendel chose varieties of pea plants that differed in seven traits that were easy to identify. For example, some strains produced round peas while others produced wrinkled peas. Some produced green peas while others produced yellow peas. Some varieties were short while others were tall. Mendel then crossbred different varieties of peas. He crossed round peas with wrinkled peas, yellow pods with green pods, and short plants with tall plants.

Mendel designated the first peas he crossbred the P generation. This stands for parental generation. He called the first generation of offspring F_1, for "first filial." *Filial* refers to sons or daughters. Each subsequent generation was designated F_2, F_3, and so on. Now look at the results of one such cross—yellow pods and green pods.

The first time Mendel crossed the yellow and green plants and planted the seeds, all of the offspring (the F_1 generation) produced green pods. The yellow pods seemed to have disappeared. Mendel then allowed the adult F_1 plants to fertilize themselves. (In pea plants, male gametes and female gametes from the same plant can fuse together and form a seed. In most plants, male gametes must fuse with female gametes from other plants.) When the pods emerged in the next generation of plants (F_2), Mendel found something very interesting. Three fourths of the F_2 plants produced green pods. The other one fourth produced yellow pods. Somehow, the F_1 plants still had the information for yellow pods. But the information remained hidden until it reappeared in the F_2 plants.

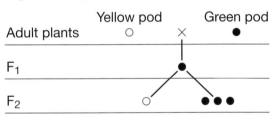

Mendel then let the F_2 plants fertilize themselves, and planted the seeds. The results became more interesting.

- Pure green and pure yellow pod plants produced all green pod plants.

- Two green pod plants produced three fourths green pod plants and one fourth yellow pod plants.

- Pure yellow pod plants produced all yellow pod plants.

Mendel found the same patterns when he crossbred strains of pea plants with those with other traits. For example, he crossed tall plants with

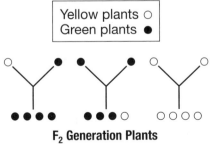

F₂ Generation Plants

short plants. All of the F_1 plants were tall. Of the F_2 plants, 25 percent were short. From these experiments, Mendel concluded the following. (Keep in mind that Mendel knew nothing about DNA, homologous chromosomes, or meiosis.)

- There are hereditary factors that determine each trait. Furthermore, there are two variants of each factor. In this case, the factor was pod color, and the two variants were yellow and green. Today, these factors are called genes. Each variant is called an **allele.**

- Each individual inherits two of each factor (or gene). One gene comes from the mother, and the other gene comes from the father.

- One variant (or allele) is dominant over the other. A **dominant** allele always shows itself. In this case, the green pod allele is dominant over the yellow pod allele. The nondominant allele (yellow) is termed recessive. A **recessive** trait will be hidden when a dominant one is present. There was a dominant allele and a recessive allele for every trait that Mendel tested.

Consider the three possible allele combinations that an individual pea plant can possess. It is standard to use the first letter of the dominant trait to symbolize each gene. The pod color gene for green will be designated G. Because the green allele is dominant, a capital G is used. The yellow allele is recessive, so a lowercase g is used.

Remember, each individual has two genes coding for the same trait. One is inherited from the mother and the other one from the father. So the possible combinations are GG, Gg, and gg. The GG individual has two green alleles, so the pods are green. The gg individual has two yellow alleles, so the pods are yellow. What about the Gg plant? Because green is dominant over yellow, the green allele hides the yellow allele. Therefore, this plant produces green pods.

A trait that you can see on an individual (green pods, wrinkled peas, short branches) is called a **phenotype.** The actual combination of alleles that code for this visible trait is called a **genotype.** In this case, there are two phenotypes—green pods and yellow pods. And there are three genotypes—GG, Gg, and gg. As you can see, you can determine the phenotype if you know the genotype. You cannot, however, always determine the genotype by looking at the phenotype. You know that plants with yellow pods have a gg genotype. But you do not know if a plant with green pods is GG or Gg.

Pure green:	GG ●
Pure yellow:	gg ○
Green:	Gg ●

Cross two P generation plants	GG ●	×	gg ○
Resulting F_1 generation	Gg ●		
Cross two F_1 generation plants	Gg ●	×	Gg ●
Resulting F_2 generation	GG/Gg ●●●		gg ○
Two possible crosses of F_2 plants	Gg ● × gg ○	OR	gg ○ × gg ○
Resulting F_3 generation	Gg ●● gg ○○		gg ○○○○

Three Possible Allele Combinations

Genotypes in which both alleles are the same (GG, gg) are called **homozygous.** Genotypes with one dominant allele and one recessive allele (Gg) are called **heterozygous.**

Genotype		Phenotype
GG	homozygous dominant	green pods
Gg	heterozygous	green pods
gg	homozygous recessive	yellow pods

■ PRACTICE 13: Mendel's Experiments

Read the following paragraph. Decide if each statement that follows is true (T) or false (F). Write the correct letter on each line.

Mendel crossed a long-stem variety of plant (tall) and a short-stem variety of plant (short). The F_1 plants were all tall. Of the F_2 plants, 75 percent were tall and 25 percent were short.

_____ 1. The dominant allele is tall.

_____ 2. The recessive allele is short.

_____ 3. If two short plants are crossed, the resulting next generation will be all tall plants.

_____ 4. The tall plants, when crossed, will produce more tall plants than short plants.

_____ 5. By the F_2 (third generation) of crossing the plants, all the plants will be tall again.

Punnett Squares

Each one of Mendel's crosses yielded a specific ratio of green pod plants to yellow pod plants. The F_1 generation contained 100 percent green pods. The F_2 generation had a ratio of three green pod plants to every one yellow pod plant. In other words, it was 3:1. To understand why these ratios occur, look at meiosis. Once again, keep in mind that Mendel did not know about chromosomes or meiosis, yet he still figured out these patterns.

As you remember, each cell contains pairs of homologous chromosomes. Each chromosome within the homologous pair contains a variation of the same gene (an allele). Both chromosomes may have a dominant allele (GG). Both chromosomes may have a recessive allele (gg). Or, one chromosome could have a dominant allele and the other a recessive allele (Gg).

Now look at what happens when a heterozygous cell undergoes meiosis and forms four haploid cells.

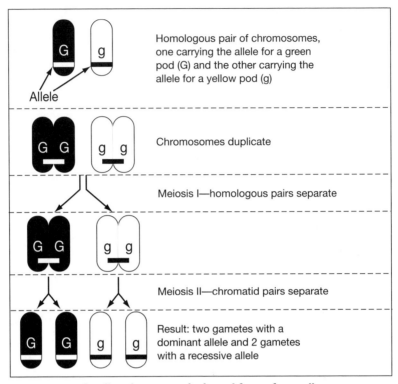

A cell undergoes meiosis and forms four cells

Now look at what happens if a heterozygous male is crossed with a heterozygous female. Each produces two gametes with dominant alleles and two gametes with recessive alleles. One of the male gametes fuses with only one of the female gametes. Which male gamete fuses with which female is completely random. There is a 50 percent chance that the male gamete that is fertilized will contain the dominant allele. Likewise, there is a 50 percent chance that the female gamete that is fertilized will contain the dominant allele. Now look at the possibilities.

- Male G fertilizes Female G = GG green pod—25%

- Male G fertilizes Female g = Gg green pod—25%

- Male g fertilizes Female G = Gg green pod—25%

- Male g fertilizes Female g = gg yellow pod—25%

Now look at the phenotype ratios—there are three green pods to every yellow pod. Does this ratio look familiar? It is the same ratio Mendel got in the F_2 generation.

TIP

You can see for yourself how these ratios work by flipping two coins. Say that heads (H) are dominant and tails (t) are recessive. Flip two coins simultaneously 100 times, and record your results. Then count the number of times HH, Hh, hH, and hh occurred. You should get roughly equal numbers of each combination.

There is an easier way to determine the probabilities of each genotype and phenotype. It is called a **Punnett square,** developed by British biologist Reginald C. Punnett. Here is how you set it up.

1. Draw a box and divide it into four equal squares.

2. On the top of the box, write the allele of each female gamete (G and g). On the left side of the box, write the allele of each male gamete (also G and g).

3. Then fill in each box with the allele combinations.

Once again, look at the genotype and phenotype ratios.

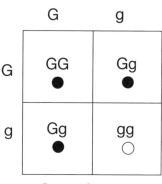

Punnett Square

Now set up a Punnett square that predicts the genotype and phenotype ratios of Mendel's first cross. As you remember, he crossed a green pod plant with a yellow pod plant. The green pod plant was homozygous dominant (GG) and the yellow pod plant was homozygous recessive (gg).

1. Set up the Punnett square. Write the possible female alleles on top and the possible male alleles on the left side. For the purpose of this square, say that the female is the green plant and that the male is the yellow plant.

2. Then fill in each square by combining the male and female alleles.

Female

	G	G
g	Gg ●	Gg ●
g	Gg ●	Gg ●

Male

Note that in this cross, all of the offspring have the same genotype. Each is heterozygous. As a result, each of the offspring has the same phenotype.

■ IN REAL LIFE

Maria had a history of cystic fibrosis in her family, so she was worried about having children. Cystic fibrosis is a recessive genetic disorder in which the lungs produce a thick mucus that inhibits breathing. Usually the life expectancy of people with cystic fibrosis is 30 years. She and her husband decided to see a genetic counselor. The genetic counselor studied the family histories of both Maria and her husband to see which relatives had had cystic fibrosis. From that information, she calculated the probability that one of their children would inherit the disease. In this case, the risk was small.

■ PRACTICE 14: Punnett Squares

Read the following sentence. Then follow the directions below to set up a Punnett square. Use GG for dominant, gg for recessive, and Gg for one dominant and one recessive allele.

A gardener crossed a male heterozygous green pod plant with a female yellow pod plant.

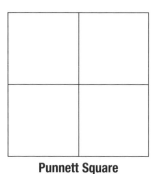

Punnett Square

1. Determine the genotype of the green pod plant. Determine the genotype of the yellow pod plant.

2. Now set up your Punnett square. What are the male alleles? What are the female alleles?

3. Now fill in the Punnett square. What are the allele combinations in each box?

4. What is the ratio of green pod offspring to yellow pod offspring? _____

Sex-Linked Traits

So far, you have studied genes that are present on autosomes. Now look at the sex chromosomes. In humans, females contain two X chromosomes and males contain an X chromosome and a Y chromosome. Using a Punnett square, you can determine the ratios of males to females.

As you can see, the ratio is 1:1. There is a 50 percent chance of the offspring being male and 50 percent chance of it being female.

What happens to genes that are present on the X chromosomes? Such genes are referred to as **sex-linked.** As you will learn, crosses produce remarkably different phenotype ratios when the genes are sex-linked than when the genes are on the autosomes. Here is why.

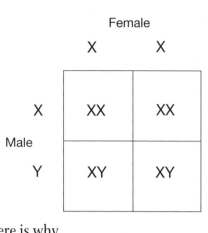

As you remember, females contain two homologous X chromosomes in their cells. Each chromosome has an allele for the same gene. Males, however, have an X and a Y. These two chromosomes are not homologous. Genes present on the X chromosome are not present on the Y chromosome. In fact, as far as is currently known, no genes are on the Y chromosome other than those that produce chemicals that make a male. Therefore, males have only a single copy of each gene.

Color blindness is a fairly common sex-linked trait. People who are color blind have difficulty distinguishing between red and green. The gene for color blindness is recessive. Here are the possible genotypes and phenotypes for males and females. B is used for normal vision and b for color blindness. Note how sex-linked traits are symbolized.

Female:	$X^B X^B$	$X^B X^b$	$X^b X^b$
	normal vision	normal vision	color blind
Male:	$X^B Y$	$X^b Y$	
	normal vision	color blind	

THINK ABOUT IT

Is it possible for a couple to have a color-blind daughter if only one of the parents is color-blind? Write your answer on a separate sheet of paper before reading on.

See how females have to inherit two recessive alleles to become color blind? Males only have to inherit one. As a result, most color-blind people are male.

Now see what happens when a homozygous female with normal vision and a color-blind male have children.

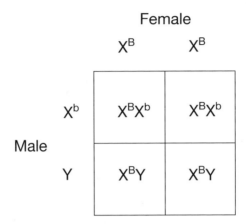

Female

	X^B	X^B
Male X^b	$X^B X^b$	$X^B X^b$
Y	$X^B Y$	$X^B Y$

All of the children have normal vision.

Now see what happens when a color-blind woman and a man with normal vision have children.

Female

	X^b	X^b
Male X^B	$X^B X^b$	$X^B X^b$
Y	$X^b Y$	$X^b Y$

Something very interesting happens. All of the girls have normal vision, but all of the boys are color blind.

■ PRACTICE 15: Sex-Linked Traits

Read the following paragraph. Then set up a Punnett square on another sheet of paper. Fill in the lines with the correct percentage based on your Punnett square. Use **GG** for dominant, **gg** for recessive, and **Gg** for one dominant and one recessive.

Hemophilia is a recessive, sex-linked trait. People with hemophilia lack an enzyme necessary for blood to clot. Therefore, they are in danger of bleeding to death every time they cut themselves. In the past, this condition was usually fatal. Fortunately, special blood transfusions have enabled hemophiliacs to live normal lives.

A normal male and a heterozygous female decide to start a family.

1. What are the chances that their daughter will have hemophilia?
   _____

2. What are the chances that the daughter will be heterozygous?
   _____

3. What are the chances that their son will have hemophilia? _____

4. If the son with hemophilia decides to start a family with a woman with hemophilia, what are the chances that his sons and daughters will have hemophilia? _____

Advances in Genetics

Mendel completed his work in 1865. Then he presented it to the local natural science society. They listened politely and quickly forgot about the presentation. Mendel received the same reaction from other established scientists. Even Charles Darwin, whose work on evolution would have benefited directly from Mendel, ignored Mendel's work. Knowing about genetics today, it seems strange that scientists during that time could overlook something that was so important. It is important to remember, however, that Mendel's approach was very different from that of his contemporaries. His methods and the way he used mathematics were radical at the time. Most scientists did not understand what he was doing.

In 1900, three scientists in different countries rediscovered his work. Sixteen years after Mendel died, he became one of the most famous scientists of all time.

The field of genetics has exploded since the 1950s discovery of DNA's role in heredity. You will now learn some of the advances in the study of genetics. You will also learn how genetics is being applied to people's lives.

Gene Interactions

When Mendel did his crosses, he purposefully chose traits that had two clear-cut alternatives. There was tall and there was short. There were green pods and yellow pods, wrinkled peas and smooth peas. Most traits are not that straightforward. Consider height in people. People are not simply tall or short. Instead, the range of heights is infinite. In this case, more than one gene is involved. Traits that are determined by more than one gene are called **polygenic traits.**

Some genes have more than two possible alleles. Of course, each person has no more than two of the alleles. One of the most important examples is blood type. There are three possible alleles—A, B, and O. Therefore, the possible genotypes are AA, AB, AO, BB, BO, and OO. It is critical that you know your blood type if you are going to receive a transfusion. That is because if you have type A blood (AA) and you get a transfusion of blood that contains a B allele (AB, BB, or BO), your immune system will attack the new blood. The results can be fatal. Likewise, if you are type B (BB) and you get a transfusion of blood with an A allele, your immune system will attack the blood that contains A. People with type O blood (OO) have the most difficulty getting a transfusion because their immune systems will attack blood that contains A or B.

IN REAL LIFE

People with type O blood cannot receive transfusions of other blood types, but they can give transfusions. If someone needs a transfusion but their blood type is not known—for example, if the person was in a car crash— doctors can safely give the person type O blood.

Blood type is also an example of a second genetic principle. This principle is called **codominance.** The A and B alleles are neither dominant nor recessive. So one does not hide the other. The O allele, however, is recessive. So A and B alleles will be dominant over the O allele. Another example of codominance occurs in some cattle. There are two alleles that determine coat color. Cows that are homozygous for one allele have red coats. Cows that are homozygous for the other allele have white coats. Cows that are heterozygous have pink or roan coats. If you look carefully, however, you will see that these coats have a mixture of red and white hairs. Both alleles are expressing themselves.

Just as a dominant gene can override a recessive allele, one gene can override, or dominate, another gene. Here is an example. In mice, there are two genes that determine coat color. The first gene can be called B for pigment. Mice with the dominant alleles (BB, Bb) are black. Homozygous recessive mice (bb) are brown. Now bring in the second gene, which can be called P for pigment. Mice with the dominant allele (PP, Pp) do produce pigment, but the color of the pigment depends on the genotype of the B gene. Mice that are homozygous recessive for the P gene (pp) do not produce any pigment. So they are white. The genotype of the B gene no longer matters because the P gene has overridden it.

Black mouse	Brown mouse	White mouse
BB or Bb and PP or Pp	bb and PP or Pp	BB, Bb, or bb and pp

Of course, not all traits are determined by genes alone. The environment is also an important factor. An oak tree may be especially tall because of its genes. But it also may be tall because it is growing in a spot where it gets plenty of nutrients, water, and sunlight.

Mapping Genes

To find the root causes of many diseases, researchers are turning to genes. They are searching for specific genes associated with genetic disorders. Not only are they finding the place on the chromosome where these genes are located, they are also decoding the nucleotide sequence. They have identified the genes for cystic fibrosis, muscular dystrophy, Tay Sachs disease, sickle-cell anemia, and, recently, have found a gene associated with breast cancer in women. Every human gene has been mapped in a project called the Human Genome Project, completed in 2003.

Understanding the genetic basis of a disease can help researchers understand how a disease works. Researchers can determine what enzyme the defective gene codes for. Such knowledge may lead to a cure. Doctors are also able to identify which people may be susceptible to certain diseases by examining their DNA for certain genes.

However, there are also potential pitfalls.

- Not all genetic conditions can be traced to a single gene. Interactions between genes can be complex. For example, a certain genotype in males may increase the risk of heart disease, while that same genotype in females may decrease the risk. Environmental factors and behaviors (eating habits, exercise) also are factors in determining a person's risk for heart disease.

- There are important privacy issues. Already, people can be tested for the presence of certain harmful genes that increase their risk of getting a disease. Who should have access to this information? Insurance companies? Employers? These are important issues that have to be dealt with as more is discovered about heredity and genetics.

■ PRACTICE 16: Advances in Genetics

Look at the list of terms below. Fill in each line with the letter of the term that correctly completes each statement.

a. codominance   **b.** Human Genome Project   **c.** polygenic

1. When alleles are neither dominant nor recessive, _____ occurs.

2. Traits that are determined by many genes are called _____ traits.

3. The massive task in which scientists mapped every human gene is called the _____.

LESSON 6: Evolution

WORDS TO KNOW

adaptation	gene pool	sexual reproduction
behavioral adaptation	natural selection	speciation
evolution	physical adaptation	species
fitness	populations	variation
fossil record	resource partitioning	

Adaptation and Variation

Adaptation

A **species** is a group of plants, animals, or fungi that share most characteristics in common. An **adaptation** is a change in a species that helps the species survive in a particular environment. When the change is physical, it is called a **physical adaptation.** For example, seals have thick layers of fat that help them survive in frigid water. Plants have colorful flowers that attract pollinators. When the change is in the way an organism acts, or behaves, it is called a **behavioral adaptation.** For example, wolves hunt most effectively in packs. Birds migrate north every spring to feed on the numerous insects.

Adaptations do not happen instantly. A giraffe cannot decide to grow a longer neck so that it can reach higher into a tree. A cheetah does not suddenly become faster so that it can catch faster prey. Adaptations develop over many generations. This gradual change in organisms over time is called **evolution.** In this lesson, you will learn about the forces that drive evolution.

Variation

No two people are the same. Everybody has a unique set of characteristics. The same is true for all organisms. No two cheetahs are the same. No two oak trees are the same. This **variation** is one of the keys to evolution—and the survival of all organisms.

To understand why these variations exist, you first need to go inside your cells. You have learned that all cells contain a chemical called DNA. In complex cells, the DNA is wrapped into tight bundles called chromosomes. These chromosomes are inside the nucleus of the cell.

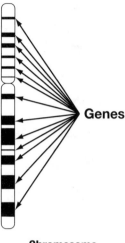

Genes

Chromosome

Think of DNA as a library of instruction books for making proteins. Your body is affected by which proteins your cells make. Chromosomes are the DNA "instruction books." Human cells contain 23 pairs of these chromosomes. Each chromosome "book" contains many "chapters" called genes. Each gene contains instructions for one individual trait. For example, there is a gene for eye color; there is another gene for how tall you grow.

Review these facts.

■ A gene is a set of DNA instructions for an individual trait, such as height or eye color.

■ Genes are contained in chromosomes.

■ Chromosomes are made from DNA.

Everybody has a unique set of genes. Therefore, no two individuals are the same. Look at how this variation comes about.

You were produced through **sexual reproduction.** In other words, you inherited half your genes from your mother and half from your father. That is why you resemble your parents. You are not, however, identical to your parents. The genes from your parents were shuffled together to form a unique combination. For example, you may have inherited your mother's eyes and your father's hair.

Now think about what would happen if you were produced asexually— in other words, if you only had a single parent. You would inherit all of that parent's genes. Therefore, you would look exactly like that parent. Your children would inherit all of your genes and would look exactly like you. If everybody was produced asexually, there would be far less variation.

TIP

You can compare your parents' sets of genes to playing cards. One parent's cards have a lot of clubs but few diamonds. The other parent's cards have a lot of diamonds but few clubs. When you shuffle them together, you come up with a new combination of suits. The new combination of cards will have roughly equal numbers of diamonds and clubs. In the same way, you are born with a new combination of genes.

You do not always inherit perfect copies of genes from your parents. Sometimes there are changes in the genes called mutations. Some mutations can drastically change an individual. Some can be helpful. Some can be fatal. Most have no effect at all. They can, however, increase variation.

Without genetic variation, there could be no evolution. Every organism would be exactly the same.

■ PRACTICE 17: Adaptation and Variation

Look at the list of words below. Fill in each line with the letter of the word that correctly completes each statement.

    a. variation   **d.** sexual reproduction
    b. genes   **e.** chromosomes
    c. mutation

1. Bundles of DNA found inside every cell are called _____.

2. DNA instructions for a single trait are called _____.

3. A change in DNA that is passed from parents to children is called a _____.

4. _____ is the difference in organisms due to the presence of different genes.

5. The process by which male and female cells from two individuals combine is called _____.

Natural Selection

Natural selection is the process that drives evolution. Over time, it causes the species with beneficial genes to increase and the species with less beneficial genes to decrease. Two British naturalists, Charles Darwin and Alfred Wallace, developed this theory. Darwin first published the theory in 1838 in *The Origin of Species.*

Darwin's theory of natural selection made four major points.

■ Not only do species differ from one another, individuals within species vary. Just as no two people are alike, no two finches, no two iguanas, and no two giraffes are exactly the same.

■ Most of this variation is inherited.

■ **Populations** (groups of plants or animals of the same species that occupy a certain area and interbreed) usually produce more offspring than the environment can sustain.

■ Only those individuals best adapted to their environment survive to produce offspring.

Natural Selection in Action

Look at an example of natural selection in action.

Cheetahs are the fastest mammals alive today. They can reach over 90 kilometers per hour over a short distance. They use this speed to chase down fast animals such as gazelles and impalas.

Cheetahs have several adaptations that allow them to reach these speeds. They have long legs. They have flexible spines that allow them to stretch as they run and to turn quickly. They have large lungs and hearts so they can take in lots of oxygen. Their claws provide extra traction when they run.

Cheetahs first appeared on the African plains 3.5 million years ago. Of course, nobody was around then to see what happened. Modern humans would not evolve for another 3 million years. But scientists have a good idea about what happened.

Grasslands had just appeared. They were filled with animals of all sizes. There were lions that hunted the larger animals. There were also saber-toothed cats, now extinct, that hunted the really big animals. The cheetahs had to chase smaller prey. However, these smaller animals were fast.

Here is what scientists think happened.

1. There was natural variation among the cheetahs. Maybe some had longer legs than others. Maybe some had larger lungs than others. The result of these variations was that some cheetahs could run faster than others.

2. The faster cheetahs had an advantage over the slower cheetahs. They could catch more prey. Therefore, they ate better, were healthier, and lived longer.

3. Because they were healthier, the faster cheetahs produced more cubs than the slower cheetahs.

4. The faster cheetahs could take better care of their cubs. They caught more food to feed the cubs. Therefore, their cubs lived to become adults.

5. This next generation of cheetahs was also fast. The fastest of these cheetahs produced the most cubs.

6. Over many generations, the number of fast cheetahs increased. The number of slow cheetahs decreased.

Now look at the theory of natural selection and how it relates to the cheetahs. Remember that all the traits discussed are controlled by genes.

■ There is genetic variation in all species. For example, some cheetahs had longer legs than others.

- Some individuals have genes that give them an advantage over other individuals. Cheetahs with longer legs ran faster and caught more animals.

- Individuals with these beneficial genes produce more young. They pass these genes on to the next generation. Individuals with less advantageous genes produce fewer young or no young at all. They do not pass their genes on to the next generation. The faster cheetahs produced more cubs, which were also fast.

- The young that inherit the beneficial genes are more likely to reproduce and pass on their genes. Over many generations, the number of individuals with the beneficial genes increases. The number with less beneficial genes decreases or disappears. The fastest of the next generation of cheetahs produced the most cubs. The number of slow cheetahs decreased.

The cheetah example shows how natural selection can drive evolution. The ability to run fast developed in cheetahs as an adaptation to life on the African plains. These changes probably occurred over thousands (or tens of thousands) of years. Here is an example of how natural selection might act quickly, perhaps over just a few generations.

Suppose a new disease is introduced into a population of moose. Most of the moose die from the disease. However, a few moose have genes that help them fight the disease. They survive and reproduce, passing the gene to their young. Eventually, all moose in the population have genes protecting them from the disease.

THINK ABOUT IT

African wild dogs live on the African plains. They live in large family groups and hunt in big packs. There are perhaps 3000 to 4000 left in all of Africa. Recently, entire packs of these dogs started dying from a disease called canine distemper. Scientists worry that because there are so few animals left, they may not be able to develop an immunity to the disease. Explain why. Write your answer on a separate sheet of paper.

Often, species do not need to experience adaptations to survive in their environments. They are doing just fine. After all, cheetahs in Africa have stayed the same for the past 3 million years or so.

Here is an example of how natural selection could actually prevent change. Arctic hares (a type of rabbit) live in the far north, where there is snow much of the year. Most of the hares have white fur that blends in with the snow. Predators, such as foxes and owls, have a difficult time seeing them. But suppose there is a mutation that turns some of the hares black. Black-furred hares are easy to spot in the white snow, so predators would have an easy time catching them. It is unlikely that a black arctic hare could live long enough to reproduce and pass on its genes. Therefore, the black gene would likely disappear from the population.

Fitness

You may have heard the phrase "survival of the fittest." Charles Darwin used this phrase when describing natural selection. This phrase is often misunderstood. People think it means that only the strongest survive, but that is not correct.

Fitness is an individual's ability to reproduce and pass on its genes. Adaptations, such as the cheetah's increased speed, increase fitness. Adaptations in trees to reduce water loss increase fitness. Adaptations in behavior, such as birds taking care of their young, increase fitness. Adaptations that help an animal attract a mate increase fitness. But no matter how strong, fast, or smart an animal is, if it fails to reproduce or if its young do not survive, its fitness is zero. It will not pass its genes to the next generation.

Fitness can only be compared among individuals within a species. A mother lion that gives birth to and successfully raises four healthy cubs a year is twice as fit as a lion that only raises two cubs. However, the fitness of a lion cannot be compared to the fitness of a mosquito that may produce many thousands of offspring.

■ PRACTICE 18: Natural Selection

Decide if the following characteristics increase fitness (**I**) or decrease fitness (**D**). Write the correct letter on each line.

_____ **1.** A cheetah runs fast, enabling it to catch more food for its young.

_____ **2.** A tree puts all of its energy into growing tall so it can absorb more sunlight. As a result, the tree has no energy to produce flowers and seeds.

_____ **3.** A deer hides during the day and feeds at night to avoid being seen by predators.

_____ **4.** A male bird has bright feathers to attract mates.

_____ **5.** A strong, aggressive wolf dominates all the other wolves. It even attacks potential mates.

Evolution in Action

Evolution and natural selection take place over a long period of time. This period of time is normally so long that scientists cannot observe it happening in their lifetimes. There are, however, some notable exceptions. An ongoing example has been developing in North America ever since colonists began arriving from Europe. When the colonists arrived, they brought plants, such as apple trees, with them from their home countries. These plants created a new source of food for species that already lived in North America.

One of those species was a fly that depended on the native hawthorn tree for its survival. The fly would deposit its eggs on the fruit of the hawthorn tree. The eggs would hatch into larvae, referred to as maggots, and the maggots would eat the fruit. The maggots would then go into a pupa stage and emerge from the pupae as adults. The adults would reproduce, and the cycle would start over.

By the 1860s, apple growers in the United States discovered that maggots hatched from hawthorn fly eggs had begun feeding on apples.

(This has led farmers and scientists to refer to the fly as the "apple maggot fly.") At some point since the introduction of apples, some of the fly population had begun to lay eggs on apples rather than on hawthorn fruit. It is likely that this happened by accident. The maggots that hatched on apples had better circumstances than the maggots hatching on hawthorn fruit. The apples provided 200 times more food. The apples also provided greater depth for maggots to burrow in. This gave them protection from birds and from a parasitic wasp.

However, the maggots that hatched on the apples also faced some challenges in their new circumstances. The apples were not as good a food source as the hawthorn fruit in terms of nutrition. Also, the maggots on the apples faced competition from caterpillars and other consumers. Maggots that hatched on hawthorn fruit continued to thrive.

Some of the maggots that hatched on apples did well, too. They lived to pass on a new generation of flies that would use apples as a food source. Over time, the life cycle of the flies adapted to match the life cycle of the apple tree. The new adults would hatch just in time for the apples to ripen. Apples ripen about a month earlier than hawthorn fruit, although there is some overlap. Because the life cycle of the flies that hatch on apples now differs from the life cycle of the flies that hatch on hawthorn fruit, the two groups no longer mate.

Presently, the two groups of apple maggot fly are considered to be the same species. They look exactly the same, and their life cycles happen in the same way. But the timing of their life cycles is completely different. Researchers believe that this is evidence that the two groups will eventually be two species.

Scientists are especially interested in how new species evolve. Remember that a species is a group of plants, animals, or fungi that share most characteristics in common. In most cases, appearance alone can determine whether two plants or two animals are members of the same species. More importantly, individuals of the same species must be able to interbreed and produce fertile offspring. In other words, members of a species share a gene pool. The **gene pool** is the whole amount of all the genotypes within the population. Dogs can breed with dogs, but they cannot breed with cats. Therefore, dog genes and cat genes do not mix. If a horse and a donkey mate, they produce a mule. Mules, however, are sterile. Therefore, horses and donkeys are considered different species.

For the most part, scientists can make pretty good guesses about which species evolved from which. One source of information is the **fossil record.** Fossils are created when the footprints or body parts of organisms are buried in sand or sediment. Over time, calcium in an organism's bone, shells, or other hard tissues becomes mineralized as the sediment is changed to rock. Scientists are able to learn a lot about what an animal or a plant may have looked like based on these fossil remains. They are also able to date the fossils based on the age of the rock in which they are found. By studying the fossil record, scientists can see the changes that took place over time.

Scientists compare traits of living organisms. Cells from plants, animals, and fungi have the same type of cell membranes, organelles, and DNA. They divide the same way. They even contain many of the same genes. Scientists can look at the evolutionary relationships between species by comparing the DNA sequences. The more similar the sequences, the closer the evolutionary relationship.

Speciation

Scientists now have a pretty good idea of how new species form. Determining why new species form is trickier. You will learn about one of the most famous examples of **speciation** (the origin of new species in evolution)—the Darwin finches of the Galápagos Islands.

Darwin made many of his observations while he was the naturalist aboard a ship called the *HMS Beagle.* The ship surveyed South America from 1831 to 1835. During Darwin's voyage on the *Beagle,* he traveled to the Galápagos Islands—a group of volcanic islands 600 miles off the coast of Ecuador. While on these islands, he collected 13 species of finches. Each species had unique diets and feeding habits. Some were ground feeders; others lived in trees. There were seed-eaters, insect-eaters, fruit-eaters, and bud-eaters. One species actually used cactus needles to probe trees for insects the same way that woodpeckers probe for insects with their bills. The differences between the finches were in their beaks. Seed-eaters had

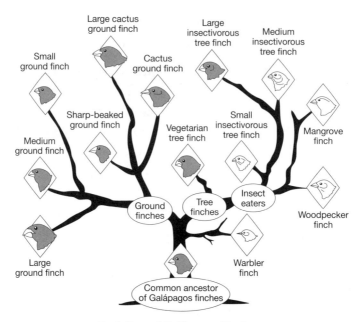

Evolution of Galápagos Finches

large, thick bills suitable for crushing seeds. Insect-eaters had smaller, delicate beaks that they used to pick off insects.

How did all these species come about? Here is what scientists think happened. About 10,000 years ago, a storm blew several seed-eating finches to the islands. Because the islands were new, the finches did not encounter any other land birds. With so much to eat, the finches thrived and colonized all of the islands. Each island contained a separate population of finches. These populations rarely interbred. Through natural selection, different bills developed in the finches that allowed them to use more resources on each island. Eventually, each population evolved to the point where they could not breed with birds from other islands. They had become separate species.

Here is the most important requirement of speciation. With few exceptions, speciation can only occur when two populations become isolated from each other and form separate gene pools. Populations can be physically isolated. For example, the finch populations were separated by water. Mountain ranges might separate other populations. Or two populations may live in different habitats. One may live in grasslands while the other lives in forests. If the two populations were to interbreed, the gene pools would mix. The changes between the two populations would become diluted, and speciation would not occur.

Eventually, all of the finch species colonized every island. Then they faced a new type of evolutionary force—competition for resources. Here is an example. Say species A has a medium-sized beak suitable for eating medium seeds. Species B has a smaller beak that allows it to eat seeds as well as a few insects. Species B arrives on species A's island. Now there are two species competing for medium-sized seeds. The supply starts to run out. But some species A individuals have slightly larger beaks than the others. They can eat seeds that are too large for species B. These individuals eat more food, produce more offspring, and pass on their genes. Likewise, species B individuals with smaller beaks are able to include more insects in their diet. They produce the most offspring and pass on their genes. After many generations, species A only eats large seeds and species B only eats insects. They no longer compete. The result on the Galápagos Islands is 13 species of finches with specialized diets.

Resource partitioning is when organisms live in the same geographic area and consume slightly different foods or use resources in slightly different ways. This is apparently quite common among plants and animals. Rather than competing with one another for the same food or space to live, they specialize.

■ PRACTICE 19: Evolution in Action

Decide if each statement that follows is true (**T**) or false (**F**). Write the correct letter on each line.

_____ **1.** Scientists can study evolutionary relationships between species by comparing DNA.

_____ **2.** According to the definition of a species, two individuals from different species cannot breed and produce fertile offspring.

_____ **3.** Speciation occurs when two populations interbreed.

_____ **4.** The Darwin finch story is an example of resource partitioning.

LESSON 7: Organizing Life

GOAL: To understand how organisms are classified

WORDS TO KNOW

ancestor	division	mnemonic
classes	families	orders
classification	genera (plural of *genus*)	phylum (plural *phyla*)
classify	kingdoms	taxonomy

Classification

Evolution is like a tree. You can start with one species. Say this ancestral species evolves into two new species. You can call them Species A and Species B. Even though A and B are now different species, they still share most of the same genes, since they evolved from a common **ancestor.** Over time, A splits into two new species, Species 1 and Species 2. B splits into Species 3 and Species 4. Species 1 and 2 share many characteristics, but they share fewer characteristics with Species 3 and 4.

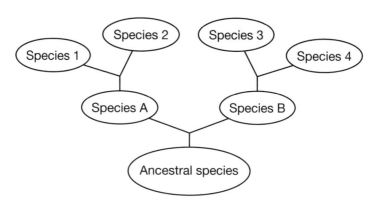

Scientists study living plants and animals and the fossils of extinct organisms, and compare their physical characteristics. Then they group together, or **classify,** those organisms that have features in common. The **classification** system used to show these relationships is called **taxonomy.**

The broadest categories are the **kingdoms.** The six basic kingdoms of life cover all living things. The kingdoms are archaebacteria, bacteria, protists, fungi, plants, and animals.

The kingdoms are divided into smaller groups. The broadest group within each kingdom is a **phylum** (plural *phyla*). Each phylum is divided into groups called **classes.** Classes are in turn subdivided into **orders,** then **families,** then **genera** (the plural form of *genus*), then species. A species is any group of organisms that can reproduce together and produce offspring that are fertile. This is the smallest group in any kingdom.

TIP

To help you remember the order of the taxonomic groups, memorize this sentence. <u>K</u>ing <u>P</u>hilip <u>C</u>ould <u>O</u>rder <u>F</u>ried <u>G</u>iraffe <u>S</u>andwiches. The first letter of each word corresponds with the first letters of <u>K</u>ingdom, <u>P</u>hylum, <u>C</u>lass, <u>O</u>rder, <u>F</u>amily, <u>G</u>enus, and <u>S</u>pecies.

The Six Kingdoms

Here is an overview of the six kingdoms. You will learn about each kingdom in detail in later lessons.

ARCHAEBACTERIA

All organisms in this kingdom are single-celled, with no cell nucleus. They include organisms that live in harsh environments, such as areas with very salty water, or those that are very hot. Most archaebacteria do not need oxygen to survive.

BACTERIA

All bacteria are also single-celled, with no cell nucleus. Some bacteria cause diseases such as Lyme disease. Some, such as the bacteria that turn milk into yogurt, are very useful.

PROTISTS

These are simple organisms, with cell walls and nuclei. Many are single-celled, but some have many cells. Protists include algae, protozoans, and slime molds.

FUNGI

These organisms have cell walls, similar to plants, but they do not produce chlorophyll. Fungi include mushrooms, molds, and yeasts.

PLANTS

Organisms in the plant kingdom have many specialized cells with cell walls. They use chlorophyll and sunlight to make food.

ANIMALS

All animals have many specialized cells. They do not have cell walls or chlorophyll. Animals do not produce their own food; instead, they eat other organisms. Animals include insects, fish, birds, and mammals.

Here is how the African lion is classified.

- Kingdom: Animalia

- Phylum: Chordata. This phylum includes all animals with backbones.

- Class: Mammalia. This class includes all animals that have fur and mammary glands.

- Order: Carnivora. This order includes meat-eating mammals, such as cats, dogs, bears, weasels, seals, and raccoons.

- Family: Felidae. This family includes all cats.

- Genus: *Panthera*. This genus also includes tigers, leopards, and jaguars.

- Species: *Panthera leo*. This species only includes the African lion.

Scientists always refer to a species by both its genus and species names. The genus name is always capitalized, and both the genus and species are written in italics. So sugar maples are *Acer saccharinum;* bald eagles are *Haliaeetus leucocephalus;* humans are *Homo sapiens. Homo* is the genus name, and *sapiens* is the species name. After you have written it once, you can shorten the genus name to the first initial: *H. sapiens.*

Classifying organisms is not always easy. Some species share similar characteristics but are not closely related. For example, both birds and bats can fly. Bats, however, are in the class Mammalia. Birds are in the class Aves. Both developed the ability to fly independently. Scientists are constantly changing how they classify organisms as they gather more information. Until recently, scientists said that fungi were plants.

IN REAL LIFE

It seems hard to believe, but Chihuahuas, poodles, and Labrador retrievers are all the same species—dog. They are just different varieties.

■ PRACTICE 20: Classification

Circle the letter of the answer that correctly completes each of the following statements.

1. The animals that share the most genes are _____.
   a. animals in the same class
   b. animals in the same family
   c. animals in the same order
   d. animals in the same genus

2. The first division in taxonomy is called _____.
   a. kingdom
   b. order
   c. genus

3. The scientific name for the humpback whale is *Megaptera novaengliae*. These two words are the whale's _____.
   a. kingdom and class
   b. order and species
   c. genus and species
   d. family and genus

4. There are _____ kingdoms in the taxonomy model that is in current use.
   a. 6
   b. 4
   c. 2

UNIT 1 REVIEW

Circle the letter of the correct answer to each of the following questions.

1. What principle(s) did Redi's and Pasteur's experiments demonstrate?
   a. All organisms require energy.
   b. All organisms come from other living organisms like themselves.
   c. Life formed between 3.5 and 4 billion years ago.
   d. Bacteria reproduce by dividing.

2. Which of the following is true about diffusion in cells?
   a. It requires the expenditure of energy.
   b. Enzymes speed it up.
   c. Molecules move from an area of low concentration to an area of high concentration.
   d. The diffusion of water is called osmosis.

3. Which of the following is true about the nucleus?
   a. It is surrounded by a single phospholipid membrane.
   b. It is where glycolysis occurs.
   c. It is the site of protein synthesis.
   d. It contains the cell's DNA and RNA.

4. Which of the following processes involves the breakdown of ATP?
   a. the light phase of photosynthesis
   b. the dark phase of photosynthesis
   c. inactive transport
   d. passive transport

5. Which nucleic acids contain anticodons?
   a. DNA
   b. mRNA
   c. tRNA
   d. rRNA

6. To which part of the DNA nucleotide do the letters A, T, C, and G refer?
   a. the phosphate group
   b. the nitrogen base
   c. the deoxyribose
   d. the amino acid group

7. Which of the following is true about the synthesis of mRNA?
   a. It occurs outside the nucleus.
   b. No enzymes are involved.
   c. It follows the assembly of amino acids into proteins.
   d. It takes place along an unraveled section of DNA.

8. Which is NOT a source of genetic variation among individuals?
   a. acquired traits
   b. mutations
   c. dominant and recessive alleles
   d. sexual reproduction

9. Which of the following situations will likely lead to speciation?
   a. Individuals from one population breed with individuals from a second population.
   b. Two populations are physically separated from each other.
   c. Two populations occupy the same habitat type.
   d. Two populations compete for the same food.

10. Which is the narrowest classification of organisms?
   a. species
   b. genus
   c. kingdom
   d. class

UNIT 1 APPLICATION ACTIVITY 1
Diffusion through a Selective Membrane

To see how diffusion works, try this experiment.

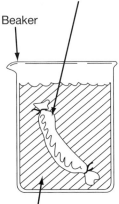

Dialysis tube with starch solution

Beaker

Fold over and tie off one end of a 30-cm piece of dialysis tubing with string. Pour a starch solution into the tube until the tube is two-thirds full. Fold over and tie off the other end of the tube with string. Weigh the filled tube bag, and record the weight in the chart below before continuing.

Fill a 250-ml beaker with distilled water. Add five drops of iodine to the water. This will turn the water a yellow-orange color. Place the tube bag into the beaker. Allow the bag to stay in the iodine water for 10 to 20 minutes. Iodine is an indicator for starch. It will turn from yellow-orange to blue-black when it comes into contact with starch.

Water with 5 drops iodine (yellow/orange color)

Remove the tubing from the water, dry it, and weigh it again. Record the weight in the chart.

Beginning weight of tube bag	
Weight of tube bag after water	

1. Observe the water in the beaker. What color is it?

_____

2. Observe the starch solution in the tube. What color is it?

_____

3. What does this tell you about the tubing as a membrane?

_____

_____

_____

4. Compare the weights of the tube before and after being put into the 250-ml beaker of water. How can you account for the weight change?

_____

_____

_____

_____

_____

UNIT 1 APPLICATION ACTIVITY 2
Comparing Plant and Animal Cells

Using prepared slides of animal and plant cells, observe each cell type under a microscope. Look at the plant cell slide, and identify the cell wall, cytoplasm, nucleus, and chloroplasts. The cell membrane will be there, but it will be very difficult to see because it is so close to the cell wall. Draw a diagram of the plant cell on a separate sheet of paper. Label the organelles you can identify.

Look at the animal cell slide, and identify the cell membrane, nucleus, and cytoplasm. Depending on the quality of your microscope and the slide, you may be able to see mitochondria. Draw the animal cell on a separate sheet of paper. Label the organelles you can identify.

On the lines on the next page, compare the two diagrams. How do they differ? (Use a separate sheet of paper if you need more space to explain.)

_____

_____

_____

_____

_____

_____

_____

_____

UNIT 1 APPLICATION ACTIVITY 3
Genetic Probability Is Like Flipping a Coin

Geneticists use probability to predict the results of genetic crosses. For this activity, you only need a coin—any coin will do. Before you toss the coin, predict the possible outcomes. Suppose you tossed the coin 20 times. Record your estimates in the chart below. Calculate the percentage of time your coin would come up heads and the percentage of time it would come up tails. (To find the percentage, divide your prediction by the total number of tosses, and then multiply by 100.)

Now test your predictions. Flip the coin 20 times. Record in the chart below the number of times the coin lands heads up and the number of times it lands tails up. Calculate and record the percentages. Combine your results with those of other learners.

	Your Toss		Combined Tosses	
	Predicted	Actual	Predicted	Actual
No. of heads				
No. of tails				
Percentage (heads)				
Percentage (tails)				

1. How accurate were your predictions? _____

2. Are the combined results closer to your predictions? _____
   _____
   _____

3. How does this coin toss relate to genetics? _____
   _____
   _____

UNIT 1 APPLICATION ACTIVITY 4
A Model of Meiosis

Construct a model of meiosis for an imaginary organism that has a total diploid number of four chromosomes.

On a sheet of paper, draw a circle 15 cm in diameter. The circle represents a parent cell that is about to undergo meiosis. Arrange four pipe cleaners, two white and two red, randomly inside the circle. The pipe cleaners represent two pairs of homologous chromosomes.

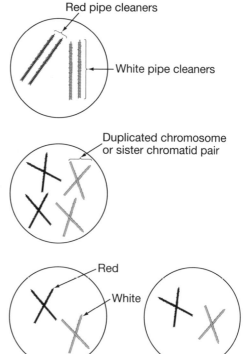

Place another white pipe cleaner next to each of the white pipe cleaners. Place another red pipe cleaner next to each of the red pipe cleaners. Pinch the pipe cleaners together. These pipe cleaners represent duplicated chromosomes—called sister chromatids. This duplication occurs before meiosis begins.

On a second sheet of paper, draw two 15-cm circles side by side. These two circles represent the two new cells produced during meiosis I. Divide the doubled "chromosomes" equally between the two new cells. Be careful to keep the "chromatids" together.

You have now separated homologous chromosomes.

Now draw four 15-cm circles side by side on a third sheet of paper. These circles represent the four sex cells that are the result of meiosis II. Separate the "chromatid pairs." Place one of each type of chromosome in each cell.

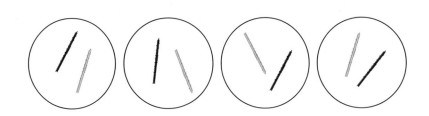

1. How do these cells compare to the cell you began with?

   _____

   _____

2. Why is it important that each sex cell have only half the normal number of chromosomes found in body cells?

   _____

   _____

3. Meiosis is often referred to as reduction division. What does this mean? _____

   _____

   _____

   _____

   _____

   _____

UNIT 2

Simple Organisms

LESSON 8: Archaebacteria and Eubacteria

GOAL: To learn about archaebacteria and eubacteria

WORDS TO KNOW

anaerobic	flagella
antibiotics	gram-negative
archaebacteria	gram-positive
bacilli (singular *bacillus*)	microscopic
bacteria (singular *bacterium*)	nucleoid
binary fission	prokaryote
cocci (singular *coccus*)	spirilla (singular *spirillum*)
eubacteria	viruses

The Oldest Life-Forms

Bacteria were probably the first life-forms on Earth. They are living things, but they are neither plants nor animals. These single-celled organisms lack most of the structures present in plant and animal cells. Yet they are still the most numerous and successful organisms on Earth. They can survive in any environment. They are found on the tops of the highest mountains and at the bottom of the deepest oceans. Some live in extremely salty water. Some live in rocks and ice. Some live in the roots of plants, or in the intestines of animals. There are more of them in your mouth right now than there are people in the world! But you have probably never seen one. This is because bacteria are microscopic. They are so small they can only be seen when magnified by a microscope.

These organisms have a cell wall, but do not have a true nucleus. The name for this kind of cell is prokaryote, which means "before nucleus." Instead of a nucleus, these cells have a nucleoid. This is a region of cytoplasm where the cell's DNA is found. DNA is usually in one long

95

strand. Some have **flagella,** or hairlike strands of protein that are used for movement. Some prokaryotes also have an extra capsule on the outside. This capsule helps protect the cell.

Scientists use the cell wall to identify different types of bacteria. They apply a special dye to the cell wall. If the cell wall reacts to the dye and turns purple, the cell is **gram-positive.** If it does not react, it is **gram-negative.**

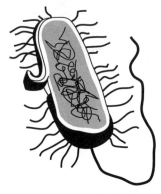

Prokaryotic Cell

⬛ TIP

The terms *gram-positive* and *gram-negative* come from the name of Christian Gram, the scientist who first developed this way of identifying bacteria.

Bacteria are grouped into two kingdoms, the archaebacteria (or "old bacteria") and the eubacteria (or "true bacteria").

Archaebacteria

The **archaebacteria** are the oldest living things. They first developed about 3.8 billion years ago. At that time, Earth's atmosphere did not contain oxygen. Archaebacteria gave off oxygen as a product of photosynthesis. Eventually, there was enough oxygen in the atmosphere for other life-forms to develop.

Archaebacteria may produce oxygen, but many of them are **anaerobic**—that is, they cannot survive when oxygen is present. However, they can survive in conditions that would kill other organisms. Unlike eubacteria, archaebacteria are not harmed by **antibiotics,** medicines that kill disease-causing bacteria.

One type of archaebacteria lives in extremely hot, acidic water. These organisms die of cold when the temperature drops to 55°C (131° F).

Another type of archaebacteria dies in the presence of oxygen. These organisms produce energy by converting carbon dioxide into methane gas. They live in areas where they are protected from oxygen, such as the mud at the bottom of swamps, or in the intestines of animals.

A third type of archaebacteria lives in extremely salty conditions. These organisms are found in places like the Dead Sea, where no plants or animals can survive—not even seaweed grows there! The pinkish color sometimes seen near the shore of very salty lakes is caused by large concentrations of these archaebacteria.

■ PRACTICE 21: The Oldest Life-Forms

Look at the list of terms below. Fill in each line with the letter of the term that correctly completes each of the following statements.

a. anaerobic   **c.** gram-positive   **e.** nucleoid
b. flagella   **d.** gram-negative

1. Scientists stain cell walls to see if the cell is _____ or _____.

2. Instead of a nucleus, prokaryotes have a(n) _____.

3. Some prokaryotes use hairlike structures called _____ to move.

4. Prokaryotes that cannot survive in oxygen are called _____.

Eubacteria

The other kingdom of bacteria is the **eubacteria,** which means "true bacteria." These are the organisms most people mean when they talk about bacteria. They are much more common than archaebacteria.

You may be most familiar with bacteria that cause diseases. Bacteria cause strep throat, tetanus, pneumonia, tuberculosis, and some sexually transmitted diseases. Most bacteria, however, are harmless. Many have positive uses and are even essential to life.

Bacteria are everywhere around you. To reduce the risk of bacterial infections, wash your hands well with soap and water or use an antibacterial hand sanitizer before you eat.

Eubacteria come in many shapes and forms. However, three shapes are most common: rod-shaped, round, and spiral.

- Rod-shaped cells are called **bacilli.** (The singular is *bacillus.*)

- Round or oval cells are called **cocci.** (The singular is *coccus.*)

- Spiral cells are called **spirilla.** (The singular is *spirillum.*)

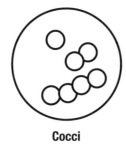
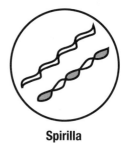

| Bacilli | Cocci | Spirilla |

Most bacteria are able to move themselves from one place to another. Different bacteria have different ways of moving. Most move by spinning their flagella. Some produce a slimy substance that they can glide along. Some bacteria do not move at all.

Like other living things, bacteria also reproduce. Most bacteria reproduce by **binary fission.** The cell makes a copy of its own DNA. Then the cell divides, and a new bacterial cell wall forms. Binary fission results in two identical daughter cells. Bacteria can reproduce very quickly. When conditions are right, they can divide once every 20 minutes.

Harmful Bacteria

Some bacteria cause diseases in humans, such as cholera and pneumonia. Some cause food poisoning, while other bacteria cause acne. They can cause diseases in plants, such as blight or cankers. Because bacteria can reproduce so quickly, just one or two bacteria can quickly become thousands of bacteria.

However, most bacteria that cause food poisoning are destroyed by heat. Cooking food properly kills these bacteria. Most disease-causing bacteria can be destroyed by antibiotics. Unfortunately, many bacteria are changing to become resistant to antibiotics. Scientists must find new ways to combat these resistant bacteria.

IN REAL LIFE

Marcia had a sore throat. She made a doctor's appointment to see if she had a bacterial infection. A friend offered her some antibiotics. Marcia knew that some bacteria have become resistant to antibiotics. The main reason is because people take antibiotics when they do not need them. She refused her friend's offer and waited until she saw the doctor.

Helpful Bacteria

Some bacteria can cause diseases. But most bacteria are not harmful. In fact, they have many important uses.

- Bacteria take nitrogen from the atmosphere and change it to a form that plants can use.

- Bacteria break down dead organisms, returning their nutrients to the soil.

- Bacteria in your stomach crowd out harmful bacteria and help you digest your food.

- Bacteria in water treatment plants help break down sewage.

- Bacteria take carbon dioxide from the air and replace it with oxygen.

- Bacteria are essential for making cheese and yogurt.

- Bacteria are used in oil spills to break oil molecules into less dangerous forms.

- Scientists use bacteria to produce medicines and for genetic engineering.

■ PRACTICE 22: Eubacteria

Circle the letter of the answer that correctly completes each of the following statements.

1. Eubacteria that are shaped like rods are called _____.
   a. bacilli
   b. cocci
   c. spirilla

2. Bacteria that cause food poisoning can be killed by _____ the food.
   a. eating
   b. freezing
   c. cooking

3. Bacteria take _____ from the atmosphere and change it so that plants can use it.
   a. methane
   b. oxygen
   c. nitrogen

4. Some bacteria are becoming _____ to antibiotics.
   a. resistant
   b. identical
   c. harmful

Viruses

Bacteria cause some diseases. But other diseases are caused by **viruses.** These are tiny particles, even smaller than bacteria. Scientists are undecided about whether or not viruses are organisms. Viruses have either RNA or DNA. But they are not cells and are not made of cells. They do not use energy, respond to the environment, or grow and develop. They cannot reproduce by themselves. They must attach themselves to a living cell in order to reproduce.

When a virus attaches itself to a cell, it injects its own genetic code into the host cell. Then it directs the cell to make copies of the virus. The virus copies are then released into the host's system. Then the new viruses attach themselves to new cells and the process begins again.

Some viruses do not seem to do any harm to the host cells. Some destroy them. This can make the host organism feel ill. If you have ever had a cold, you have had a disease caused by a virus. Other diseases caused by viruses include mumps, polio, and HIV, or human immunodeficiency virus. You will learn more about viruses in Lesson 17, Fighting Invaders.

■ PRACTICE 23: Viruses

Decide if each statement that follows is true (**T**) or false (**F**). Write the correct letter on each line.

_____ **1.** Viruses are larger than bacteria.

_____ **2.** Scientists are undecided about whether or not viruses are organisms.

_____ **3.** Viruses have most of the characteristics of living things.

_____ **4.** Once it enters a host organism, a virus grows and develops rapidly.

_____ **5.** Viruses must infect a host cell in order to reproduce.

_____ **6.** All viruses destroy host cells.

_____ **7.** The common cold and HIV are both caused by viruses.

LESSON 9: Protists

GOAL: To learn about the different classes of protists

WORDS TO KNOW

algae (singular *alga*)	parasites	pseudopod
algal bloom	plasmodium	spores
cilia	protist	toxin
eukaryote	protozoans	

Protists

The next kingdom of life is the **protist** kingdom. This kingdom includes organisms that are like plants, organisms that are like animals, and organisms that are like fungi. Some protists are single-celled, but some are multicelled. Some are microscopic in size. Some are very large. One thing that all protists have in common is that they need a wet environment. Protists live either in water or in very wet areas.

Although some protists are single-celled, they are very different from the bacteria you studied in Lesson 8. Bacteria are prokaryotes; their cells do not have nuclei. But protists do have nuclei. A cell that has a nucleus is called a **eukaryote,** or "true nucleus." A eukaryotic cell has organelles such as mitochondria and endoplasmic reticulum, which are not found in prokaryotic cells.

Many protists are very different from one another, although they are grouped in the same kingdom. For a long time, the different kinds of protists were classified as parts of other kingdoms. Some scientists still think that some protists should be classed as plants or animals. Other scientists think that the protist kingdom should be split into smaller kingdoms, with each major type of protist as its own separate kingdom. But for now, eukaryotes that are not plants, animals, or fungi are classed as protists.

Plantlike Protists

Some protists resemble plants. Like plants, they have chlorophyll and undergo photosynthesis. However, they develop differently from plants and have some different cell structures.

Most of the plantlike protists are algae. When you think of algae, you may think of a slimy green growth floating in a stagnant pond. Algae, however, come in a variety of sizes and shapes. Some consist of only a single cell, while some algae reach 60 meters in length. Some algae are green, while others can be red or brown.

Algae live everywhere. Most thrive in oceans, lakes, and rivers. Some live in hot springs and in snow. There are also algae that grow in soil and on trees. Some algae live on animals such as polar bears, turtles, and sloths. Some even live in clouds.

Single-Celled Algae

Single-celled algae are found in both the ocean and freshwater. They are an important food source for marine organisms. The rate at which these algae grow depends on the chemical makeup of the water. Certain chemicals, like those from detergents, can cause algae to grow very quickly. This high rate of growth is called an algal bloom.

Diatoms are one of the most abundant types of single-celled algae. Many organisms depend on them for food. Diatom cell walls contain the same material found in sand and glass. Most diatoms live in salt water. Over millions of years, countless diatoms have died and settled to the ocean bottom. The glassy shells accumulate in the sediment. This sediment is collected and used to filter fruit juices, beer, and wine. It is also an ingredient in toothpaste, cleansers, and polishes.

Diatom

Most dinoflagellates also live in salt water. These single-celled algae have two flagella that they use to move through the water. Some dinoflagellates release a chemical that produces light in the water. At night, people on the shore can sometimes see a greenish glow in the waves. At times, dinoflagellates give off a **toxin,** or a poison. This toxin can make shellfish, such as clams and oysters, dangerous to eat. This is especially true when dinoflagellates experience an algal bloom. So many algae can be found in one place that their reddish coloring makes the water look red. This is called a red tide.

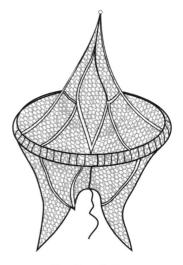

Dinoflagellate

IN REAL LIFE

Juan liked to gather shellfish along the beach. His family had done so for generations. Before he went one morning, he called the local fisheries department to see if it was safe to eat the shellfish. They told him that there was a red tide. It would be dangerous to eat shellfish from the area for the next few weeks. Juan saw other people coming back from the beach carrying mussels they had harvested. He warned them about the red tide and told them they should throw away the mussels.

The algae with which most people are familiar are the euglenas. These microscopic, single-celled algae live in freshwater. Most euglenas are green. When the weather is warm, they may form a pale green scum on the surface of the water.

Euglena

Multicelled Algae

The best-known multicelled algae are kelp and seaweed. These algae take many forms. They can be stringlike, tubular, branched, feathery, or sheetlike.

Most multicelled algae live underwater. The water filters the sunlight, so the type of light that reaches the algae differs from the type of light that reaches plants on land. Therefore, many algae have different-colored pigments to capture this light. Scientists have grouped these algae based on their colors.

Brown algae live mostly in cold, coastal waters. They are the type of algae most often referred to as seaweed. One group of brown algae, called kelp, can grow up to 90 meters in length. Extracts from brown algae are used in ice cream to prevent ice crystals from forming. They are also used as thickeners in syrups and salad dressings.

Red algae live mostly along warm, tropical shores. One type, however, lives in snow, coloring the snow red. Red algae are important food crops, especially in Japan. Red algae are also the source of agar and carrageen. Both are used as stabilizing ingredients in food.

■ PRACTICE 24: Plantlike Protists

Look at the types of algae listed below. Fill in each line with the letter of the type of algae that best completes the statement.

a. Red algae   **c.** Diatoms
b. Dinoflagellates   **d.** Brown algae

1. _____ cause red tide.

2. _____ are a source of agar and carrageenan.

3. _____ grow in cool, coastal waters; they sometimes reach 90 meters in length.

4. _____ contain the same material found in glass.

Animallike Protists

The second large groups of protists are those that have things in common with animals. They are called **protozoans,** which means "early animals." These organisms are not, in fact, animals. All animals are multicellular. Protozoans are all single-celled. But protozoans behave very much like animals in many ways.

Scientists group protozoans based on the way they move. Some protozoans such as the amoeba move by extending a **pseudopod,** or "false foot." This is a fingerlike projection from the protist's body. The protozoan uses the pseudopod to pull itself along a surface. Some protozoans such as the trypanosome use flagella that they move in a whiplike motion. Some protozoans such as the paramecium use **cilia,** short, hairlike structures. They move by beating the cilia in one direction.

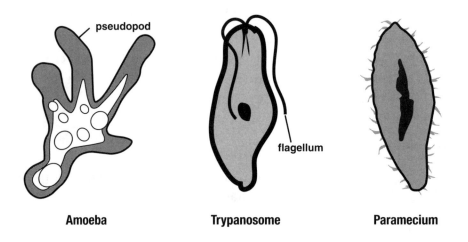

Amoeba   **Trypanosome**   **Paramecium**

Some protozoans do not move at all in their adult form. Instead, they attach themselves to another organism. These protozoans are **parasites.** They use the host organism for food, often harming the host. Some of these protists cause serious diseases such as malaria. For example, a mosquito, tick, or biting fly contains the young form of the organism in its saliva. When it bites an animal, it passes the young protozoan into the blood of the animal. The young protozoan moves through the blood until it reaches the organ to which it will attach. In the disease malaria, that organ is the liver. Over time, the infected liver cells rupture, releasing young protozoans into the bloodstream over and over.

■ PRACTICE 25: Animallike Protists

Circle the letter of the answer that correctly completes each of the following statements.

1. Protozoans are classified according to _____.
   a. the way they move
   b. whether or not they are parasites
   c. the diseases they cause

2. Some protozoans use a _____, or "false foot," to move.
   a. cilia
   b. flagella
   c. pseudopod

3. Some protozoans move by beating _____, short, hairlike structures.
   a. cilia
   b. flagella
   c. pseudopod

Funguslike Protists

Some protists seem a lot like fungi. These are slime molds and water molds. They are not classified as fungi because each fungus cell has a special function, which you will learn about in Lesson 10. This is not true of the funguslike protists. Also, unlike fungi, slime molds are able to move.

Slime molds live in water, in damp soil, or on decaying plants or animals. Slime molds are often brightly colored. Some are bright orange, blue, or purple. Some slime molds have only one cell. Other slime molds form a community. They lose their cell membranes but have many nuclei. A community of slime molds is called a **plasmodium.** The individual organisms inside the plasmodium reproduce sexually and form **spores,** small reproductive bodies. The spores are released and form new slime molds.

Water molds are found in freshwater and near the top of moist soil. They consume decaying tissue, like rotting logs. Occasionally, they attack living plants. Since water molds spread quickly to nearby plants, this can cause a great deal of damage to crops. A water mold in the mid-1800s wiped out the potato crop in Ireland. Since many people depended on potatoes for their food, many people starved to death. This was known as the Great Potato Famine. Water molds also cause diseases in other plants, such as trees and grapes. They can even cause diseases in fish and fish eggs.

IN REAL LIFE

Water molds have been particularly destructive to crops. You have just read about the Great Potato Famine. In the late 1870s, a water mold was brought from the United States to France on grape vines by accident. The American vines were supposed to be bred with existing French vines. This process would strengthen them. This is called *hybridization.* Instead, the mold infected the French vines and nearly ruined the French wine industry.

■ PRACTICE 26: Funguslike Protists

Circle the letter of the term that best completes each sentence.

1. Some _____ cause diseases in both plants and animals.
   a. slime molds
   b. water molds
   c. spores

2. A community of _____ is called a plasmodium.
   a. slime molds
   b. water molds
   c. spores

3. Slime molds reproduce sexually by means of _____.
   a. plasmodium
   b. water molds
   c. spores

LESSON 10: Fungi

GOAL: To learn about the structure, function, and diversity of fungi

WORDS TO KNOW

filament	lichen
fungi (singular *fungus*)	mycelium
germinate	symbiotic
hypha (plural *hyphae*)	

What Are Fungi?

Fungi include mushrooms, yeasts, and molds. They were once classed as plants. Today, scientists consider them as different from plants as they are from animals.

Some fungi are only a single cell, but most fungi are multicelled. Like plants, they have cell walls. But unlike plants, they do not have chlorophyll. This means that they cannot photosynthesize. Instead, they absorb their food from other organisms. Some fungi are parasites. They feed on living organisms. But most fungi feed on dead organic material, such as plants or animals. Fungi help break down dead organisms and return the nutrients to the soil.

Most fungi grow in filaments. A **filament** is a long, threadlike chain of cells. An individual filament is called a **hypha.** (The plural is *hyphae*.) The hyphae grow by getting longer and branching out at the tips. As they grow, they form an interwoven mat called a **mycelium.**

Filaments

TIP

If you take a look at bread mold, you will be able to see a tangle of individual hyphae. The tips of the hyphae penetrate the bread, absorbing nutrients. Mushrooms are a mass of tightly woven hyphae. The individual filaments are hard to distinguish.

To absorb energy for all this growth, the fungus uses the material in which it is growing. Fungi eat by absorbing nutrients. Fungi release enzymes into the dead animal or plant. These enzymes digest the food outside of the fungus. Then the fungus absorbs the food. Nutrients that the fungus does not need go back into the soil.

The growth of the hyphae and mycelium takes place under the surface of the material the fungus is using for food. As the mycelium develops, it may produce spore-bearing structures. Because most spores are carried by air currents, the spore-bearing structures usually grow above the surface. When spores are released, they float on the wind or in water. They reach a place where conditions to grow are good. Then they **germinate,** or start to grow, and a new hypha appears.

Mushrooms are a familiar type of fungus. The mushrooms you see above ground are the spore-bearing structures. The spores come from under the mushroom cap. But the mushrooms are only a small part of the whole fungus. Most of the fungus is underground. A single fungus can sprout many mushrooms.

IN REAL LIFE

Most fungi spores are too small to be seen. They are floating in the air in your kitchen. To keep fungi away, you can keep bread and other baked goods in a refrigerator. Most bread molds cannot grow unless the temperature is warm.

The Role of Fungi

Fungi have a bad reputation. Some fungi, such as mushrooms from the genus *Amanita,* are extremely poisonous. Just a bite can kill a person.

Some fungi are parasites, living on other organisms. These fungi can cause diseases in plants and animals. Athlete's foot is caused by a fungus that grows on human skin. As the fungus multiplies, it causes itching and burning. The skin looks flaky and cracked. A fungus carried by beetles caused Dutch elm disease. This disease has killed more than half the elm trees in the United States. Some fungi grow as mold. Mold in the air can cause breathing problems.

Ellen was given a book on identifying mushrooms. Ellen loved the taste of mushrooms, so she hurried out to the woods to pick some for dinner. She found several mushrooms and got out her book. Identifying them was harder than she thought. Some of them looked like edible mushrooms, but they also looked like poisonous mushrooms. Some mushrooms are deadly. Ellen decided to be safe. She stopped her search for edible mushrooms.

Fungi also have many positive uses.

- Like bacteria, fungi break down organic matter, releasing nutrients into the soil.

- As you will learn in Unit 3, some fungi grow in the roots of plants. They help the plants absorb nutrients.

- Fungi are sources of many important medicines. The antibiotic penicillin comes from a fungus. It revolutionized the treatment of bacterial diseases.

- Yeast, a single-celled fungus, is used to bake bread and make beer. The yeast feeds on sugars and releases alcohol and carbon dioxide. The carbon dioxide causes the bread dough to rise and adds fizz to the beer.

- Some fungi are good to eat.

Symbiotic Relationships

Some fungi are parasites. They harm the organism they live on. But some fungi have a different relationship with other organisms.

If you walk through the woods or in a park, you may see a crusty, funguslike growth on trees or rocks. This growth is called **lichen**. Lichen is actually an association between fungi and algae. The fungi absorb water from the air, providing moist conditions for the algae. The algae photosynthesize and provide the fungi with sugars and vitamins. Both organisms benefit from the association. This type of relationship is called a **symbiotic** relationship. The organisms in a symbiotic relationship depend on each other to stay alive and healthy.

TIP

The word *symbiotic* comes from two Greek words. The first part, *sym*, means "together." The second part, *biotic*, means "having to do with life." Other words from the same root include *biology*, which is the study of life, and *biography*, which is the story of one person's life.

Lichens can grow on practically any surface anywhere in the world. They are especially successful in harsh environments where few plants grow. These areas include mountaintops and polar regions. In northern Canada and in Lapland, caribou and reindeer depend on lichen for food.

■ PRACTICE 27: What Are Fungi?

Decide if each statement that follows is true (**T**) or false (**F**). Write the correct letter on each line.

_____ **1.** Fungi are a type of plant.

_____ **2.** Fungi use sunlight to convert carbon dioxide into sugar.

_____ **3.** The cell walls of fungi are made mostly of chlorophyll.

_____ 4. There are both single-celled and multicelled fungi.

_____ 5. Lichen are made up of algae and fungi.

_____ 6. Fungi are vital to the ecosystem because they break down dead organisms.

UNIT 2 REVIEW

Circle the letter of the answer that correctly completes each statement.

1. An organism that has a cell wall but does not have a true nucleus is called a _____.
   a. flagella
   b. prokaryote
   c. fungi
   d. mold

2. Archaebacteria are not harmed by _____.
   a. antibiotics
   b. bacteria
   c. bacilli
   d. protozoans

3. Most bacteria reproduce by _____.
   a. spirilla
   b. antibiotics
   c. binary fission
   d. viruses

4. Viruses have either RNA or DNA, but they are not made of _____.
   a. cells
   b. cytoplasm
   c. spores
   d. algae

5. Organisms that have a true nucleus are called _____.
   a. spores
   b. cilia
   c. prokaryotes
   d. eukaryotes

6. Algae photosynthesize, but they are not plants, they are _____.
   a. bacteria
   b. viruses
   c. protists
   d. chloroplasts

7. Some protists use whiplike structures called _____ to move.
   a. bacteria
   b. cilia
   c. algae
   d. flagella

8. A community of slime molds is called a _____.
   a. plasmodium
   b. spore
   c. cilia
   d. mildew

9. An organism that uses another organism for food, harming the host organism, is called a _____.
   a. prokaryote
   b. water mold
   c. slime mold
   d. parasite

10. The only parts of a fungus that usually grow above the ground are the _____.
    a. hyphae
    b. spore-bearing structures
    c. mycelium
    d. filaments

UNIT 2 APPLICATION ACTIVITY 1
Yeast Population Analysis

Look at the diagrams below. They illustrate a sample of a yeast population over five days. Assume that each dot represents 1000 yeast cells.

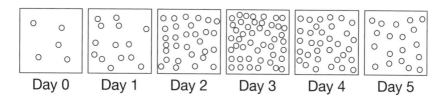

Day 0   Day 1   Day 2   Day 3   Day 4   Day 5

Count the number of yeast cells for each day, and record your data in the table below. (Remember: 1 circle = 1000 yeast cells.)

Day	Number of Cells
0	
1	
2	
3	
4	
5	

Construct a graph that compares the number of yeast cells to the time.

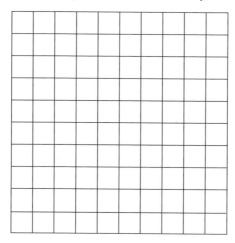

1. Between which days was there the most growth?

   _____

   _____

   _____

2. Between which days was there the least growth?

   _____

   _____

   _____

3. When did the yeast population seem to reach its maximum number?

   _____

   _____

   _____

4. What can you conclude about the population decrease?

   _____

   _____

   _____

UNIT 2 APPLICATION ACTIVITY 2
Bacteria Shapes

Bacteria have three different shapes. Bacteria whose name ends in -*cocci* or
-*coccus* are little spheres or ovals. Bacteria whose name ends in -*bacilli* or
-*bacillus* are rod-shaped. Bacteria whose name ends in *-spirilli* or *-spirillum*
are spiral-shaped.

In this activity, you will look for bacterial shapes under a microscope and try to tell whether the bacteria you see organize in a cluster, in a chain, or in pairs.

Materials

microscope

slides and coverslips

iodine

sample of pond water

Procedure

1. Drop one drop of pond water on a slide. Put a tiny drop of iodine on the slide. This will color the bacteria so you can see them better.

2. Cover the drop with a coverslip.

3. Place the slide under a microscope at low power until you see a group of bacteria.

4. Switch to high power.

5. Move the slide around until you can see three bacterial shapes.

6. On another sheet of paper, draw pictures of the bacteria and their arrangements.

Label each shape by its scientific name, and identify whether it is arranged in pairs, clusters, or chains.

UNIT 2 APPLICATION ACTIVITY 3
Grow a Bread Mold

Bread molds are fungi. They are very easy to grow. You might end up with two different kinds of fungi. One is a black or green bread mold. Another is a fuzzy, gray bread mold.

Materials

slice of bread

reclosable sandwich bag

sprinkle of soil

sprinkle of water

Procedure

1. Put a tiny bit of soil on a slice of fresh bread.

2. Sprinkle the bread with water until it is moist to the touch.

3. Place the bread in the sandwich bag, and close it tightly. There can be a little air in the bag.

4. Place the bag in a warm place.

5. In just a few days, you will see mold growing. Can you grow both kinds?

6. When you have finished observing, throw the bread and the mold away without opening the bag. Bread mold is harmless if you eat it, but it may cause problems if you breathe in the spores.

Draw a picture of the molds you grew.

UNIT 3

The Plant Kingdom

LESSON 11: Plant Biology

GOAL: To learn about the structure and function of plants

WORDS TO KNOW

bud	phloem
cambium	phototropism
cellulose	roots
fibrous root system	stem
geotropism	stomata (singular *stoma*)
hormones	taproots
hydrotropism	transpiration
leaves	tropism
legumes	xylem

Plant Cells

Think about houseplants. They have many of the same requirements you have. They need water. They need energy to grow. They need nutrients. But houseplants cannot walk to the sink to get a drink of water from a faucet. They cannot go to the refrigerator to get something to eat. They must stay where they are. In this lesson, you will learn about the structure of plants and how they get what they need while rooted in one place.

Plant and animal cells are similar in many ways. Both have a cell membrane, which controls what enters and leaves the cell. Both have a nucleus, where DNA is stored and bundled up into chromosomes. Both have organelles, including mitochondria, endoplasmic reticulum, Golgi complex, and ribosomes. Both have a cytoskeleton. But there are also major differences.

Cell Walls

As you know, plant cells are surrounded by a cell wall. These walls are made out of a complex sugar called **cellulose.** Cellulose fibers are extremely strong. When you eat a vegetable, the crunch is from the cellulose in the cell walls.

A plant's cell walls maintain the shape of the cell and keep it from swelling and bursting. They protect the inside of the cell. However, they also have additional functions.

- Cell walls provide structural support for plants. Plants do not have bones like people. Without rigid cell walls, plants would collapse. The cell walls in tree trunks are especially strong and thick. These walls also have other compounds, including lignin, which further strengthen them.

- Cell walls contain chemicals that help the plants resist diseases caused by bacteria and fungi.

- Cell walls prevent water loss.

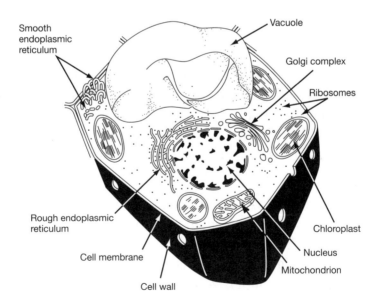

Plant Cell

Vacuoles

Plant cells contain large structures called vacuoles. Vacuoles sometimes take up 90 percent of a cell. They are filled with a liquid called cell sap. The juice from an orange or a lemon is cell sap stored inside vacuoles. Cell sap is made up of mostly water. However, it contains other chemicals as well. Plant cells store salts, sugars, and proteins in vacuoles. Vacuoles also have the same functions as lysosomes in animal cells. They contain chemicals that break down worn-out parts of the cell.

Chloroplasts

Most importantly, plant cells have organelles called chloroplasts. Inside chloroplasts, one of the most important series of chemical reactions on Earth—photosynthesis—takes place. As you learned in Lesson 2, this process uses sunlight, air, and water to produce energy.

■ PRACTICE 28: Plant Cells

Circle the letter of the answer that correctly completes each of the following statements. (*Hint*: There may be more than one correct answer.)

1. Both plant and animal cells have _____.
    a. cell walls
    b. a nucleus
    c. mitochondria
    d. chloroplasts

2. The function of plant cell walls is to _____.
    a. give the plant structural support
    b. store DNA
    c. protect the inside of the cell
    d. help plants resist disease

3. Cellulose is _____.
    a. the most common component of cell sap
    b. a complex sugar found in cell walls
    c. part of the endoplasmic reticulum
    d. found both in plant and animal cells

4. Vacuoles _____.
   a. are found in plant cells
   b. can fill up to 90 percent of a cell
   c. can perform the same function as lysosomes in animals
   d. can perform the same function as mitochondria in animals

Photosynthesis

As you know, photosynthesis begins when chlorophyll absorbs sunlight. The energy from the sunlight then starts a long series of chemical reactions. The air and water taken in through the plant's roots change carbon dioxide to glucose. The energy from the sun is now stored in the glucose. When the plant needs energy, the cells break down glucose in the mitochondria.

Photosynthesis makes all of life on Earth possible. It is the source of your food. Think of where you get your energy. You either eat plants that get their energy from photosynthesis, or you eat animals that get all their energy from eating plants.

There is another reason photosynthesis is critical to life on Earth. Oxygen is released during the early stages of photosynthesis. This is the source of all the oxygen you breathe. Almost all organisms require oxygen for respiration.

THINK ABOUT IT

In some parts of the world, huge areas of forest have been cut down. The loss of so many trees increases the amount of carbon dioxide in the air. Why do you think this is? Write your answer on a separate sheet of paper.

■ PRACTICE 29: Photosynthesis

Decide if each statement that follows is true (**T**) or false (**F**). Write the correct letter on each line.

_____ **1.** Photosynthesis uses sunlight to convert oxygen to proteins.

_____ **2.** Oxygen is a product of photosynthesis.

_____ **3.** Chlorophyll is the green pigment that absorbs sunlight.

Leaves

Plants need sunlight and carbon dioxide for photosynthesis. The more of these resources they can collect, the more sugars they can produce. But a plant in the shade cannot move to a sunnier spot. It must make the best use of the resources available to it. **Leaves** are perfectly designed to gather as much light and carbon dioxide as possible. The cells in leaves are crammed with chloroplasts that gather light. However, the shapes of leaves are even more important. Leaves are flat and thin. This leaf shape ensures that as many cells as possible are exposed to sunlight. A leaf is almost all surface area. In other words, because it is flat and thin, more of its surface is in direct contact with the environment than an object that is knobby and thick.

To understand why shape is so important, imagine a leaf shaped like a cube (drawing **a** below). A cube has a small surface area. The cells on the outside of the cube would be exposed to the sun. The cells on the inside, however, would not. Slice that cube 1000 times, so that each slice is as thin as a leaf (drawing **b** at the right). When the cube is cut up into thin slices, cells on the inside are also exposed to the sun. Now the cube has a much greater surface area.

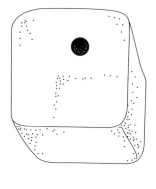

a

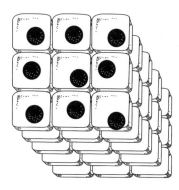

b

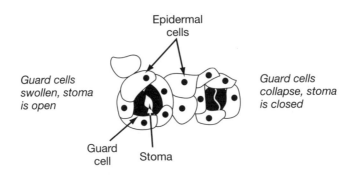

Epidermal
cells

Guard cells
swollen, stoma
is open

Guard cells
collapse, stoma
is closed

Guard
cell

Stoma

Stomata

Carbon dioxide enters a leaf through small openings called **stomata.** Stomata are usually located on the bottom of the leaf. They are surrounded by guard cells that open and close the stomata. Because the leaf is thin, the carbon dioxide does not need to travel far to reach the cells that need it for photosynthesis.

There are trade-offs, however. This flat, thin shape causes leaves to lose a lot of water. Plants need water to keep cool for many reasons, including photosynthesis, and even for structural support. You may have noted that if you do not water a plant, it quickly begins to droop.

To reduce water loss, most leaves are covered with a waxy substance. But this does not stop water loss completely. Leaves must constantly balance water loss with the uptake of carbon dioxide. When leaves open their stomata, carbon dioxide enters, but water escapes.

TIP

To see how a greater surface area leads to faster water loss, get two sponges that are several centimeters thick. Split one of the sponges in half so that you have two sponges that are half as thick as the first sponge. Place the three sponges side by side. Soak the intact sponge and the two halves of the split sponge in water. Place them in the sun, and see which sponge dries faster.

Many trees in temperate climates have other strategies for reducing water loss. For example, trees drop their leaves in the fall. During cold weather, the air becomes dry. Water loss increases. Because the water in the ground may be frozen, the trees cannot take up more water to compensate (make up) for the increased dryness. By dropping their leaves, trees have far less surface area through which they can lose water.

Again, there are trade-offs. Trees cannot photosynthesize without leaves. They must also spend a lot of energy to grow new leaves in the spring. In cold climates where the growing season is short, trees cannot afford to spend that much energy. That is why you see mostly evergreens, such as spruce and fir, in northern forests.

Trees that shed their leaves do conserve some of their resources, however. Before the leaves fall, the chlorophyll breaks down and moves into the stem. Then you can see the red and yellow pigments (colors) in the leaves. The color is hidden by the green chlorophyll during the warmer months. That is why leaves change color in the fall.

■ PRACTICE 30: Leaves

Circle the letter of the answer that correctly completes each of the following statements.

1. An increase in the surface area of leaves _____.
   a. increases the amount of sunlight the plant collects
   b. increases water loss
   c. increases photosynthesis
   d. all of the above

2. Carbon dioxide _____.
   a. is needed for photosynthesis
   b. enters the leaves through the chlorophyll
   c. comes from the soil
   d. all of the above

3. To conserve water, _____.
   a. plants have stomata on top of their leaves
   b. leaves are often covered in a waxy substance
   c. some trees drop their leaves in the winter
   d. all of the above

Roots

Now you will learn about the **roots,** the parts of the plant that grow under the ground. Roots have three purposes.

- Roots anchor the plant in the soil and keep it upright, even in strong winds.

- Roots store food reserves. Plants do not immediately use all the glucose they produce during photosynthesis. They convert the sugars into complex sugars, such as starch. Beets, carrots, and sweet potatoes are three examples of roots that store complex sugars. These storage reserves in the roots allow plants to regenerate (produce again) if they lose their stems or leaves to animals, fire, winter cold, or lawn mowers. Not all underground storage structures are roots. Potatoes are actually part of the stem. Bulbs, such as onions and tulips, are also parts of stems.

- Roots absorb water and nutrients from the soil. Because plants lose so much water through their leaves, the roots must grow continuously, seeking water. In desert climates, roots can reach down over 45 meters in search of water. The tips of the roots are covered with a thick layer of cells called a root cap. The root cap keeps the tips from being damaged as they push through the soil.

There are two patterns of root growth. Many plants, such as trees, grow long **taproots** that branch off. These roots can go deep into the soil. If you ever try to pull up dandelions, you will discover that they have long taproots. Other types of plants, such as grass, have a **fibrous root system.** These plants have many stringy roots that cling to the soil.

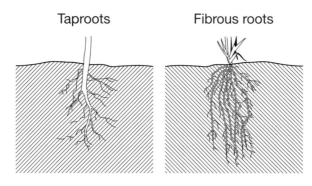

Taproots   Fibrous roots

The ends of roots are covered with tiny growths called root hairs. These greatly increase the surface area of roots. Just as a greater surface area on leaves lets plants collect more sunlight, a greater surface area on roots lets them collect more water.

IN REAL LIFE

Edwin could not keep houseplants alive. He killed his first plants by not watering them enough. When he got some new houseplants, he decided that he was not going to make the same mistake, so he constantly soaked the soil. These plants also died. He had given them too much water. Roots need energy to grow, take up nutrients, and maintain themselves. They also need oxygen for respiration. When Edwin put too much water in the soil, the roots could not get enough oxygen.

As you have learned, roots take up nutrients from the soil. Just as you need nutrients in your diet, plants need nutrients to maintain their cells, make proteins, and carry out other life functions. The nutrients that plants need include nitrogen, phosphorus, calcium, potassium, and magnesium.

Roots have help taking in nutrients. A type of fungus called mycorrhiza grows on the roots. The mycorrhiza feed on sugars that the roots provide. In return, the mycorrhiza help the roots absorb phosphorus from the soil. Without these fungi, the plants would not get enough phosphorus and would grow poorly.

Some types of plants, called **legumes,** have a similar relationship with a type of bacterium called rhizobium. These bacteria live in the roots of legumes such as alfalfa, soybeans, peas, and clover. They, too, get sugars from these plants. In return, they convert nitrogen from the air into a form that the plants can use. Nitrogen that the plants do not use is released into the soil, making the soil more fertile. Farmers often plant legumes in certain fields for one year, enriching the field with nitrogen. The next year, they may plant non-legumes, such as corn, in those fields. Because there is so much nitrogen in the soil, the crops grow better.

PRACTICE 31: Roots

Circle the letter of the correct answer to each of the following questions. (*Hint*: There may be more than one correct answer.)

1. What are the functions of roots?
   a. to convert carbon dioxide to glucose
   b. to anchor the plant in the soil
   c. to store food
   d. to absorb water and nutrients from the soil

2. What are root caps?
   a. a protective layer of cells at the tips of roots
   b. the part of the root that contains chlorophyll
   c. the part of the root in which food is stored
   d. the part of the root that protects the tips of the roots as they push through the soil

3. What are mycorrhiza?
   a. a type of fungus that grows on plant roots
   b. a fungus that helps the plant take up nutrients, especially phosphorus
   c. bacteria that convert nitrogen from the air into nitrogen the plant can use
   d. an organism that feeds on sugars from the plant's roots

Stems

The **stem** is the structure between the roots and the leaves. It holds a plant's leaves high in the air, exposing them to the sun. A tree can gather more sunlight if it grows taller than its neighbors.

Stems also serve as passageways for water and sugar. Water must travel through the stem to get from the roots to the leaves. Sugars must travel through stems to get from the leaves to the roots. You will now examine how water and sugar move through the stem.

Water Transport

Consider the center of a tree. The wood in the tree is made up of long, thin cells stacked end to end. The walls of these cells are thick and hard. They provide structural support for the stem (the tree "trunk"). If you look at these cells through a microscope, you will see that they have no nucleus, organelles, or cytoplasm. They are dead. In fact, these cells function as pipes. They have openings at both ends. They form a continuous passageway for water to travel from the roots to the leaves. These hollow, water-conducting cells form a kind of tissue called **xylem.** Xylem is in the stems, roots, and leaves. The veins in leaves contain xylem, too.

For many years, scientists debated how water moves through the xylem. By traveling from the bottom of a tree to the top, this process seems to defy gravity. Some thought that there were pumps in the stem that pushed up the water, but xylem cells are dead. Others thought that the roots pushed up the water, but this requires energy. Plants with dead roots (or no roots at all) still take up water. Scientists finally determined that the water is pulled up through the top of a plant or a tree by solar energy.

TIP

You can see how water moves up through a plant. Place some dye in a cup of water. Then cut off a small piece of stem from a flower or a vegetable with leaves attached, such as celery. Place the remaining flower or vegetable, stem down, in the colored water. (It is best to cut the stem underwater to prevent air from entering the xylem.) You can then trace the path of the colored liquid as it moves up the stem or stalk and enters the leaves.

To understand how water moves up a plant, you first need to know a little more about water. You have seen how water beads up on a window when it rains. That is because the water molecules stick together. Molecules are like tiny magnets. The bonds between water molecules are quite strong.

Here is how the sun pulls up water through the tree. The sun shines on the leaves. This causes water to exit the leaves through the stomata, or openings on the leaves. The water molecules that go from the leaves to the air pull other water molecules behind them. These molecules pull the ones behind them, and so on down the entire stem to the roots. This process is called **transpiration.** The faster water evaporates from the leaves, the faster it moves up through the stem.

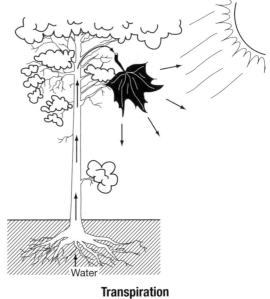

Transpiration

Food Transport

If you look at bark through a microscope, you will see long, thin cells stacked end to end. Unlike cells in the xylem, though, these cells are alive. They have a cytoplasm, but no nucleus. Each of these cells has a small companion cell that keeps it alive. These cells, called **phloem,** carry sugars from the leaves— or the food storage areas in the roots and stem—to the rest of the plant. In trees, phloem is located near the outside of the trunk, or bark. In herbs, the phloem is bundled with xylem on the inside of the stem. The phloem also extends into the roots and leaves.

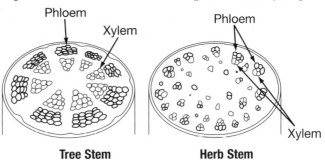

Tree Stem   **Herb Stem**

Scientists also found it difficult to determine how sugars move through the phloem. They now believe that this is what happens.

1. Through photosynthesis, the plant loads sugars into the phloem cells in the leaves. This process requires energy.

2. As more sugars are loaded into phloem cells, water from the nearby xylem rushes in. This creates a sugar solution.

3. As more water rushes in, the pressure inside the phloem cells builds. This pressure pushes the sugar solution through the phloem cells, into the stem, and down to the roots.

TIP

Think of a balloon. When you blow up a balloon, the pressure of the air inside the balloon is higher than the pressure outside the balloon. When you let go of the end of the balloon, the air rushes out. It moves from high pressure to low pressure, and the balloon falls. Water pressure works in the same way. As water moves into phloem cells in the leaves, the pressure builds. The pressure in adjacent, or nearby, phloem cells is lower. Therefore, the water moves into these cells as well.

Plant Growth

In the winter, after a tree has lost its leaves, look at the end of one of its twigs. You will see a tightly packed bundle called a **bud.** In the spring, this bud will open up into a new leaf. A new bud will start to form at the base of this leaf. New growth occurs at the end of the stem or shoot.

Plant Growth

Woody plants, such as oak trees, not only grow longer, they also grow wider. Inside the tree trunk, between the phloem and the xylem, there is a layer of dividing cells called **cambium.** The cells that divide toward the inside of the tree become xylem. The cells that divide toward the outside become phloem. If you slice through the trunk of a tree, you will see tree rings. Each ring represents a year of secondary growth. People can determine how old a tree is by counting these rings.

Many factors control how a plant grows. Environmental factors include how much direct sunlight a plant is getting, the air temperature, and the length of the day. Plants also produce small amounts of chemicals called plant **hormones.** These hormones control how quickly cells divide, how many branches the plant grows, the direction in which the branches grow, the growth of flowers, the ripening of fruit, and many other factors.

■ PRACTICE 32: Stems

Decide if each statement that follows is true (**T**) or false (**F**). Write the correct letter on each line.

_____ **1.** Cells in the xylem contain some cytoplasm.

_____ **2.** Water is pulled up from the roots to the leaves.

_____ **3.** Xylem and phloem are only in the stem.

_____ **4.** The movement of sugars from the leaves to the roots requires energy.

_____ **5.** In woody plants, growth occurs only at the end of the stem.

_____ **6.** Plant hormones are chemicals that control growth in plants.

Tropism

Have you ever noticed that the leaves on houseplants always seem to face toward the window? This is not an accident. Plants are able to change the way they grow in response to the environment. This kind of change is called **tropism.**

There are several different kinds of tropism. Each kind is designed to make sure the plant gets the light, nutrients, and water it needs to grow.

The first kind of tropism is the one plants show when their leaves face toward a window. This is called **phototropism,** or movement in response to light. Plants need sunlight for photosynthesis. To fulfill this need, their leaves and stems grow toward the light.

A second important tropism is called **hydrotropism.** This is movement in response to water. Plants need water for photosynthesis. A plant's roots will grow in the direction of water.

A third important tropism is **geotropism.** This is movement in response to gravity. The roots of a plant grow downward, toward the source of gravity.

Tropisms can be either positive or negative. If the tropism is positive, the plant grows toward the source of the stimulus. If the tropism is negative, the plant grows away from the stimulus. Growth can be affected by both kinds of tropism at the same time. For example, a plant's stem grows upward. It is affected by positive phototropism, or growth toward the light. It is also affected by negative geotropism, or growth against the pull of gravity. The plant's roots grow downward. They are affected by positive geotropism and negative phototropism.

Scientists think that all these changes are the result of plant hormones. These hormones cause cells on one side of a plant's roots, stem, or leaves to grow more quickly than cells on the other side. This causes the plant part to bend. In a houseplant on a windowsill, the cells on the side of the stem that faces away from the window will grow more quickly than the cells on the sunny side. This makes the stem bend toward the light.

■ PRACTICE 33: Tropism
Look at the list of terms below. Fill in each line with the letter of the term that correctly completes each of the following statements.

a. tropism   **b.** geotropism   **c.** hydrotropism   **d.** phototropism

1. A plant's stem grows toward the light. This is an example of positive
   _____.

2. A _____ is change in response to a stimulus.

3. A plant's roots grow downward, toward water. They show both
   positive _____ and positive _____.

LESSON 12: Plant Diversity

GOAL: To learn about the major groups of plants in the world today

WORDS TO KNOW

anthers	lycopods	prothallus
conifers	monocot	rhizomes
dicot	nectar	sepals
embryo	nonvascular plants	stigma
ferns	ovary	style
filaments	petals	succulent
fronds	pistil	vascular plants
gymnosperms	pollen	
horsetails	pollination	

The Earliest Plants

If you take a walk in the woods or through a park, you will see a great variety of plants. Most of the plants you see today produce flowers and seeds, but that was not always true. If you were able to go back in time, the forests would look a lot different. When dinosaurs were alive between 100 and 350 million years ago, there were no flowering plants. Relatives of spruce, fir, and pine filled the forests. If you went back further in time, before the dinosaurs, you would have been walking through vast swamps shaded by giant ferns and lycopods. Today, many of these ancient types of plants still exist among the flowering plants.

Plants first appeared on land about 400 million years ago. Life on land posed new challenges for these plants.

- Water loss became a problem.

- Land plants had to develop ways to extract water and minerals from the soil.

■ Water no longer supported their weight. Plants needed to develop structures to support themselves.

Plants solved these problems in different ways. Some developed specialized cells to move water and food through the plant, and to store water and food until needed. These cells make up xylem and phloem tissues. Plants that have a system to store and transport water and nutrients are called **vascular plants.** Plants that cannot store and transport water are called **nonvascular plants.**

Nonvascular Plants

The first land plants were probably nonvascular plants. These plants include about 25,000 different species of mosses and worts. Nonvascular plants can live in almost any kind of environment. You may have seen moss growing between cracks in a sidewalk, or on the shaded side of a tree. Some have adapted to living in the desert. Most plants that survive in the tundra are worts or mosses.

Like other plants, nonvascular plants use photosynthesis to make energy. But unlike other plants, they do not have true leaves, true roots, or flowers. They do have underground stems that anchor them to the soil, but these stems cannot supply water and food to the plant. Instead, the plant absorbs nutrients over its entire surface.

Because they cannot store or transport food and water, nonvascular plants are limited in size. However, they often grow in such close-packed groups that they seem to form a continuous carpet. Growing close together like this helps the plants retain water. The plants shade one another and keep air from circulating. This reduces water loss by evaporation.

Life Cycle of Nonvascular Plants

Mosses and worts begin life as a spore, floating on the wind. If the spore lands in a moist place, it can germinate, or start to grow. It produces a green, leafy-looking plant. This is the first stage in the plant's life cycle. This leafy-looking plant produces gametes, or sex cells. Some plants produce only sperm, or male gametes. Some produce only eggs, or female gametes. Some produce both. When raindrops wash the sperm into the egg, fertilization occurs.

The fertilized egg grows into a new plant, on top of the old one. The new plant does not produce sex cells. Instead, it produces spores. Eventually, the new spores are carried away by the wind. If a spore lands in a moist place, germination can occur, starting the cycle again.

The Role of Nonvascular Plants

Although mosses and worts are small, they play an important role in the environment. Their carpetlike growth helps prevent erosion by covering the surface of the soil. They break down other dead plants, adding nutrients to the soil. They act as a filter by absorbing pollutants before they can reach the soil or water. They provide food for animals—especially important in areas like the tundra, where caribou rely on them as an energy source. Even dead mosses have a use. They are an excellent growth medium for other plants and can be used as fuel.

■ PRACTICE 34: Nonvascular Plants

Circle the letter of the answer that correctly completes each of the following statements.

1. Plants that do not have xylem and phloem are called _____.
    a. vascular plants
    b. nonvascular plants
    c. carpetlike

2. Nonvascular plants begin as a(n) _____, carried by the wind.
    a. spore
    b. root
    c. egg

3. Nonvascular plants are important because they _____.
    a. produce grains for humans to eat
    b. prevent erosion
    c. have beautiful flowers

Vascular Plants

Plants that contain xylem and phloem are called vascular plants. Because vascular plants can move water from the ground to the rest of the plant, they no longer have to absorb water through their leaves. Therefore, they can live in drier climates. Also, xylem and phloem enable plants to grow bigger.

Lycopods

Some of the first vascular plants were the **lycopods.** They were probably the most common land plant 400 million years ago. Some grew over 30 meters tall. In fact, much of the coal that is burned today is made of the remains of these plants.

Most of these lycopods are now extinct, but there are still some around. If you walk through the woods, you may see small plants that look like baby spruce trees growing in moist soil. You may also see a clublike structure on top of each plant. These plants are called club mosses. The clublike structures on top of the plants contain spores.

Club Moss

If you dig around a club moss, you will find a network of underground stems called **rhizomes.** These rhizomes connect the club mosses. So if you see a group of club mosses, they may all be part of a single plant.

Horsetails

Horsetails are another vascular plant that dominated the swamps 300 million years ago. Today, there are just a few types of horsetails left. You can find them in wet areas alongside ponds, roads, and railway beds. Horsetails look like reeds with joints evenly spaced along their stems. Sometimes branches come out of the joints. A little cone on top contains spores. Some of the cell walls in horsetails contain silica, the same

Horsetails

material found in diatoms. These plants were once used to scrub pots and were therefore called scouring rushes. Horsetails also have rhizomes.

Ferns

Ferns are the most familiar of the ancient vascular plants. Ferns grow all over the world and thrive in most climates. Ferns come in a variety of forms. Some water ferns look like clover. In New Zealand, you can find large tree ferns.

Typical Fern

The most common ferns have large, feathery leaves called **fronds.** Rhizomes connect these fronds together.

Some ferns have separate stems that contain spores. Other ferns carry the spores on the underside of the fronds. If you turn over a frond, you may see rows of raised brown dots. These dots contain the spores.

■ PRACTICE 35: Vascular Plants

Circle the letter of the answer that correctly completes each of the following statements.

1. Vascular plants are unlike nonvascular plants because they _____.
   a. can move water from the ground to the rest of the plant
   b. use photosynthesis
   c. do not have roots

2. Ferns reproduce by producing _____.
   a. cones
   b. fruit
   c. spores

3. Club mosses and horsetails _____.
   a. have structures on the bottom that contain spores
   b. have underground stems called rhizomes
   c. are examples of nonvascular plants

Seed Plants

All the plants discussed so far do not produce seeds. However, most of the plants you see today do. Every tree, shrub, grass, and wildflower produces seeds. The diversity of seed plants is amazing.

Plant Life Cycles

To understand why seed plants are so successful, you will first need to learn about plant life cycles.

All plants reproduce sexually. Two cells, a male gamete (or sperm) and a female gamete (or egg), fuse together to form a single cell. This process is called fertilization. The new cell divides rapidly, forming first an **embryo**— a tiny plant developing within a seed—then an adult plant.

Lycopods, horsetails, and ferns produce special cells called spores. These spores scatter in the wind, land in the soil, and begin to grow. But the plants they grow into do not look like the adult plants at all. In ferns, for example, the spores grow into tiny heart-shaped plants called **prothallus.** These tiny plants produce new specialized cells—the male and female gametes. For fertilization to occur, the male gamete must swim to the female gamete. The fused cell then grows into the fern plant with which you are familiar. It produces spores, and the cycle begins again.

Now look at the life cycle of seed plants. The adult seed plants produce spores, just as nonseed plants do. These spores, however, do not scatter in the wind. They stay on the adult plant. Some spores develop into fine yellow grains called **pollen.** Each pollen grain produces male gametes. Other spores develop into structures that produce female gametes.

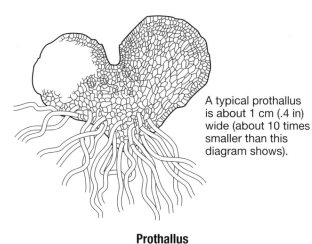

A typical prothallus is about 1 cm (.4 in) wide (about 10 times smaller than this diagram shows).

Prothallus

For fertilization to take place, the pollen grains that contain male gametes must travel to the female gametes. This process is called **pollination.** For some plants, the wind carries the pollen. For other plants, animals, especially insects, carry the pollen.

This type of life cycle gives seed plants a big advantage over nonseed plants. Remember that in ferns and other nonseed plants, the male gamete must swim to the female gamete. Therefore, these plants must grow in wet areas. In seed plants, the male gamete does not need to swim. It is carried inside the pollen, either by the wind or by animals. Therefore, seed plants can grow in dry areas as well as in wet areas.

In seed plants, the plant embryo is enclosed in a seed. The outside of the seed, called the seed coat, is hard and waterproof. It protects the embryo and keeps it from drying out. A seed also contains food reserves that help the embryo withstand harsh conditions. As the embryo grows, it bursts out of the seed.

THINK ABOUT IT

Wind-pollinated plants produce huge quantities of pollen. This airborne pollen causes allergies in many people. Why must these plants produce so much pollen? Write your answer on a separate sheet of paper.

Conifers

There are two major groups of seed plants. The oldest group is the **gymnosperms.** A gymnosperm is a plant that produces uncovered seeds. Today, the most common gymnosperms are the **conifers,** or cone-bearing plants. Conifers include pines, spruces, firs, cedars, and redwoods. Conifers are well adapted to cold and dry environments. Conifers are especially abundant on mountaintops and in northern climates. Most conifers have leaves shaped like needles. These leaves have a thick waterproof layer, so they lose very little water. Remember that in cold climates, the air becomes dry. Most conifers do not drop their leaves in the fall.

Conifers produce male and female gametes inside cones. Male cones contain pollen. Female cones, which are much larger than the male cones, contain the female gametes. Wind carries the pollen from the male cone to the female cone, so fertilization takes place in the female cone. The tough, woody scales on the female cones protect the developing seeds.

Flowering Plants

Eighty percent of all plant species on Earth are seed plants. Ninety-five percent of all seed plants are flowering plants. You can find flowering plants on almost any land in the world. They are the major food source for all land animals, from insects to elephants. Almost all the plants grown for food are flowering plants. The animals humans eat depend on flowering plants to survive.

Flowering plants are divided by the number of seed-leaves each seed has. The seed leaf is the first leaf or leaves that will emerge when the seed germinates. If a plant has one seed leaf, it is a **monocot.** If it has two, it is a **dicot.** There are more dicots than monocots. However, the grasses, including all the cereal grains, are monocots, making them a very large group. Other monocots include orchids, lilies, and palm trees. Nearly all other plants, except conifers, are dicots. Conifers have many seed leaves.

The next way flowering plants are divided is by the type of fruit they set. Not all fruit is like the kind you buy in the store. Fruits like apples, pears, and raspberries are all members of the same family, which also includes the roses. These plants make a juicy, or **succulent,** fruit. Peas and a few other garden vegetables are members of a family that also produces succulent fruits. These are usually called legumes.

Other plants, such as the grain plants, make a dry fruit. The wheat your bread is made from came from a dry fruit. All the tree nuts, such as walnuts, are dry fruits.

There are many fruits you probably do not even think of as fruits. Maple trees make fruits that humans do not eat. They are produced in sets of two and can fly away from the parent tree like little helicopters. Oaks produce acorns, which can be eaten, but are very bitter. Both are dry fruits.

Fruits, whether succulent or dry, are nothing more than the ripened ovary of a flower. Flowers are the reproductive organs of plants.

Flower Parts

If you peek inside a flower, you will see a flask-shaped structure called the **pistil.** The pistil is the female part of the flower. The rounded bottom is the **ovary.** Fertilization takes place in the ovary. The neck of the flask is called the **style.** The top of the flask is called the **stigma.**

The male structures surround the pistils. They are a series of thin stalks called **filaments,** with lobes on top called **anthers.** The anthers contain pollen.

Colorful **petals** surround the flower. The colors attract animals, such as insects, that pollinate the flower. Flowers may also produce a sugary substance called **nectar** to attract animals. Another set of leaflike structures called **sepals** also surround the flower. In some plants, they are colorful like petals. In other plants, they are small and green.

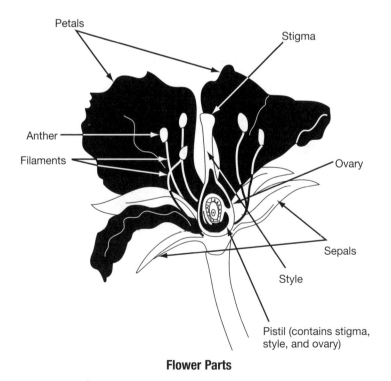

Flower Parts

Note that many flowers do *not* contain all these structures. Some plants have male and female flowers. Wind-pollinated flowers do not need petals to attract animals.

Pollination

The following is what happens in a bee-pollinated flower.

1. A bee, attracted by the bright petals and sweet smell, lands on a flower and feeds on the nectar.

2. While eating, the bee brushes against the anthers and covers itself with pollen.

3. The bee flies to another flower to feed. Some of the pollen on the bee from the last flower rubs off on the stigma.

4. The pollen on the stigma sprouts long tubes. These tubes grow down through the style and into the ovary.

5. Male gametes from the pollen travel down the tubes into the ovary. They join with the female gametes and form embryos.

6. Once fertilization occurs, the flower starts to change. The petals and anthers drop off. Inside the ovary, a seed develops around each embryo. The ovary itself turns into a fruit.

Fruits are important adaptations for plants. They help the plant disperse the seeds. Some fruit, such as the fluffy dandelion fruit, gets caught up in the wind. Many fruits are edible. When animals eat the fruit, the seeds pass through the animals' digestive systems unharmed. Some fruit have barbs that stick to animals that brush by. The animals then carry the seeds to a new location. Coconuts may fall into the ocean and float to new islands.

■ PRACTICE 36: Seed Plants

Look at the list of words below. Fill in each line with the letter of the word that correctly completes each statement.

a. pollen   **c.** fruit   **e.** anthers
b. stigma   **d.** fertilization   **f.** cones

1. When a male and female gamete fuse together, it is called _____.

2. The structures in conifers that contain the seeds are called _____.

3. The fine yellow powder containing the male gametes is called _____.

4. The three parts of the flask-shaped pistil are called the _____, style, and ovary.

5. The structures of the flowers containing pollen are the _____.

6. After fertilization, the ovary turns into a(n) _____.

UNIT 3 REVIEW

Look at the list of words below. Fill in each line with the letter of the word that correctly completes each statement.

a. oxygen   **c.** surface area   **e.** leaves
b. roots   **d.** water   **f.** carbon dioxide

1. In photosynthesis, plants use sunlight to convert _____ and _____ to glucose.

2. Plants pay a price for having a high amount of surface area to collect sunlight. They lose a lot of _____.

3. Water flows through the xylem from the roots to the _____.

4. Root hairs help a plant take up more water because they increase the _____ of the roots.

5. A plant's _____ anchor the plant in the soil, absorb water and nutrients, and store food reserves.

Circle the letter of the item that correctly answers each of the following.

6. The rhizobium bacteria that live in the roots of legumes _____.
   a. convert carbon dioxide to glucose
   b. help the plants take up water
   c. convert nitrogen from the air into a form the plant can use

7. By closing their stomata, plants _____.
   a. prevent water loss, but can no longer take up carbon dioxide
   b. prevent water loss, but can no longer take up phosphorus
   c. prevent water loss, but can no longer gather sunlight

8. Which of the following do mosses lack?
   a. waterproof leaves
   b. xylem and phloem
   c. roots

9. Why do conifers differ from flowering plants?
   a. They do not have vascular tissue.
   b. They are not seed plants.
   c. They have cones instead of flowers.

10. Which of the following is true of the ovary in flowering plants?
    a. It attracts pollinators, such as bees.
    b. It develops into the fruit.
    c. It contains pollen.

UNIT 3 APPLICATION ACTIVITY 1
Photosynthesis

Photosynthesis is going on all around us. The following activity will help you understand how the process of photosynthesis works.

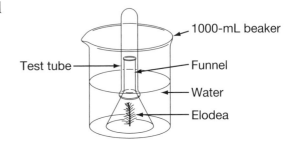

1000-mL beaker

Test tube

Funnel

Water

Elodea

Pour 500 ml of water in a 1000-ml beaker. Allow the water to sit overnight. (This allows chlorine or other additives that may be in the water to evaporate.)

The next day, dissolve 3 grams of sodium bicarbonate (baking soda) in the water.

Place a single sprig of elodea plant in the bottom of the beaker. Put a funnel over the plant, as shown in the diagram above.

Fill a test tube with water. Place your thumb securely over the mouth of the tube. Turn the tube upside down, and place it over the top of the funnel.

Set the beaker in direct sunlight. Count the number of gas bubbles that appear in the test tube. Record in the chart the number of bubbles that appear after 30, 60, 90, 120, 150, 180, and 210 seconds.

Time (seconds)	Number of Bubbles
30	
60	
90	
120	
150	
180	
210	

After several hours, remove the test tube from the water. Immediately put your thumb over the mouth of the test tube. Have your instructor, or a partner, light a wooden splint. Then blow out the flame so the splint is still glowing. Remove your thumb from the mouth of the test tube and immediately place the glowing splint into the test tube.

Observe and explain what happens.

_____

_____

_____

Graph your results on a separate sheet of paper. The graph shown at the right is an example.

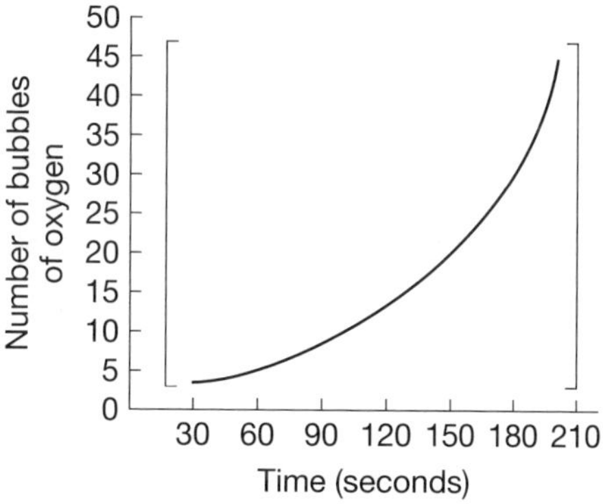

How are your results related to photosynthesis?

_____

_____

_____

_____

_____

_____

What conclusion can you draw from your graph?

_____

_____

_____

_____

UNIT 3 APPLICATION ACTIVITY 2
Plant Overcrowding

Place equal amounts of soil in each of three 15-cm (6-inch) pots. The soil should be no higher than 2.5 cm (about 1 inch) from the top of the pot. Label the pots A, B, and C. In pot A, plant three lima beans; in pot B, plant seven lima beans; in pot C, plant ten lima beans. Place the pots in good

		Diameter of Stem	Number of Leaves	Width of Largest Leaf	Weight Day 1	Weight Day 2
Pot 1	1					
	2					
	3					
Pot 2	1					
	2					
	3					
	4					
	5					
	6					
	7					
Pot 3	1					
	2					
	3					
	4					
	5					
	6					
	7					
	8					
	9					
	10					

light, and water them every two or three days. Allow plants to grow 10 cm. Then cut the plants off at soil level. Be sure to keep track of which plants come from which pot.

In the chart on page 150, record, *for each plant from each pot,* the following data: diameter of stem; number of leaves; width of largest leaf at widest point; and weight. Dry the plants overnight, and weigh them again the next day. Record the data on the chart on page 150.

Make a bar graph to compare plant weights. Use the sample on the right as a guide. (Use a separate sheet of paper.)

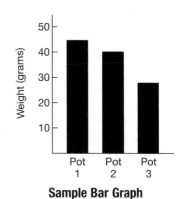

Sample Bar Graph

1. Which plants did best?

2. Which plants did worst?

_____

3. What conditions were the same for all three pots?

_____

4. What did you notice about the seeds in Pot C? Why?

_____

_____

5. When planting a garden, why is it necessary to thin out plants after they emerge from the soil?

_____

_____

UNIT 4

The Animal Kingdom

LESSON 13: Invertebrates

GOAL: To survey the major groups of animals that lack backbones

WORDS TO KNOW

abdomen	crustaceans	platyhelminthes
amoebocytes	exoskeleton	polyp
annelids	gastropods	pores
antennae	gills	poriferan
arachnids	hemocoels	pseudocoelom
arthropods	insects	secrete
bivalves	invertebrate	shell
carapace	larvae (singular *larva*)	sponges
cephalopods	mantle	tentacles
cephalothorax	medusa	thorax
chelicerae	mesoglea	trachea
chelicerates	mollusks	unirames
chitin	molting	valves
choanocytes	mucus	visceral mass
closed circulatory system	muscular foot	worm
cnidarian	nematodes	
coeloms	pedipalps	

Characteristics of Animals

Now you will explore the animal kingdom. On the next page are some key characteristics of animals.

- All animals are multicellular.

- Animals do not photosynthesize. Instead, they must take in food and break it down.

- Animal cells do not have cell walls.

In this lesson and the next, you will survey the major phyla in the animal kingdom. First, you will look at phyla of animals that do not have backbones. An animal that does not have a backbone is called an **invertebrate**.

Poriferan and Cnidarian

The two simplest phyla include the **poriferan** phylum, which contains the sponges. It also includes the **cnidarian** phylum, which contains the jellyfish and corals. These animals have specialized cells and tissue, but lack organs. Despite their simplicity, they have survived for hundreds of millions of years.

Poriferan

Poriferans, or **sponges,** are found in oceans throughout the world. A few species live in freshwater. Sizes range from a couple of centimeters to over 3 meters in diameter. Sponges spend their entire lives in one spot. Most sponges attach themselves to rocky surfaces. Some live on top of other animals. The backs of crabs are often covered with sponges. The sponges help to camouflage the crabs.

Sponges are one of the earliest examples of cells working together. In many ways, however, they more closely resemble a colony of individual cells rather than an animal. Only some of the cells join together to form tissue. Other cells move independently inside the sponge.

Sponges have a flexible skeleton made of proteins and minerals. This gives sponges their shape and is an attachment site for the individual cells. These skeletons are the original sponges that people used to clean their kitchens and bathrooms. Today, most household sponges are made out of synthetic materials.

Sponges are shaped like vases. They are hollow on the inside and have a large opening on top. A single layer of tissue covers the outside of the sponge. Some of the cells in this layer have **pores,** or tiny openings. Water flows through the pores to the inside of the sponge.

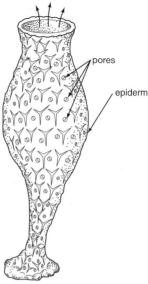

A Sponge

Behind this layer is a jellylike layer that contains cells called **amoebocytes.** These cells are not connected. They can move independently. Some amoebocytes **secrete** (form) the skeleton. Others produce sperm and eggs.

Lining the inside cavity of the sponge are another group of cells called **choanocytes.** Each has a whiplike flagellum. By beating the flagellum, the choanocytes create a current of water that flows in through the pores and out through the opening at the top of the sponge. The cells then extract oxygen and food (mostly bacteria and algae) from the water.

Cnidarians

The phylum of cnidarians forms an important part of ocean ecosystems, especially in the tropics. Cnidarians include jellyfish, sea anemones, and coral. Some species are so small you need a microscope to see them. Others weigh over a ton.

Cnidarians are the first animals that possess specialized tissues. They have two layers of tissue, as opposed to the one layer in the poriferans. Muscles enable them to move around. Nerves enable them to sense their environment and to coordinate their movements. As a result, cnidarians can live in a wider range of conditions than the sponges.

Cnidarians' bodies are shaped like cups. There is a hollow cavity inside where food is digested. This cavity opens up into a mouth. **Tentacles**— long, flexible structures used for feeling or grasping—surround the mouth and capture and draw in food.

There are two layers of tissue. The outer layer contains muscle cells and nerve cells. The inner layer surrounds the inner cavity. The cells in the inner layer are involved in digestion.

Between the two layers is a fluidlike substance called the **mesoglea.** The mesoglea acts as a skeleton, giving the animal its shape.

TIP

To understand how a fluid can act like a skeleton, find a hose and attach it to a faucet. Squeeze and bend the hose. Now block the open end of the hose and turn the water on. The water pressure will make it much harder to bend and squeeze the hose. Thus, when a liquid is contained in a tightly enclosed space, it provides enough support for that space to work as a skeleton.

Cnidarians come in two forms—the polyp and the medusa.

POLYPS

A **polyp** is an invertebrate that has a hollow, tubelike body. The tube is closed at one end and attached to a surface. The open end consists of a mouth surrounded by tentacles. The tentacles snare food that floats by.

MEDUSAS

A **medusa** resembles an upside-down bowl or umbrella. The medusa's mouth and tentacles face down. Unlike polyps, medusas float or swim. The medusas include jellyfish.

Some cnidarians spend the first part of their lives as polyps and the second part as medusas. The **larvae,** or early forms of the organism, settle to the bottom of a body of water and grow into polyps. The polyps will bud, creating free-swimming medusas. (These medusas have genes that are identical to the polyp from which they budded.) The medusas produce eggs and sperm.

Corals are formed by huge colonies of polyps. Each polyp surrounds itself with a skeleton made of calcium carbonate. As the polyps die, other

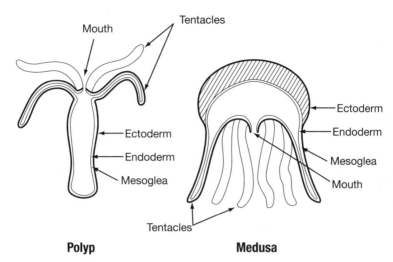

Polyp	**Medusa**

polyps settle on top of these skeletons, then build their own skeletons. Eventually, these corals can become huge, growing reefs that can stretch for kilometers. In the tropics, coral reefs are a vital part of the ocean ecosystem. Fish and other marine organisms live in these reefs. Unfortunately, many corals are dying. Scientists suspect that pollution may be killing the polyps that form the coral.

IN REAL LIFE

Jorge took his friend Peter snorkeling to the reefs off the Florida Keys. The beauty of the coral astounded Peter. He started to break off a piece of coral to take home. However, Jorge stopped him. He explained that the coral was a living colony of tiny animals. The reefs were already in bad shape. If everybody who visited the reef took home a souvenir, there would not be any left.

Cnidarians hunt for food. Small cnidarians eat single-celled organisms. Larger ones capture small fish. Cnidarians use stinging cells to capture their prey. When brushed, these cells eject tiny poisonous darts that pierce the victim. Most cnidarians are not dangerous to humans, although they can be painful. Sea wasps, which live off the Australian coast, are one of the few cnidarians that can deliver a fatal sting.

■ PRACTICE 37: Poriferan and Cnidarian

Decide if the following phrases describe a poriferan (**P**) or a cnidarian (**C**). Write the correct letter on each line.

_____ **1.** has just a single layer of tissue

_____ **2.** has nerve and muscle cells

_____ **3.** forms coral reefs

_____ **4.** contains stinging cells

_____ **5.** filters food from water

_____ **6.** spends its life in one place

The Worms

A **worm** is a long, softbodied invertebrate. Worms usually move by creeping or crawling. In this section, you will learn about three phyla of worms—the platyhelminthes (flatworms), the nematodes (roundworms), and the annelids, which include earthworms and leeches.

These phyla represent major advances in complexity.

■ They all have a front end and a back end. The front end contains a mouth, most of the major sense organs, and the central nervous system or brain. As a result, the animal always moves in a single direction.

■ These phyla, and all the others you will study from now on, have three layers of tissue. Remember that the poriferans have one layer and the cnidarians have two layers.

■ These phyla have organs.

Flatworms

The simplest of these animals are the **platyhelminthes,** or flatworms. As their name implies, flatworms look more like ribbons than tubes. A flatworm has a simple set of organs. It has an intestine in which it digests food, organs that excrete waste, and organs used for reproduction. It also has true muscle fibers and a primitive central nervous system. It absorbs oxygen through its skin.

TIP

To remember that platyhelminthes is another name for flatworms, look at the first part of the name: *plat-*. This comes from a word that means "flat." The words *plate* and *flat* come from the same source. Plates are flat—and so are platyhelminthes.

Flatworms range in length from a quarter of a centimeter to over 9 meters. They live both in the water and in moist soils, where they hunt for food. Some types of flatworms that live in warm, shallow oceans are beautifully colored.

Most flatworms, however, are parasites. A parasite is an organism that feeds on another living organism. Parasitic flatworms spend most of their lives feeding and reproducing inside the host organism. They can weaken and sometimes kill their hosts, but killing the host is not to a parasite's advantage. If the host organism dies, the parasite also dies.

Many flatworms can infect people. Most can be treated with medicine. One of the most common parasites is the tapeworm. Tapeworms lodge in the host's intestine and absorb nutrients.

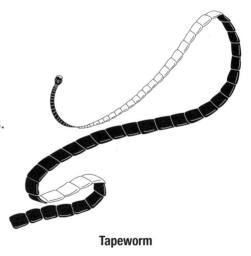

Tapeworm

They can grow over 3 meters long. Because their food has already been digested by the host, tapeworms do not have (or need) a digestive tract. The body of the tapeworm is made of many segments, each of which contains reproductive organs. The segments break off and leave the host through the feces. Each segment can then grow into a new tapeworm. People get tapeworms by eating infected meat. Tapeworm is now uncommon in the United States because most of the meat is inspected. Cooking the meat long enough will also kill the parasite.

Flukes are an especially dangerous group of parasitic flatworms. They can live in the host's liver, lungs, intestines, or brain, causing extensive damage. Most flukes go through several phases and infect more than one type of animal. Schistosomiasis is a common disease in parts of Africa, Asia, and South America. The fluke that causes it spends part of its life in humans and part of its life in snails. The adult flukes live in the blood vessels around the intestines and liver of humans, where they lay up to 2000 eggs each day. The eggs pass out with the feces and develop into larvae. The larvae then burrow into the digestive organs of snails and develop further. When humans wade in water where the snails are, the larvae leave the snails, burrow into the skin of humans, and finally enter the bloodstream where they will grow and lay eggs.

Roundworms

The **nematodes,** or roundworms, are some of the most abundant animals on Earth. They are everywhere. An acre of soil or an acre of ocean contains billions of roundworms. The vast majority are not harmful. Most nematodes feed on organic matter and other roundworms. But some types are parasitic and can severely damage plants and animals.

Like flatworms, roundworms have muscle fibers and primitive brains. They also have the same types of organs. Here are some of the differences.

- Flatworms have only a single opening in their digestive tracts. Wastes must pass out through their mouths. Roundworms have two openings—a mouth in the front and an anus in the back. This efficient digestive system may be the reason roundworms are so successful.

Unit 4: The Animal Kingdom • Biology

- Flatworm bodies are solid. Roundworms have a cavity, or hollow place, outside the digestive tract called the **pseudocoelom.** This cavity is filled with fluid that helps to cushion the digestive tract. The fluid also serves as a skeleton, giving the roundworm its shape.

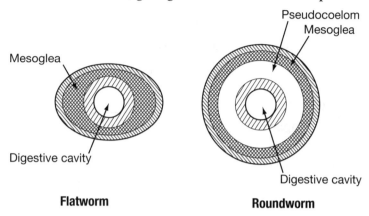

Flatworm   **Roundworm**

There are about 50 species of parasitic roundworms that infect humans. They include the hookworms, pinworms, and filarial worms. Some of the most dangerous roundworms are the *Trichinilla*, which cause the disease trichinosis. People get trichinosis by eating undercooked pork or wild game, such as bear, that contains *Trichinilla* worms. Inside the body, the worms bore into muscles. If not treated, trichinosis damages the muscles. It can be very painful and sometimes fatal.

Annelids

There are three classes of **annelids,** or segmented worms: the marine worms, which live in the ocean; the earthworms; and the leeches. Like roundworms, annelids have a mouth and an anus. They also have a brain, nerves, and muscles. Their muscles and organs, however, are more highly developed. Here are some of the characteristics that distinguish annelids from flatworms and roundworms.

- Annelids' bodies are divided into segments, or sections. Each segment contains its own sets of nerves and muscles. These segments enable the worm to move much more efficiently. Watch the segments of an earthworm as it moves. You will see different segments expanding and contracting as the worm pulls itself along.

- Annelids have fluid-filled body cavities called **coeloms.** The coeloms are similar to the pseudocoeloms in roundworms. They contain organs, including waste-removal organs and male and female reproductive organs. The fluid inside the coelom serves as a skeleton.

- Annelids have several hearts that pump blood through closed veins. This is called a **closed circulatory system.** As a result, blood can move quickly, circulating nutrients and oxygen to the entire body.

THINK ABOUT IT

Compare the impact of xylem and phloem in plants with the impact of hearts and veins in animals. Write your answer on a separate sheet of paper.

MARINE WORMS

Marine worms are the most beautiful of the annelids. Some are very colorful. Others live in tubes burrowed into the sand on the ocean floor. The marine worm partially emerges from the tube and extends a crown of feathery gills into the water. These gills absorb oxygen and trap food particles.

EARTHWORMS

Earthworms are the most familiar of the annelids. Some tropical earthworms can grow 2 meters long and almost 5 centimeters in diameter. Earthworms burrow through the soil and eat organic matter. Farmers and gardeners love earthworms, because the worms break up and aerate the soil, making it easier for plant roots to grow.

LEECHES

Leeches are the most notorious of the annelids. They live in ponds and streams and feed on the blood of larger animals. They are not, however, dangerous. While feeding, leeches secrete a powerful chemical that keeps the blood flowing. For hundreds of years, doctors used leeches to bleed patients. Today, doctors use this chemical—and the leeches themselves—to prevent blood from clotting during surgery.

■ PRACTICE 38: The Worms

Circle the letter of the correct answer to each of the following questions.

1. Which of the following phyla includes animals with a digestive tract that has only a single opening?
   a. platyhelminthes
   b. nematodes
   c. annelids
   d. all of the above

2. Which of the following phyla includes animals with a pseudocoelom?
   a. platyhelminthes
   b. nematodes
   c. annelids
   d. all of the above

3. Which of the following phyla includes animals with hearts?
   a. platyhelminthes
   b. nematodes
   c. annelids
   d. all of the above

Mollusks

Who would have thought that slugs, clams, and octopuses had anything in common? All three belong to the phylum Mollusca. **Mollusks** are a diverse group of animals that live in the ocean, in freshwater, and on land.

Despite their many differences, mollusks have certain features in common.

- All mollusks have a **muscular foot.** Many mollusks use this foot to move, to grip surfaces, and to dig into the ground.

- The area containing the internal organs is called the **visceral mass.** The organs include a heart, a digestive system, excretory organs that get rid of wastes, and reproductive organs. A mollusk also has a head that contains a brain and sense organs.

- All mollusks have a sheet of tissue called a **mantle** that covers the visceral mass. In most mollusks, the mantle secretes a **shell,** or hard outer covering.

Now you will learn about the three major classes of mollusks—the gastropods, the bivalves, and the cephalopods.

Gastropods

The **gastropods** are mollusks with either a single shell or no shell at all. Gastropods include snails and slugs. They live in freshwater, in salt water, and on land. A shallow bay or a wet field can contain billions of snails or slugs. Most gastropods have coiled shells. They retreat into their shells for protection or to prevent water loss. Still, these shells are light enough to carry around. Slugs have either reduced internal shells or no shells at all.

On land, a gastropod uses its muscular foot to move. Both snails and slugs glide on top of **mucus,** a slippery substance that they secrete. Most gastropods graze on plants and algae. A few snails hunt other animals. Some marine species drill holes in the shells of clams and other snails to get at the meat. The poisonous cone snail injects fish with a poison that is so powerful it can actually kill humans.

Bivalves

The **bivalves** include clams, mussels, oysters, and scallops. Most live in the ocean, although there are a few freshwater species. Bivalve shells are split in half. These halves are called **valves** (hence the name *bivalve*). A powerful muscle holds the two halves closed. If you were to open up a clam and peel away the mantle, you would see its internal organs and small head. Many bivalves, such as clams, use their muscular foot to bury themselves in the mud. Others, such as mussels and oysters, attach themselves to rocks.

Most bivalves have **gills** that filter food and oxygen from the water. The deep-water scallop has a unique way of feeding. When it detects prey swimming by, it opens its shell. Water rushes in, sweeping in the prey. The scallop then closes its shell, trapping its meal.

When some species of oysters find a foreign substance in their mantle, they surround it with a hard, shiny substance. The results are pearls. Today, most commercial pearls are formed around bits of shell that people insert in the oysters.

Cephalopods

The **cephalopods** include squid, octopuses, and cuttlefish. They only live in the ocean. Cephalopods are best known for the eight arms surrounding their heads. Squid have eight arms plus two tentacles. Unlike the gastropods and bivalves, many cephalopods can move fast. The foot of a squid is modified into a funnel that expels water, creating a powerful jet. The squid uses this speed to chase down prey. Squid also have small internal shells that help them maneuver in the water. Octopuses do not have shells. They prefer to lie low, although they can move quickly over short distances to catch prey or escape enemies.

Cephalopods are by far the smartest invertebrates. They have big heads, big eyes, and big brains. Scientists have trained octopuses to run mazes and to distinguish between different shapes and colors.

Giant squid, which can reach over 18 meters long, are the largest invertebrates in the world. Their eyes are the size of car headlights. They live hundreds of meters deep, so they are rarely seen. Scientists have found evidence that sperm whales eat giant squid. Although nobody has ever seen it, it is fun to imagine the epic battles that take place between these two giants at the bottom of the ocean.

■ PRACTICE 39: Mollusks

Circle the letter of the correct answer to each of the following questions.

1. Which mollusks have mantles surrounding their internal organs?
   a. gastropods
   b. bivalves
   c. cephalopods
   d. all of the above

2. Which mollusks use their muscular foot to burrow into the mud?
   a. clams
   b. slugs
   c. squid
   d. all of the above

3. Which is true of ALL mollusks?
   a. Their mantles secrete protective shells.
   b. They have a muscular foot.
   c. They have large, complex eyes.
   d. They are filter feeders.

4. What is the main feature that defines bivalves?
   a. They are missing most internal organs.
   b. Their shells are split in half.
   c. They use their shells for protection.
   d. They are good to eat.

Arthropods

If phyla were to be judged by the number of species they contain, the arthropods would win easily. **Arthropods** are invertebrates with segmented bodies and jointed limbs. They include insects, spiders, centipedes, crabs, and lobsters. Scientists have identified almost a million species so far, and there may be as many as 10 million species. That is more than the number in all other animal phyla put together.

Arthropods most likely evolved from annelids. Like annelids, arthropods have segmented bodies and a similar nervous system. They also have a body cavity called a coelom. However, the similarities end there.

The most important difference between the annelids and arthropods is that arthropods have a coat of armor called an **exoskeleton.** It contains a rigid substance called **chitin.** The exoskeleton helps protect the arthropods from enemies, but that is only the beginning.

- The exoskeleton is waterproof. It prevents arthropods from drying out. It also prevents water from entering arthropods that live in the water. Many scientists believe that this waterproof coat enabled arthropods to be the first animals to colonize land.

- Groups of specialized muscles are attached to the exoskeleton. These muscles power the arthropods' legs, wings, antennae, and body segments. The result is that arthropods can run fast and are powerful fliers. If you have ever watched an ant carry a large load, you know how strong these muscles can be.

If you have ever worn a suit of armor, you know it can cause some problems. Here is how arthropods have solved these problems.

- It is difficult to move around in a coat of armor. Arthropods can move because their body segments and their appendages (legs, antennae, and mouth parts) have hinges or joints. In fact, *arthropod* means "jointed feet."

- It is difficult to grow when you are wearing a suit of armor. Arthropods have adapted by shedding their coats when they have outgrown them. This process is called **molting.** Arthropods may molt several times during their lives. Many insects look completely different after they molt. A caterpillar changes into a butterfly. A grub changes into a wasp. A nymph changes into a dragonfly.

■ THINK ABOUT IT

Why is molting such a dangerous time for arthropods? Write your answer on a separate sheet of paper.

Arthropods have complex senses that allow them to move and respond quickly to the environment. Like annelids, arthropods have hearts that pump fluid containing oxygen and nutrients to all parts of their bodies. However, in arthropods, the fluid does not flow through a closed set of veins. Instead, it flows through a series of cavities called **hemocoels.**

Arthropods are divided into three groups. They are the chelicerates, the crustaceans, and the unirames. A fourth group, the trilobites, dominated the oceans 500 million years ago. They are extinct now, but many trilobite fossils remain.

Chelicerates

The biggest class within the chelicerates are the arachnids. This class includes spiders, scorpions, mites, and ticks. The bodies of the arachnids are divided into two sections—the cephalothorax in front and the abdomen in back. Chelicerates have two clawlike mouthparts called chelicerae. Spiders use their chelicerae to inject poison into their victims. They also have a second pair of mouthparts called pedipalps. In scorpions, the pedipalps form large claws that the scorpions use to capture and hold prey. All arachnids have eight legs.

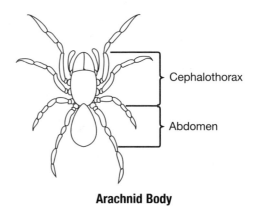

Arachnid Body

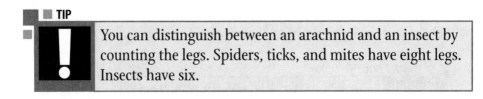

TIP

You can distinguish between an arachnid and an insect by counting the legs. Spiders, ticks, and mites have eight legs. Insects have six.

Most arachnids hunt for their food. They eat insects, including many pests. The giant bird spiders in South America actually eat small birds. Scorpions, and some spiders, ambush or chase down their prey. Many spiders spin silken webs to capture their prey. Both spiders and scorpions poison their victims. Scorpions have a stinger on the end of their tails. Although spider bites and scorpion stings can be irritating or even painful, few are dangerous to people.

Ticks and many types of mites are parasites. Ticks attach themselves to larger animals and drink their blood. Some species of ticks can transmit dangerous diseases. Two common tick-borne diseases in the United States are Rocky Mountain spotted fever, which is transmitted by wood ticks and dog ticks, and Lyme disease, which is transmitted by tiny deer ticks.

IN REAL LIFE

It was a hot summer day, and Maurice was out hiking wearing shorts and sandals. On his way home that afternoon, he cut through a stand of trees and shrubs. That night, he found a creature the size of a poppy seed on his leg. It had eight legs. Maurice quickly brushed his leg and scanned the rest of his body. He found two more deer ticks. Fortunately, they had not attached themselves to his skin. The next time he cut through the woods, he would wear long pants and hiking boots. He would also tuck the cuffs of his pants into his socks.

Crustaceans

Crustaceans include lobsters, crabs, and shrimp. Most live in the ocean. Some, such as crayfish, live in freshwater. If you turn over a rotting log, you will likely see sow bugs, another crustacean.

Crustaceans have two pairs of **antennae** that they use to sense the environment. They also have distinctive mouthparts that they use for biting and chewing. The body of the crustacean is covered with a hard, protective shield called a **carapace.** If you have ever eaten lobster, you know how hard the carapace can be.

Lobsters, crabs, and shrimp are the best known crustaceans, but they are not the most important. The oceans are filled with tiny crustaceans called copepods. They may be the most abundant animal on Earth. Marine animals, from fish to giant whales, feed on copepods.

Unirames

The **unirames** include centipedes and millipedes, but by far the most important class are the **insects.** You cannot get away from insects unless you dive into the ocean. They are underground, in the air, in freshwater, and in your house. There is an astounding variety of insects. They eat plants, other insects, dead animals, and the blood of live animals. There are 300,000 species of beetles alone.

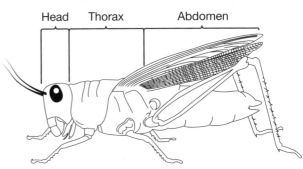

Insect Body

An insect's body is divided into three distinct regions—the head, the **thorax,** and the abdomen. All insects have one pair of antennae and six legs. Except for fleas and a few other small groups, all insects have two pairs of wings for at least part of their lives. Ants start off with wings, but chew them off.

If you have ever watched a housefly or a dragonfly buzzing around tirelessly, you know that insects use a lot of energy. Insects have a unique way of taking in oxygen. The circulatory system does not carry the oxygen. Instead, the oxygen goes directly to the cells through a network of tubes called **trachea.** This ensures that oxygen reaches the cells quickly.

Insects affect people in many ways. Insects eat all types of plants, including important crops. Farmers use pesticides to try to control them. Insects also spread dangerous diseases. In the Middle Ages, fleas spread bubonic plague, which killed one third of all Europeans. Mosquitoes transmit deadly diseases such as malaria, yellow fever, and encephalitis.

But insects are also essential to life on Earth. Bees and butterflies pollinate plants. If they suddenly disappeared, many flowering plants, including the ones you eat, would not produce seeds. Insects are also a critical food source for many animals, including birds.

■ PRACTICE 40: Arthropods

Circle the letter of the answer that correctly completes each of the
following statements.

1. The major difference between arthropods and annelids is that
   arthropods _____.
   a. are not segmented
   b. do not have a coelom
   c. have an exoskeleton
   d. have a closed circulatory system (blood is pumped through a
      network of closed veins)

2. Hard carapaces are found on _____.
   a. spiders
   b. crabs
   c. beetles
   d. all of the above

3. Chelicerates are distinguished by _____.
   a. their clawlike mouthparts called chelicerae
   b. their six legs
   c. their three body regions
   d. all of the above

4. Copepods are _____.
   a. chelicerates with enlarged pedipalps
   b. tiny crustaceans that live in the ocean
   c. wingless insects
   d. unirames

5. Insects take in oxygen through a network of tubes called _____.
   a. thorax
   b. trachea
   c. antennae
   d. hemocoels

LESSON 14: Vertebrates

GOAL: To learn about chordates and their most important class, the vertebrates

WORDS TO KNOW

amphibian	jawless fish	reptiles
bony fish	mammal	sense organs
cartilage	mammary glands	skeleton
cartilaginous fish	marsupial	spinal cord
chordates	metamorphosis	swim bladder
coldblooded	nervous system	vertebrae (singular *vertebra*)
fetus	notochord	
gill slits	placental	vertebrates
		warmblooded

Chordates and the First Vertebrates

In this lesson, you will learn about one more phylum—the chordates. This phylum accounts for only one tenth of one percent of the animal kingdom, yet these animals dominate the land, the ocean, and the sky. They have given rise to the largest, the fastest, the strongest, and the most intelligent animals in the world.

Just what is a chordate? **Chordates** include organisms such as fish, birds, snakes, and humans. These organisms are different in many ways. But they all share some things. Here are some features that all chordates have in common.

- All chordates have **gill slits.** In fish, these gill slits contain structures that filter food and oxygen from the water.

- At some point in their development, all chordates have a stiff rod called a **notochord** running through their bodies. The notochord provides support for the body.

- All chordates have a central nerve cord or **spinal cord.** This nerve cord helps send messages from the brain to the rest of the body.

By now, you may be confused. You have a spinal cord, but you do not have a notochord, and you certainly do not have gill slits. The fact is that you do not now, but you did once. During the earliest stages of development inside your mother's womb, you had both a notochord and gill slits. These structures disappeared before you were born.

As they mature, most chordates develop a backbone. This is made up of a series of small bones called **vertebrae** (singular *vertebra*). These bones surround the nerve cord. They protect the nerve cord and provide support. Animals with backbones are called **vertebrates**—that is, animals with vertebrae. Here are some other features vertebrates have in common.

- They have a closed circulatory system. A heart pumps blood through a network of blood vessels. This system distributes oxygen and nutrients to all tissues, even in the largest bodies.

- They have a highly developed **nervous system,** including a complex brain.

- They have highly developed **sense organs,** such as eyes and ears.

Coldblooded and Warmblooded

You probably know that the normal temperature for the human body is about 98.6°F or 37°C. Your body has ways to keep the temperature about the same all the time. Your body temperature is controlled from the inside. Organisms that control their body temperature from inside are called **warmblooded.** These animals keep their body temperatures constant. Warmblooded organisms usually need to eat extra food to create the energy they need to keep warm. They can remain active over long periods of time in both hot and cold weather.

Some vertebrates do not control their body temperature in this way. Instead, they take on the temperature around them. If they are in cold air or water, then their bodies are cold. If the air or water is warm, their bodies are warm. These organisms are called **coldblooded.** They can only control their body heat by taking in heat from the outside, or by being very active. They must bask in the sun to warm up, then retreat into the shade to cool down. They are only active in short spurts. Like a car engine without coolant, a coldblooded animal will overheat if it is active for too long.

Fish—The First Vertebrates

The first vertebrates were jawless fish that did not have skeletons. Instead, they had bony plates under their skin and around their brains. Their gill slits contained structures that filtered oxygen from the water. Jaws were the next major step in the evolution of vertebrates. Fish with jaws could eat larger prey by biting off chunks of food. Therefore, these fish could grow larger. Eventually, the fish lost their bony plates and developed a skeleton—bones that support the body and give it shape.

Today, there are three major classes of fish.

JAWLESS FISH

Jawless fish, closely related to the first vertebrates, do not have true jaws. Because of this, they usually eat by suction. Some, like lampreys, suck the blood from live fish. Others, like hagfish, feed on dead or dying fish. Jawless fish do not have scales. Their skeletons are made of **cartilage,** a strong connective tissue that is lighter and more flexible than bone. Jawless fish are found in both freshwater and salt water.

CARTILAGINOUS FISH

Fish in this second major class have skeletons made of cartilage. This class includes sharks, skates, and rays. **Cartilaginous fish** live in salt water only. They have a long history; the first fish in this class appeared about 135 million years ago! Sharks are fierce predators that maneuver quickly in the water. A shark has two pairs of fins on its body and a large fin on its tail. Fins enable it to swim and change directions quickly. In skates and rays, one pair of fins is enlarged, forming wings.

BONY FISH

The last major class of fish includes almost 30,000 species, in all shapes and sizes. Tiny herring and giant tuna are both members of this class. As the name suggests, these fish have skeletons made of bone. **Bony fish** live in both salt water and freshwater. Like sharks, these fish use fins to maneuver through the water. But bony fish also have a gas-filled organ called a **swim bladder** that allows them to float at any depth.

TIP

The classes of fish are sometimes called by their scientific names: agnatha, chondrichthyes, and osteichthyes. These are just Greek versions of the common names. *Agnatha* means "jawless." *Ichthyes* means "fish." *Chondri* means "cartilage." And *ostei* means "bony." So agnatha are jawless fish, chondrichthyes are cartilaginous fish, and osteichthyes are bony fish.

Although there are thousands of species of fish, most fish have many things in common. Except for jawless fish, their bodies are covered in scales. They have a skeleton made of either bone or cartilage. They have sense organs, such as eyes and nostrils. They have fins and a tail for swimming, and gills to absorb oxygen from the water. They are coldblooded. Most fish reproduce by laying eggs.

■ PRACTICE 41: Chordates and the First Vertebrates

Circle the letter of the answer that correctly completes each of the following statements.

1. Chordates that have gill slits include _____.
   a. fish only
   b. vertebrates only
   c. reptiles only
   d. all chordates, although the gill slits may disappear before birth

2. Cartilaginous fish _____.
  a. live only in salt water
  b. have skeletons made of cartilage
  c. include fierce, fast-swimming predators
  d. all of the above

3. Bony fish _____.
  a. live only in freshwater
  b. have a swim bladder
  c. have bony plates instead of a skeleton
  d. all of the above

Amphibians

By 350 million years ago, the seas were getting crowded. There was strong competition for food. Also, there were so many animals that oxygen in the sea was being used up faster than it could be replaced. A new type of fish crawled out of the water to feast on the insects. These fish walked on muscular fins. Instead of just relying on gills, they used lungs to draw oxygen from the air. These vertebrates eventually gave rise to the amphibians.

An **amphibian** is an organism that can live both in water and on land. Amphibians include frogs, toads, salamanders, and newts. They live in or near freshwater. Most amphibians spend the first part of their lives in the water. They spend the second part on land, where they feed on insects and other invertebrates. They return to the water to reproduce.

The first amphibians were not fully adapted to life on land. They had to go back to the water to reproduce. The offspring of amphibians had gills. When they grew into adults, the animals developed lungs. But as juveniles, they had to live in the water.

Also, like fish, amphibians are coldblooded. They take on the temperature of the surrounding environment. In the water, the temperature does not change much, even in the winter. On land, the temperature of the air changes a great deal. Amphibians spend a lot of time in the water to regulate their body temperature.

These early amphibians also faced other challenges. Adaptations occurred that handled these challenges.

- Water no longer supported their bodies. They needed strong bones and muscles so they could stand up and move around. They developed a skeleton made of bone, not cartilage, to support their bodies.

- They needed a new way to take in oxygen. They developed several different ways to get oxygen. Young amphibians, which live in the water, use gills. As they mature, they develop lungs. Unlike human lungs, amphibian lungs cannot expand to take in air. Instead, the amphibian gulps in air, which is less effective. To increase their oxygen intake, they adapted to absorb oxygen through their skin.

- Sound travels differently through air than through water. Amphibians developed ears that let them detect sound on land.

- Amphibian eggs are like fish eggs. They dry out in the air. Amphibians return to the water to lay their eggs.

Amphibians are different from fish in other ways, too. Their circulatory system is more complex. Amphibian hearts have three chambers, not just two. Amphibians also have kidneys to remove waste from the blood.

The ability to change form as they mature developed in amphibians as an adaptation to living on land. This kind of change is known as **metamorphosis.** Most amphibians go through a complete metamorphosis. The adult lays eggs in water, fertilizes them, and leaves them to hatch. The young amphibians come out of the egg as tadpoles. Tadpoles have gills and a tail, but no legs. Slowly, the tadpole's tail shortens, and it grows legs. It develops lungs. Once this process is complete, the adult amphibian is able to leave the water. Still, because amphibians' skin must stay moist, amphibians spend their lives near water or in damp places.

■ PRACTICE 42: Amphibians

Decide if each statement that follows is true (**T**) or false (**F**). Write the correct letter on each line.

_____ **1.** Most amphibians spend their whole lives in water.

_____ **2.** Amphibians have hearts with three chambers.

_____ **3.** Young amphibians are tiny versions of adults.

_____ **4.** Once an amphibian's lungs develop, it relies on them for all its oxygen.

_____ **5.** Most amphibians go through a complete change, or metamorphosis.

Reptiles

Forty million years after the first amphibians came on shore, some vertebrates started venturing away from the water. These were the first **reptiles.** These coldblooded vertebrates had adaptations that allowed them to live in dry climates.

- Their eggs are surrounded by a waterproof shell, so they can survive on land.

- They have expandable rib cages, so—unlike amphibians—they can breathe in air by expanding their lungs. Therefore, reptiles do not have to absorb oxygen through their skin.

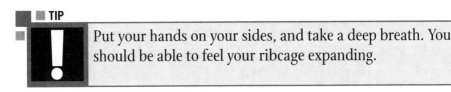

TIP

Put your hands on your sides, and take a deep breath. You should be able to feel your ribcage expanding.

- Because reptiles do not have to absorb oxygen through their skin, their skin does not have to be wet. Instead, waterproof scales cover their skin.

These changes meant that reptiles no longer had to live near water. Entire new habitats opened up to them. From 300 million years ago to 65 million years ago, reptiles ruled Earth. The most dominant group of reptiles were the dinosaurs.

Scientists learned about dinosaurs from the fossils of their bones. From these bones, scientists have a good idea of what these creatures looked like. Some were only the size of chickens. Others, like *Tyrannosaurus rex*, were giant, jagged-toothed meat-eaters. Others had armor or giant horns. Some of the long-necked dinosaurs reached 27 meters long and weighed 80 tons. Dinosaurs also colonized the oceans and the air.

About 65 million years ago, dinosaurs suddenly disappeared. There are many theories explaining why. Most theories blame a drastic change in the climate. One popular theory states that a huge meteor struck Earth. This meteor, scientists say, started tremendous fires and threw so much dust and ash into the air that sunlight was blocked from Earth for several years. Scientists have found a giant crater off the coast of Mexico, lending further support to this theory.

Reptiles Today

There are three orders of reptiles living today.

CROCODILES, ALLIGATORS, AND CAIMANS

The crocodiles and their relatives, the alligators and caimans, are fierce meat-eaters that live in or near the water. They are the closest living relatives of the dinosaurs.

TURTLES AND TORTOISES

Turtles and tortoises are distinguished by their protective shell. They live on land and in freshwater and salt water.

LIZARDS AND SNAKES

Lizards and snakes are the most successful reptiles. They live in a variety of habitats, from deserts to woodlands to swamps to jungles. Snakes evolved from lizards. They slither along, using their dry scales for traction. All snakes hunt for their food. They either strangle their prey or kill them with poison. Then they swallow their prey whole.

■ PRACTICE 43: Reptiles

Circle the letter of the correct answer to each of the following questions.

1. Why was the development of an expandable rib cage so important in reptiles?
   a. They could eat more.
   b. Their lungs became more efficient.
   c. It led to the development of dry, scaly skin.
   d. both *b* and *c*

2. How do scientists know what dinosaurs were like?
   a. Scientists study the dinosaur species that are still alive today.
   b. Scientists study the written records they left.
   c. Scientists study the fossils of their bones.
   d. Scientists study other reptiles that are very similar to dinosaurs.

3. Which of the following is NOT true about snakes?
   a. They evolved directly from lizards.
   b. They are slimy.
   c. Their eggs have shells.
   d. They swallow their prey whole.

Birds

Reptiles and amphibians are coldblooded, which means they cannot control their body temperatures. Birds and mammals are warmblooded. They can keep their body temperatures constant. Producing all that heat, however, takes energy. Just as you need to feed the furnace to keep your house warm, warmblooded animals need a lot of food to keep their bodies warm. In contrast, a rattlesnake needs to eat only a few meals per year.

Birds and mammals have also evolved feathers and fur to keep heat from escaping from their bodies.

You cannot go anywhere in the world without seeing birds flapping or gliding through the air. Birds evolved from reptiles. Many scientists think that birds evolved directly from dinosaurs. Still, scientists are unclear exactly how flight evolved. The following are some of the major adaptations that had to occur for creatures to fly.

- Birds' bones are light. Some are filled with air. Still, they are strong enough to support birds' powerful wing muscles. These muscles are attached to the breastbone and pull the wings up and down.

■ TIP

Have you ever had a meal of roast chicken or turkey? Did you find that there was more light meat than dark? Even though chickens and turkeys cannot fly long distances, they have the same amount of flight muscle as other birds. In these birds, the white meat is flight muscle. The dark meat is leg muscle. This should give you some idea of how large a bird's flight muscles need to be.

- Feathers act like sails, catching drafts of air. Feathers also keep the birds warm. The feathers of ducks and other water birds keep the birds dry. Colorful feathers and fancy plumes also attract mates.

- Flight requires a lot of energy. Birds have efficient lungs and circulatory systems that quickly distribute oxygen to all parts of the body.

■ Birds must have excellent eyesight. They need to see well in order to maneuver quickly in the air, find and grab food while flying, and land on branches.

The ability to fly enables birds to travel great distances. Most birds spend the winter in warm climates such as the tropics. In the spring, many birds fly north to nest and take advantage of swarms of insects that hatch. Some birds migrate many thousands of miles. More amazing still, they return to the exact same nesting site every summer. Birds typically lay between one and five eggs, although some species lay more. One or both parents tend the eggs and take care of the young.

The diversity of birds is reflected in their beaks, which come in all shapes and sizes. Different beaks are designed to probe the mud for food, catch insects, crack open seeds, pry open shells, scoop up fish, and rip flesh.

■ PRACTICE 44: Birds

Circle the letter of the answer that correctly completes each of the following statements.

1. Birds' bones are _____.
   a. light and strong
   b. made of flexible cartilage
   c. denser than the bones of other animals

2. Birds use their _____ for warmth, flight, protection, and to attract mates.
   a. beaks
   b. feathers
   c. eyes

3. Birds evolved directly from _____.
   a. dinosaurs
   b. amphibians
   c. fish

Mammals

Sixty-five million years ago, the age of dinosaurs ended and the age of mammals began. A **mammal** is a warmblooded vertebrate that has body hair and produces milk to feed its young. Small, shrewlike mammals lived at the same time as dinosaurs. When the dinosaurs disappeared, the mammals diversified. Today, they range from tiny moles that live underground to the great blue whale—the largest animal that has ever lived. Many adaptations have contributed to the success of mammals.

- Mammals are warmblooded, so they can survive in a large range of conditions. Most mammals are covered with fur to prevent heat loss. Layers of fat or blubber also keep mammals warm and serve as food reserves.

- Most mammals give birth to live young rather than lay eggs. The developing young mammal is called a **fetus.** Mammals have **mammary glands** that produce milk to feed their young.

- Mammals have a variety of teeth that are designed to eat different types of food. Carnivores, such as wolves and cheetahs, have sharp canine teeth for tearing meat. Horses, deer, and bison have flat molars for grinding up grass. Beavers have large incisors for gnawing wood.

- Mammals have specialized limbs. Some have long legs so they can run fast. Bats have wings. Whales and seals have flippers for swimming. Primates have long limbs for swinging through trees.

- Mammals have large brains that are capable of learning.

There are two major groups of mammals, the marsupials and the placentals.

Marsupials

The **marsupial** fetus partially develops in the uterus inside the mother. When it is still the size of a lima bean, it crawls down the birth canal and enters an exterior pouch, where it completes its development. Most marsupials live in Australia. They include kangaroos, koala bears, and opossums. One marsupial, the opossum, lives in North America.

Placentals

Most mammals are placental. The fetuses of **placental** mammals complete their development inside the uterus. The fetus is attached to an organ called a placenta, which provides it with food and oxygen. In many placentals, the animals can walk right after they are born.

Modern humans, *Homo sapiens*, are relative latecomers in the mammal world. Still, their impact has been astounding. They evolved in Africa only 75,000 years ago. They spread through Africa, then through Europe and Asia. About 12,000 years ago, people crossed from Siberia to Alaska, then spread through North and South America. Today, humans occupy all parts of the world, and their numbers are increasing rapidly. They have brought many changes, which have affected other species, habitats, and perhaps even the climate.

■ PRACTICE 45: Mammals

Decide if each statement that follows is true (**T**) or false (**F**). Write the correct letter on each line.

_____ **1.** Mammals are warmblooded, meaning they cannot control their body temperatures.

_____ **2.** Mammals have a variety of teeth, which means they can eat different types of food.

_____ **3.** Layers of fat in mammals serve as food reserves and prevent heat from escaping.

_____ **4.** Marsupial newborns are far more mature than placental newborns.

_____ **5.** Modern humans were alive during the time of the dinosaurs.

UNIT 4 REVIEW

Look at the list of phyla below. Write the letter of the correct phylum on the line before each description.

a. poriferan   **b.** cnidarian   **c.** platyhelminthes

_____ **1.** digestive tract has only a single opening

_____ **2.** does not have nerve or muscle cells

_____ **3.** has two body forms—the medusa and the polyp

Circle the letter of the answer that correctly completes each of the following statements.

4. If you take a trip to the desert, you will see many arthropods, but few, if any, mollusks and annelids. That is because _____.
     a. there is more for arthropods to eat in the desert
     b. arthropods have jointed appendages
     c. arthropods have a waterproof exoskeleton that keeps them from drying out
     d. mollusks and annelids only live in the ocean

5. _____ are by far the smartest class of mollusks.
     a. Gastropods
     b. Bivalves
     c. Cephalopods
     d. none of the above

6. _____ allowed fish to eat bigger prey and thus grow bigger.
     a. A closed circulatory system
     b. Fins
     c. Jaws
     d. A large brain

7. Reptiles differ from amphibians because _____.
   a. most reptiles are now extinct
   b. reptiles are coldblooded
   c. most reptiles do not lay eggs
   d. reptiles do not absorb oxygen through their skin

8. Different mammals are capable of eating a variety of foods because they _____.
   a. are warmblooded
   b. have mammary glands
   c. have specialized teeth
   d. have specialized limbs

9. Warmblooded animals have an advantage over coldblooded animals because warmblooded animals _____.
   a. do not have to eat as much
   b. can live in a greater variety of climates
   c. have lighter, cartilaginous skeletons
   d. do not have to worry about water loss

10. Modern *Homo sapiens* _____.
   a. are marsupials
   b. evolved in Africa relatively recently
   c. live only in cold parts of the world
   d. have had little impact on other species

UNIT 4 APPLICATION ACTIVITY 1
Earthworms and Plant Growth

Mix two parts potting soil with one part peat moss. Divide the mixture between two 15-cm pots. Plant three seedlings of houseplants in each pot (coleus or spider plant work well). To one of the pots, add three to six medium-sized earthworms. Place gauze or a fine wire mesh

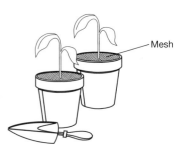

Mesh

screening over the pot to prevent the worms from crawling out. Do not add worms to the other pot.

Place the pots in indirect, but good, sunlight. Water them with equal amounts of water on a regular basis. Observe the general growth of the plants daily for about two or three weeks.

Explain the differences in growth patterns of the two sets of plants.

_____

_____

_____

_____

_____

Why is it important not to overwater the plants?

_____

_____

_____

_____

_____

UNIT 4 APPLICATION ACTIVITY 2
Comparing Vertebrates

Using photographs, encyclopedias of animals, reference books, or the Internet, observe five different animal specimens. Write the names of the animals in the chart on page 190.

Now answer the questions on the following page, and record your answers in the appropriate places in the chart.

Animal					
Body covering					
Number of heart chambers					
Warmblooded/ coldblooded					
Milk glands to feed young					
Brain size (ratio of fish brain to all others)					
Category					

What type of body covering does each animal have?

How many heart chambers does it have?

Is the organism warmblooded? Is it coldblooded?

How does each animal feed its young?

What is its approximate brain size?

In which category does each animal belong (fish, amphibian, bird, mammal, reptile)?

Consider the information collected in your chart. Think about how brain size might be related to each organism's ability to cope with changes in its environment. On a separate sheet of paper, write a paragraph explaining your conclusions.

UNIT 4 APPLICATION ACTIVITY 3
Comparing Variations in Humans

Work with a partner. Measure your height. Next, measure the length of your left index finger. Finally, measure the length of your left forearm from elbow to wrist. Enter your measurements in the chart below. Express all measurements in centimeters. Compile the same data for your partner and for all of the learners in your group. Enter the data in the chart.

	Learner						Class Average
	1	2	3	4	5	6	
Height (cm)							
Length of left index finger (cm)							
Length of left forearm (cm)							

Make a bar graph *for each of the measurements* for each learner, using the sample on the right to guide you. Make your graph on a separate sheet of paper.

What are the average measurements for height, finger length, and forearm length for the learners in your group? Enter them in the chart above.

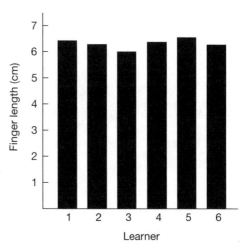

Sample Bar Graph

UNIT 5

The Human Body

LESSON 15: Digestion and Excretion

 GOAL: To learn about the organs and glands of the digestive system; to learn about the function of the kidneys

WORDS TO KNOW

antioxidants	feces	pepsin
anus	food pyramid	peristalsis
appendix	gallbladder	pharynx
bile	glomerulus	rectum
bladder	glucagon	renal artery
Bowman's capsule	glycogen	renal pelvis
capillaries	hydrochloric acid	renal vein
cecum	ileum	saliva
chyme	insulin	salivary glands
coenzymes	jejunum	serum proteins
collecting duct	kidneys	stomach
colon	large intestine	taste buds
cortex	lipase	tongue
digestive tract	liver	urea
duodenum	loop of Henle	ureter
epiglottis	maltose	urethra
esophagus	medulla	villi (singular *villus*)
essential amino acids	nephrons	water-soluble
fat-soluble	pancreas	

The Human Body

Perhaps you have seen an old movie in which a steam engine thunders down the train tracks, spewing black smoke through its stack. Inside the steam engine, a man tirelessly shovels coal into a red-hot furnace. The energy that the burning coal releases turns water into steam. The steam powers the pistons in the engine and propels the train forward. Burning the coal also produces wastes, which exit through the smokestack.

Your body is a little like a steam engine. To power your body, you must put food into your mouth. Your body breaks the food down into energy. This process also creates wastes that your body must dispose of.

But here is where the analogy ends. If your body burned food as a steam engine burned coal, not only would you waste most of the energy, you would be burned to a crisp. Instead, your body carefully extracts energy-rich compounds along with other important chemicals from the food you eat. As you learned in Unit 1, your body distributes these compounds to your cells. There, through a series of complex reactions (respiration), they get broken down into energy and carbon dioxide. But, when you take in food, you also take in other compounds. These are compounds that your body cannot use or that may even be toxic. So many chemical reactions in your body also produce wastes that your body must get rid of.

THINK ABOUT IT

You have already learned about chemical reactions that produce waste. Can you name a reaction and the waste it produces? Write your answer on a separate sheet of paper.

In this lesson, you will learn how your body breaks food down into materials it can use. And you will learn how your body processes and excretes (gets rid of) wastes.

The Digestive Tract

In this section, you will follow the journey a meal takes through your **digestive tract**. It truly is a long journey, because the typical human digestive tract is over 9 meters long. During this journey, enzymes break food down into the four basic organic molecules you learned about in Unit 1. These four basic organic molecules are monosaccharides, lipids, amino acids, and nucleic acids. Your digestive tract also absorbs other important chemicals including water, vitamins, and minerals.

The Mouth

Digestion begins as soon as you put food in your mouth and begin to chew. Your lips close and form a tight seal.

TIP

To understand the role that your lips play in chewing and swallowing, try eating without closing your lips. You might only want to attempt this exercise if there is nobody else in the room!

Your tongue then positions the food between your teeth. The **tongue** is a remarkable muscular organ that manipulates the food inside your mouth. It also enables you to form the sounds necessary for speech. The tongue is filled with sensory nerves that monitor the texture of the food. It also has special chemical sensors called **taste buds** that monitor the chemical nature of the food. These sensors alert you to any substance that should not be swallowed. There are four different types of taste buds that sense four different tastes: sourness, bitterness, sweetness, and saltiness.

Three **salivary glands** produce a fluid called **saliva.** The saliva contains mostly water, ions, and mucus. The saliva moistens and lubricates the food and makes it easier to swallow. The ions in the saliva help prepare the food for digestion. They may even kill bacteria in the food. The saliva also contains an enzyme that begins the process of breaking starch into simpler sugars. Because food does not remain in the mouth for very long, this enzyme works mostly on food that gets caught in the teeth.

Chewing breaks food into smaller pieces, making the food easier to swallow. Chewing also exposes more of the food to digestive enzymes. Therefore, it speeds digestion. There are four types of teeth. You use incisors in the front of your mouth to bite and cut the food. The sharper canine teeth tear food such as meat. When you chew and grind up the food you use the flatter premolars and molars in the back of your mouth. Each tooth is covered with a material called enamel, which is the hardest substance in your body.

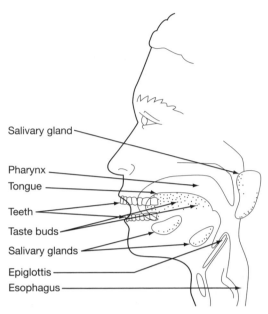

Salivary gland

Pharynx

Tongue

Teeth

Taste buds

Salivary glands

Epiglottis

Esophagus

The Mouth

Swallowing is a tricky process because of what can only be described as an evolutionary design flaw. Both the windpipe and the **esophagus** (the tube that leads to the stomach) open up into the region in the back of the mouth called the **pharynx.** As you know, you can choke if the food goes down the wrong tube. When you swallow, your tongue rolls the chewed, moistened food into a ball called a bolus. Then the tongue pushes the bolus to the pharynx. A flap called the **epiglottis** seals off the windpipe and prevents the food from entering it. The tongue and muscles in the pharynx then push the food into the esophagus.

From here on, the digestive process goes from voluntary (consciously controlling your chewing and swallowing) to automatic. Special types of muscles in the esophagus squeeze in wavelike contractions and push the food toward the stomach. Mucus lines the esophagus and smooths the way. These coordinated muscle contractions are called **peristalsis.** You cannot consciously control these contractions.

TIP

To understand peristalsis, think of squeezing the final bit of toothpaste from the end of the tube out the front. The muscles in the esophagus push food toward the stomach in a similar manner.

The Stomach

The **stomach** is a large, J-shaped chamber that serves as a temporary storage site. The stomach can stretch to hold almost 4 liters of food.

The stomach is also where the major part of chemical digestion begins. Special cells in the stomach secrete **hydrochloric acid** (molecular formula HCl). This powerful acid serves several purposes. First, it kills potentially harmful bacteria present in the food. Second, it causes proteins in the food to unravel, making it easier for enzymes to break the proteins apart. Finally, the acid actually activates a protein-cutting enzyme called **pepsin.**

Food passes from the esophagus to the stomach through a one-way valve. This valve prevents the hydrochloric acid from splashing up into the esophagus. The presence of food in the stomach stimulates the production of the acid and enzymes. The food then stays in the stomach for a few hours. Smooth muscles in the stomach wall churn the stomach and mix food, acid, and enzymes together into a milky substance called **chyme.** The chyme then passes through a second valve at the other end of the stomach and into the small intestine.

The fact that the stomach produces such a powerful acid can be problematic. If you poured the same concentration of hydrochloric acid on your skin, you would severely burn yourself. Cells in your stomach, however, secrete a thick mucus that coats the stomach wall. This coating protects the stomach from the acid and pepsin. Occasionally, this mucous layer breaks down. This can lead to heartburn or acid reflux. If the cardiac sphincter weakens, acid can enter the esophagus, especially after a big meal. In most instances,

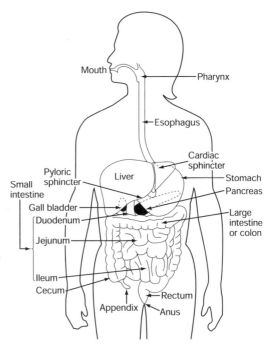

The Digestive Tract

heartburn is simply uncomfortable. But, in chronic cases, the acid can severely damage the esophagus. Over-the-counter antacids neutralize the hydrochloric acid. Other more powerful medications reduce the amount of acid the stomach produces. However, aspirin, which is a type of acid, can make heartburn worse.

The Small Intestine, Pancreas, and Liver

The small intestine is a winding 6- to 8-meter tube. Peristaltic contractions of muscles inside the walls of the small intestine push the food through. The small intestine is divided into three sections. The first 30 centimeters is called the **duodenum.** It contains numerous enzymes that nearly complete the breakdown of the food.

Cells in the small intestine secrete some of these enzymes. Two separate organs are also involved in digestion. One of these organs is the pancreas. The **pancreas** secretes several types of enzymes. These enzymes break proteins down into individual amino acids. They also break nucleic acids down into individual nucleotides, starches into simple sugars, and fats into their smallest components (fatty acids and glycerin). These enzymes travel from the pancreas to the duodenum. The pancreas also produces bicarbonate, which neutralizes any stomach acid that seeps into the small intestine.

THINK ABOUT IT

Just as the stomach releases pepsin in an inactive form, the pancreatic enzymes are also inactive when they are released. Once they reach the small intestine, they are activated by another enzyme. Why is it important that stored digestive enzymes are inactive? Write your answer on a separate sheet of paper.

The second organ involved in the digestive process is the **liver.** As you will see, this large organ is truly a multipurpose structure. The liver does not secrete any enzymes that are directly involved in digestion. It does, however, secrete a substance called **bile,** which aids in the digestion of fats. Fats do not dissolve in water. The bile, which contains salts, cholesterol, amino acids, and pigments, breaks the fats into tiny globules. This happens in much the same way that laundry detergent breaks down dirt in clothes. Bile is stored in a small organ called the **gallbladder.** From there, it travels to the duodenum.

The other two sections of the small intestine are the **jejunum** and **ileum.** These 3-meter-long sections are involved in the absorption of food into the bloodstream and lymph tissues. If you were to look closely at the inner wall of the small intestine, you would see that it is folded into fingerlike projections called **villi.** The villi greatly increase the surface area through which food is absorbed. In fact, if you were to flatten out the small intestine, it would cover an entire tennis court. These villi wave quite vigorously and mix the food with the enzymes. Inside each villus (singular of *villi*) are tiny blood vessels, called **capillaries,** and lymph vessels that take up the digested food.

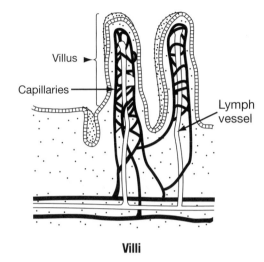

Villi

The Large Intestine

The remaining undigested food passes from the small intestine through another one-way valve into the **large intestine** or **colon.** The first part of the large intestine is called the **cecum.** A fingerlike structure called the **appendix** extends from the cecum. The appendix appears to be an evolutionary "leftover." It probably had a function many years ago, but it has no apparent function now. Occasionally, a piece of food may get caught in the appendix. Bacteria that occur naturally in the large intestine may then multiply and infect the lining of the appendix. This can cause it to swell. The result is severe pain. In some cases, the appendix may burst and create a life-threatening situation. Therefore, it is important that surgeons remove an infected appendix before it reaches that point.

Several processes occur throughout the rest of the large intestine, which is about 1.5 meters long. Water and dissolved minerals are absorbed through the walls of the large intestine. The large intestine contains a large quantity of bacteria, particularly *Escherichia coli (E. coli)*. These bacteria feast on the food that the small intestine was unable to process. They also synthesize (create and integrate) important vitamins such as vitamin K, biotin, and folic acid. These vitamins are absorbed through the large intestine. Peristaltic muscle contractions push the remaining wastes, called the **feces,** to a storage area at the end of the large intestine called the **rectum.** The feces consist of the remaining undigested food, bile, and dead bacteria. The feces are then eliminated through the **anus.**

■ PRACTICE 46: The Digestive Tract

Look at the list of terms below. Fill in each line with the letter of the term that correctly completes each statement.

a. appendix   **e.** peristalsis

b. epiglottis   **f.** gall bladder

c. liver   **g.** small intestine

d. fats

1. The _____ seals off the windpipe when you swallow.

2. The wavelike muscle contractions in your esophagus, small intestine, and large intestine are called _____.

3. Fingerlike projections called villi occur in the _____.

4. A now useless fingerlike projection protruding from the cecum is called the _____.

5. Bile, which is synthesized by the _____ and stored in the _____, breaks up _____.

Absorption of Nutrients

The human body is constantly changing. Every minute of every day, cells within the body are being broken down. The body needs to manufacture thousands more cells to replace them.

To do that, the body needs the correct materials. It needs nutrients such as protein, vitamins, and minerals. The best way to get these nutrients is to eat a balanced diet that includes foods rich in carbohydrates, vitamins, and minerals.

One way to make sure your diet is balanced is to use the guidelines prepared by the USDA (United States Department of Agriculture). To show how many servings of different kinds of foods you should get every day, the USDA developed a **food pyramid.** A healthy diet includes more of the foods at the lower levels of the pyramid than the ones above them.

Here is the USDA food pyramid.

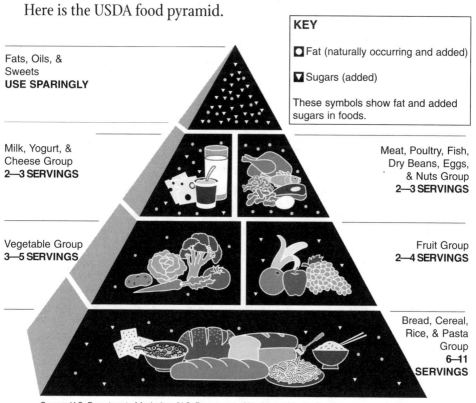

KEY

☐ Fat (naturally occurring and added)

▼ Sugars (added)

These symbols show fat and added sugars in foods.

Fats, Oils, & Sweets
USE SPARINGLY

Milk, Yogurt, & Cheese Group
2—3 SERVINGS

Meat, Poultry, Fish, Dry Beans, Eggs, & Nuts Group
2—3 SERVINGS

Vegetable Group
3—5 SERVINGS

Fruit Group
2—4 SERVINGS

Bread, Cereal, Rice, & Pasta Group
6—11 SERVINGS

Source: U.S. Department of Agriculture/U.S. Department of Health and Human Services

USDA Food Pyramid

Now take a closer look at the fate of each type of nutrient as it passes through the digestive tract. The digestive tract is quite efficient at using the nutrients it liberates during digestion. Ninety-five percent of the fats and ninety percent of the amino acids that are broken down during digestion are absorbed.

Carbohydrates

Your body uses carbohydrates mostly as an energy source. As you have already learned, your cells extract energy from glucose through a complex series of reactions called respiration. Many of the carbohydrates you eat contain more than one type of sugar. They include simple sugars such as sucrose (table sugar) and lactose (from milk). Carbohydrates also contain more complex sugars such as starch and glycogen. Most of these starches come from grains, such as bread, pasta, and cereal, and from vegetables, such as potatoes and turnips. The breakdown of starch begins in the mouth, where an enzyme splits the starch into a sugar called **maltose.** The maltose then moves down to the small intestine where an enzyme produced by the pancreas starts to work. Other enzymes that the small intestine secretes break the maltose into glucose. This is then actively loaded into the blood vessels in the villi. As you have already learned, active transport requires energy and is powered by the molecule ATP.

The level of glucose in the bloodstream usually remains constant. Two hormones, **glucagon** and **insulin,** control the sugar level. If the blood sugar level is too high, insulin triggers the liver to remove the glucose. The insulin then assembles the glucose into a substance called **glycogen.** Both your liver and your muscles store the glycogen. If the blood sugar level is too low, glucagon triggers your liver to release the glucose back into your bloodstream. From there, the glucose gets distributed to the cells that need it. If you eat a lot of sugar, however, your body converts all the excess carbohydrates into fat.

Sam had missed lunch and needed some fast energy to get through the rest of his classes. So he stopped at the chocolate shop, bought a box of fudge, and ate it in one sitting. At first, the fudge had its desired effect. Sam was alert and felt as though he could sprint around the campus. Then, halfway through his class, his energy level plummeted. As hard as he tried, he could not fight off sleep. By eating the fudge, he had flooded his bloodstream with sugar. To compensate, his pancreas released insulin, which triggered his liver to remove the sugar from his blood. His body, however, overcompensated and removed too much glucose. As a result, Sam had little energy.

Fats

Despite its bad reputation, fat is an essential nutrient. It is one of the essential components of cell membranes and of some types of hormones. Many essential vitamins, including A, D, E, and K, are stored in fat. Layers of fat help insulate your body. Fat also contains a lot of energy. But, like all foods, consuming too much fat is unhealthy. A diet too high in fats, especially in saturated fats and cholesterol, may contribute to serious health problems such as heart disease.

The digestion of fat takes place in the small intestine. As you have already learned, bile breaks the fat into smaller droplets. **Lipase,** an enzyme produced by the pancreas, breaks the fats into fatty acids and glycerol. Bile droplets containing these subunits are small and easily absorbed into the villi cells of the small intestine. This is accomplished without the cells' using any energy to absorb the droplets. Once inside these cells, the fatty acids and glycerol are reassembled into tiny triglyceride droplets. These droplets then enter the lymph vessels. Eventually, the fat enters the bloodstream.

Fat makes excellent energy reserves. It yields almost twice as much energy as the equivalent amount of carbohydrates and proteins. Fat reserves are stored in fat cells. Each person has a set number of fat cells throughout the body. These cells will increase in size in order to store more fat. The liver monitors the amount of cholesterol in the blood. It removes and stores excess cholesterol. If your cholesterol level is too low, your liver can manufacture its own cholesterol. If you eat too much cholesterol, however, your liver may not be able to keep up. In Lesson 16, you will see how high levels of cholesterol in the bloodstream can lead to heart disease.

Proteins

Your body needs 20 types of amino acids to manufacture proteins. Your body can synthesize 12 of these amino acids. The remaining eight, often referred to as essential amino acids, must come from proteins in your diet. Meat contains a complete set of the amino acids you need. Seeds, such as beans, rice, and other grains, do not have a full complement of **essential amino acids.** So vegetarians must make sure they eat the correct combinations of grains in order to get all the amino acids they need. Because your body is not good at storing amino acids, you need to eat proteins regularly.

Because proteins are so complex, breaking them down requires many steps and many enzymes. As you have already learned, hydrochloric acid in the stomach unravels the proteins and activates the first enzyme, pepsin. The pepsin slices the long amino acid chains into smaller chains. In the small intestine, a whole group of enzymes remove different types of amino acids. The molecules of these amino acids are large. Therefore, the villi cells are required to expend energy to take in these molecules and send them into the small blood vessels.

Once in the bloodstream, the amino acids are distributed to the cells that need them. The liver then takes up the remaining amino acids. The liver uses some of the amino acids to create its own proteins. It uses others to manufacture nucleic acids. Still others are assembled into **serum proteins,** which are an important component of blood. Some are used as energy. The remaining amino acids are converted into a yellow liquid called **urea.** The urea is excreted from the body.

Vitamins and Minerals

You also require a variety of other chemicals, such as vitamins and minerals. The absence of any of these substances can lead to serious diseases. You can manufacture vitamin D. Remember that bacteria in the large intestine synthesize vitamin K. The rest of the required vitamins and minerals must come from the food you eat. Most of the vitamins you need act as coenzymes. **Coenzymes** activate enzymes by binding to them and changing their shape. Coenzymes needed in respiration are manufactured from B vitamins (niacin, thiamin, and riboflavin). These are the vitamin coenzymes that are needed for several functions:

- formation of eye pigments (A)

- production of blood cells (B12, folic acid)

- blood clotting (K)

- formation of connective tissue (C)

- the absorption of calcium (D)

- active transport across cell membranes (B6)

Some vitamins, notably C and E, are known as **antioxidants.** These vitamins bind to, and deactivate, harmful chemicals in the body.

There are two major classes of vitamins. **Fat-soluble** vitamins (A, D, E, and K) are linked to fat molecules. These vitamins are stored in the liver. Because they remain in the body for a long time, overdoses of fat-soluble vitamins, especially A and D, are toxic. **Water-soluble** vitamins (C and B vitamins) dissolve in the blood. Excess water-soluble vitamins are excreted in the urine.

Important minerals include iron, calcium, sodium, potassium, and phosphorus. Minerals may be needed in large amounts, such as calcium and iron, or in trace amounts. These are some of the minerals that are needed by the human body:

- calcium—needed for bone growth, blood clotting, and muscle contraction

- iron—needed for oxygen transport in the blood

- iodine—needed in trace amounts to prevent thyroid problems

- fluoride—needed for healthy teeth and bones

- zinc—needed for certain enzymes

■ PRACTICE 47: Absorption of Nutrients

Look at the list of terms below. Fill in each line with the letter of the term that correctly completes each statement.

a. insulin   **b.** coenzymes   **c.** liver   **d.** glucagon

1. Glycogen, amino acids, cholesterol, and fat-soluble vitamins are stored in the _____.

2. The hormones that control the level of glucose in the blood are _____ and _____.

3. Vitamins that activate enzymes are called _____.

Processing Wastes

When you eat, you inevitably take in substances that the digestive tract cannot process. These substances get passed out in the feces. However, you may also eat toxic substances. Sometimes the sense of smell and the sense of taste act as a warning and the toxin is spit out. Sometimes the stomach rejects the substance, and the toxin is vomited out. However, toxic substances sometimes make it past these initial defenses and are absorbed into the bloodstream. Many of these toxins, including alcohol, drugs, and pollutants such as benzene, end up in the liver. Enzymes in the liver then break down the toxins into less harmful compounds that can be excreted from the body. But even the liver can get overworked. Several substances can scar the liver, such as chronic drinking of alcohol and drug use. The condition of scarring the liver is called cirrhosis of the liver, one of the leading causes of death in the United States.

The body also produces wastes. These wastes include discarded hormones and excess proteins. Remember that enzymes in the liver convert excess amino acids into urea. The urea, along with other toxins that the liver processes, enters the bloodstream. The body now faces a problem. How does it get rid of these water-soluble wastes while conserving water and other water-soluble compounds that the body desperately needs?

The answer lies in two bean-shaped organs called the **kidneys.** The kidneys, which are the size of fists, are located just above the waist on either side of the spine. The kidneys filter wastes from the blood. The kidneys also produce hormones and monitor the amount of water and salts in the body. Kidneys are involved in controlling blood pressure.

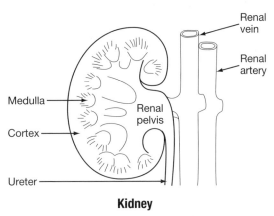

Kidney

Each kidney contains two major structures—the cortex and the medulla. The **cortex** contains about a million tiny filtering structures called nephrons. The **medulla** contains ducts that collect the filtered waste, or urine. The urine is temporarily stored in a hollow area in the center of the kidney called the **renal pelvis.** The waste is then emptied into a tube called the **ureter.**

Blood that needs to be filtered enters the kidney through a giant blood vessel called the **renal artery.** The cleansed blood exits through the **renal vein.**

Now examine the filtering units, or **nephrons.** Each nephron is a winding tube with a bulb on the end. The bulb is called the **Bowman's capsule.** Inside the Bowman's capsule is a knot of tiny blood vessels called the **glomerulus.** In the middle of this winding nephron, there is a large

U-shaped loop called the **loop of Henle.** The other end of the nephron joins a collecting duct in the medulla. Small blood vessels wind around the entire length of the nephron.

Now look at the process by which urine is filtered from the blood. You may also want to review the section on diffusion and osmosis in Lesson 2.

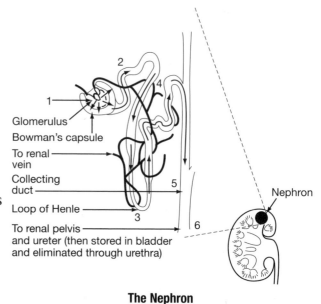

Glomerulus
Bowman's capsule
To renal vein
Collecting duct
Loop of Henle
To renal pelvis and ureter (then stored in bladder and eliminated through urethra)

Nephron

The Nephron

1. Blood enters the glomerulus (the knot of blood vessels inside the Bowman's capsule) under tremendous pressure. This pressure forces small molecules, such as water, salt, monosaccharides, and urea, out of the blood vessels and into the Bowman's capsule. Large molecules and red blood cells cannot pass through the walls of the blood vessels. So they remain behind.

2. The fluid, or urine, in the Bowman's capsule then enters the first part of the nephron. At this point, the urine contains far more water and salts (sodium chloride or table salt) than the body can afford to lose. Therefore, the blood must somehow reabsorb the water and salt. Three things happen. First, the blood vessels surrounding this first part of the nephron contain a higher concentration of solutes, and therefore a lower concentration of water, than the urine. Remember that water will cross a membrane from an area of high concentration to an area of low concentration. This process is called osmosis. Therefore, water moves out of the nephron and into the blood. Second, sodium chloride gets actively pumped out of the nephron. Third, large toxic chemicals in the blood are actively pumped into the nephron. These chemicals include ammonia (NH_3), which comes from the breakdown of proteins.

3. The urine then enters the loop of Henle. At this point, the urine contains less water and salt than it did when it left the Bowman's capsule. But it still has too much. The membranes cannot actively pump water out. But they can pump the salt out. By pumping out the salt, the water concentration inside the nephron increases and the water concentration outside the nephron decreases. The water, therefore, moves out of the nephron and is absorbed into the blood.

4. The urine then exits the loop of Henle and enters the final stretch of the nephron. More salt gets pumped out, and the water follows. At the same time, more wastes, such as ammonia, are pumped in.

5. The urine then enters the **collecting duct,** which runs through the medulla to the ureter. More water may passively flow out of the collecting duct. This depends on how much water the body needs to conserve. At this point, the amount of water the body removes from the urine is controlled by a hormone that the kidney produces.

6. The urine moves through the ureter and is stored in the **bladder.** It is then eliminated (voluntarily) through a tube called the **urethra.**

▪ PRACTICE 48: Processing Wastes

Look at the list of terms below. Fill in each line with the letter of the term that correctly completes each statement.

a. urethra   **c.** glomerulus   **e.** bladder
b. liver   **d.** sodium chloride

1. Toxic chemicals such as alcohol are processed in the _____.

2. Water and other small molecules are forced from the _____ into the Bowman's capsule.

3. To induce water to leave the nephron, _____ is actively pumped out.

4. Urine is stored in the _____ then released through the _____.

LESSON 16: Respiration and Circulation

 GOAL: To learn about the lungs and gas exchange; to learn about the components of the circulatory and lymphatic systems

WORDS TO KNOW

alveoli

aorta

arteries

arterioles

atmospheric pressure

atrium (plural *atria*)

bronchi (singular *bronchus*)

bronchioles

carbonic acid

cilia

coronary arteries

diaphragm

diastolic pressure

heart

hemoglobin

larynx

lymph

lymph nodes

lymphatic system

mucous membrane

nodes

pacemaker

partial pressure

pulmonary artery

pulmonary veins

red blood cells

systolic pressure

thoracic cavity

thoracic duct

trachea

valves

veins

ventricle

venules

vocal cords

The Respiratory System

In Lesson 15, you learned how your body takes in and processes energy-rich compounds. But remember that cells need oxygen (O_2) in order to convert these compounds into energy. You also learned that the chemical reactions in respiration produce a waste product—carbon dioxide (CO_2). Too much carbon dioxide is toxic. Therefore, your body must get rid of it. In this section, you will learn how oxygen travels from the air to your cells. You will also learn how carbon dioxide travels from your cells to the air.

Properties of Gases

Both oxygen and carbon dioxide are gases. Gas is matter in the same way that solids and liquids are matter. Each gas molecule contains a certain amount of energy that causes it to move around randomly—just as molecules in liquids move around randomly. These moving gases continually collide with one another and with solids and liquids. These constant collisions create pressure. The pressure that the gas molecules in the air exert is called **atmospheric pressure.**

Jar of gas molecules moving around

Say you have a sealed jar filled with gas. You want to increase the pressure inside the jar so that it is greater than the atmospheric pressure. There are three things you can do. First, you can heat up the gas and force the molecules to move faster. Second, you can increase the number of gas molecules in the jar. Finally, you can decrease the volume of the jar while keeping the same number of gas molecules inside.

Now, what happens when you open the jar? Air rushes out. This is because gas always moves from an area of higher pressure to an area of lower pressure.

The air pressure inside a balloon is greater than the atmospheric pressure outside the balloon. You can pop a balloon by heating it up, or by increasing the number of gas molecules by blowing more air into it. Or you can decrease the volume by squeezing it. If you prick the balloon with a pin, the pressurized air rushes out.

Breathing

The movement of air in and out of your lungs is due to pressure differences between the inside and outside of your body. Your lungs are a pair of expandable bags that are located in the thoracic cavity. The **thoracic cavity** is the hollow area of your chest. A flexible rib cage surrounds the thoracic cavity. A dome-shaped muscle called the **diaphragm** forms an airtight seal at the bottom. Take a deep breath. You have just flexed the muscles in your chest and caused your rib cage to expand. You have also flattened your diaphragm. These actions have increased the amount of space inside the thoracic cavity. Therefore, the air pressure inside the thoracic cavity has decreased. Because the air pressure outside the thoracic cavity is now greater than the pressure inside, air rushes into the lungs. Now exhale. You have relaxed your rib-cage muscles and diaphragm. The space inside the thoracic cavity has decreased. The air pressure inside is now greater than the atmospheric pressure, and air rushes out of the lungs.

The Respiratory Tract

Now, look at the passageway through which the air travels to reach the lungs. The air first enters your nose and mouth. The inside of the nasal passages is lined with a type of tissue called the **mucous membrane.** Beds of tiny blood vessels just below the surface of the mucous membrane warm the air in your nasal passages. Cells in the mucous membrane secrete mucus. This mucus moistens the air and traps airborne particles, including dust, pollen, and potentially harmful microorganisms such as bacteria and viruses. Many of the surface cells contain tiny, hairlike protrusions called **cilia.** The cilia sweep the mucus and trapped particles toward the throat.

The mucus and particles then get swallowed and destroyed by stomach acids.

The moistened and cleansed air from the nose and mouth enter the pharynx and then the windpipe. The boxlike entrance to the windpipe is called the **larynx.** When you swallow, muscles push the larynx upward. This action causes the flap called the epiglottis to

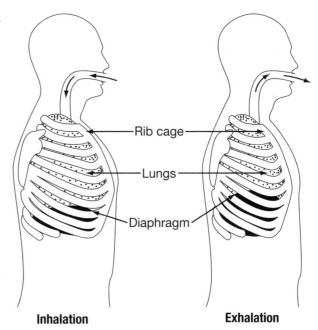

Inhalation　　　　**Exhalation**

seal the windpipe and prevent food from entering. The larynx is also the structure that produces your voice. Two ligaments (connective tissues that join bone to bone) called **vocal cords** stretch over the entrance of the larynx. These ligaments produce sound when they vibrate. Muscles in the larynx control the position and tension of the vocal cords. This is what enables you to create a variety of sounds.

From here, the respiratory tract resembles an upside-down tree. A tube called the **trachea** descends from the larynx. The trachea resembles a vacuum cleaner hose. Rings reinforce the hose and prevent it from collapsing when the vacuum is turned on. In the same way, cartilage rings reinforce the trachea and prevent it from collapsing when you inhale. The bottom of the trachea separates into branches, or **bronchi** (singular *bronchus*). Each primary bronchus enters a lung, then branches into secondary bronchi. These in turn branch into small tubes called **bronchioles.**

Each bronchiole inside the lungs ends in a cluster of tiny sacs called **alveoli.** These alveoli are what expand when the lung inflates with air. The adult human lung contains about 350 million alveoli. Capillaries, the tiny blood vessels you learned about in the last lesson, surround the alveoli. Oxygen from the air you breathe moves from the alveoli to the blood.

Carbon dioxide moves from the blood to the alveoli, and from there is eventually exhaled out through the lungs.

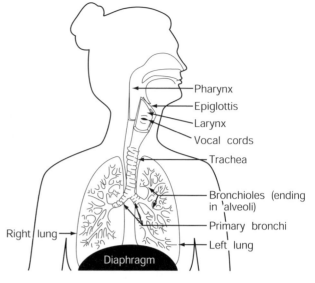

Pharynx
Epiglottis
Larynx
Vocal cords
Trachea
Bronchioles (ending in 'alveoli)
Primary bronchi
Right lung
Left lung
Diaphragm

Gas Exchange

The air you breathe is made up of a variety of gases. Nearly 80 percent of the gas is nitrogen. About 21 percent is oxygen, and 0.4 percent of the air is carbon dioxide. When you inhale, or breathe in, however, you selectively remove 25 percent of the oxygen from the air. When you exhale, or breathe out, you release carbon dioxide back into the air.

To understand how this process works, you need to examine the movement of individual gases. So far you have looked at the cumulative pressure exerted by all the gases in the air. Remember that air moves from an area of high pressure to an area of low pressure. But you can also look at the pressure exerted by each individual gas. For example, you can calculate the pressure exerted by just the oxygen or just the carbon dioxide. The pressure exerted by each individual gas is called the **partial pressure.** Just as air moves from an area of high pressure to an area of low pressure, individual gases move from an area of high partial pressure to an area of low partial pressure.

Think back to the sealed jar on page 213. The total air pressure inside the jar is equal to the atmospheric pressure outside it. However, the air inside the jar is 80 percent oxygen. The partial pressure of oxygen inside the jar is therefore four times greater than the partial pressure outside the jar. (Remember that air normally contains only about 20 percent oxygen.) If you open the jar, there will be a net movement of oxygen out of the jar.

The flow would stop when the partial pressure of oxygen inside the jar equals the partial pressure of oxygen outside the jar.

THINK ABOUT IT

Will the total air pressure inside the jar change? Write your answer on a separate sheet of paper.

Now look at what happens to the oxygen inside the alveoli. The blood entering the capillaries surrounding the alveoli is high in carbon dioxide and low in oxygen. The partial pressure of oxygen inside the alveoli is higher than the partial pressure of oxygen in the blood. Likewise, the partial pressure of carbon dioxide in the blood is higher than the partial pressure of carbon dioxide in the alveoli. As a result, oxygen passes from the alveoli into the blood vessels. And carbon dioxide passes from the blood vessels to the alveoli.

Oxygen and Carbon Dioxide Transport

Inside the capillaries there are special types of cells called **red blood cells.** Unlike most cells in your body, red blood cells do not have a nucleus. They are, however, filled with a protein called **hemoglobin.** Each hemoglobin protein contains four regions that bind to oxygen. Each region contains an iron atom. The iron is provided by the foods you eat.

The red blood cells whisk the oxygen to cells that need it for respiration. But how do the red blood cells know where to release the oxygen? The answer is fascinating. The cells that need oxygen the most are the ones that are producing the most energy. When they produce energy, cells also produce carbon dioxide. Some of the carbon dioxide released during respiration reacts with water to form an acid called **carbonic acid.** Remember that acids can change the shape of proteins. In this case, the carbonic acid changes the hemoglobin and causes it to release the oxygen.

The oxygen then diffuses into the cells, and the carbon dioxide diffuses into the blood. The beauty of this mechanism is that oxygen is only released where it is needed. Cells that are not active do not produce much carbon dioxide, so the hemoglobin does not release any oxygen to them.

Carbon dioxide enters the blood vessels so it can begin its journey to the lungs. Some of the carbon dioxide dissolves in the fluid of the blood. Some binds to the hemoglobin. The rest forms carbonic acid. Other chemicals in the blood help neutralize the acid. By the time the blood returns to the lungs, an enzyme converts the carbonic acid back into carbon dioxide. Then the carbon dioxide can diffuse into the alveoli.

Regulating Breathing

Take a deep breath, hold it for 10 seconds, then let it out. You have just proved to yourself that breathing is voluntary. You can control the timing and size of each breath—but only to a point. For example, you can only hold your breath a certain length of time before you have to let it out. When you exercise, you uncontrollably start breathing faster and deeper.

Two areas in the brain control breathing. One of these breathing centers controls your automatic breathing when you are at rest. That is why you take regular breaths without thinking about it and why you continue to breathe when you sleep.

So what happens when you start exercising? Your cells start burning oxygen and producing carbon dioxide. The carbon dioxide reacts with water and produces carbonic acid. Sensors in your blood vessels detect the increased acidity and signal the second breathing center in your brain. This center forces you to exhale more forcefully to expel the extra carbon dioxide. Meanwhile, the first breathing center triggers you to inhale faster and deeper so that you can take in more oxygen. Once you stop exercising, your cells stop producing as much carbon dioxide. Then the acidity in your blood drops, and you return to breathing normally.

Lung Disorders

You cannot avoid breathing air that contains harmful particles. The warm, moist conditions inside the lungs provide a perfect environment for bacteria and fungi. Therefore, the lungs must protect themselves. As you have already learned, cells in the respiratory tract secrete mucus that traps harmful particles and microorganisms. Cilia then sweep the mucus up to the throat. As you will learn in Lesson 17, special cells clean up any bacteria or fungi that get through.

However, you can weaken your lungs' defenses by smoking. The damage takes place over a long period of time. Some of the damage is reversible. The lungs of people who quit smoking usually recover. Some of the damage, however, is not reversible. Here is what happens to the lungs of smokers.

- Tobacco smoke irritates the cells in the lining of the lungs and stimulates them to produce more mucus.

- Tobacco smoke destroys the cilia that sweep the mucus out. As a result, the mucus accumulates in the lungs. The trapped mucus is responsible for smokers' cough.

- Microorganisms, such as bacteria, and other harmful chemicals trapped in the mucus remain in the lungs. Therefore, smokers are more susceptible to lung infections. Cigarette smoke also kills the cells that fight infections.

- Cigarette smoke contains a chemical called carbon monoxide (CO). This chemical permanently binds to the hemoglobin in the red blood cells. As a result, these cells can no longer carry oxygen.

- The accumulation of mucus permanently destroys the alveoli. This condition is called emphysema. People with emphysema can no longer take in as much oxygen. People with severe emphysema need an oxygen mask to get enough oxygen and usually do not have enough energy to get out of bed.

- Toxic chemicals in the tobacco smoke get trapped in the mucus. They irritate basal cells in the lining of the lung. This irritation causes the cells to multiply at an abnormal rate. Eventually, these rapidly dividing cells break through the lining of the lungs. They start to crowd out and kill other cells. Some of these cells may enter the bloodstream and travel to other parts of the body, where they begin to multiply. This disease is called lung cancer.

Each year, about 172,000 people in the United States are diagnosed with lung cancer. Because it is so difficult to treat, lung cancer is often fatal. Smoking causes eighty percent of lung cancer cases.

■ PRACTICE 49: The Respiratory System

Look at the list of terms below. Fill in each line with the letter of the term that correctly completes each statement.

a. cilia   c. high   e. primary bronchi

b. low   d. release oxygen

1. Individual gases, such as oxygen, will move from an area of _____ partial pressure to an area of _____ partial pressure.

2. The bottom of the trachea branches into two _____.

3. _____ sweep away the mucus that the lungs secrete.

4. The presence of carbonic acid causes the hemoglobin to _____.

The Circulatory System

So far, you have learned how blood carries nutrients from the intestines and oxygen from the lungs to all the cells in your body. You have learned about the role of red blood cells, one of the main constituents of blood. Like all vertebrates (fish, reptiles, birds, mammals), humans have a closed circulatory system. This means that the blood always remains inside the blood vessels. In this section, you will learn about the system of vessels through which the blood travels. You will also learn about the engine that pumps the blood through these vessels.

The Heart

Blood must travel a long way. First, it must go to the lungs to pick up oxygen. Some blood must travel to the brain to leave oxygen and glucose. Blood must travel to the intestines to pick up nutrients. It must pass through the liver to drop off nutrients and toxins for processing. It must travel through the kidneys to get filtered. It must travel to every cell in your body to leave oxygen and nutrients and pick up carbon dioxide and other wastes. Then blood must return to the lungs once again.

The engine forcing the blood through the circulatory system is a fist-sized pump called the **heart.** The heart is actually a double pump. The left side of the heart receives oxygenated blood from the lungs and pumps it to the rest of the body. The right side of the heart collects deoxygenated blood from the rest of the body and pumps it to the lungs.

Structure of the Heart

Now take a closer look at the structure of your heart. The heart is divided into four chambers. Each upper chamber is called an **atrium** (plural *atria*). Each lower chamber is called a **ventricle.** Each chamber is made of a powerful type of muscle. **Valves**—flaps of tissue that open and close—control the flow of blood between the chambers.

The left side of the heart is divided into the left atrium and the left ventricle. Oxygen-rich blood from the lungs enters the left atrium through large blood vessels called **pulmonary veins.** The left atrium contracts and squeezes the blood through a one-way valve. The blood then flows into the left ventricle. The left ventricle contracts an instant after the left atrium and propels the blood through a second valve. The blood then flows into a giant blood vessel called the **aorta.**

The right side of the heart is also divided into two chambers—the right atrium and the right ventricle. Blood from the head and body enters the right atrium through large blood vessels. The right atrium contracts at the same time as the left atrium and sends blood into the right ventricle. A one-way valve separates the right atrium from the right ventricle. The right ventricle contracts at the same time as the left ventricle and sends blood through another valve. Then the blood flows into the **pulmonary artery,** and on to the lungs.

When you listen to your heart, you will hear a "lub dub" sound. The "lub" is the sound of the valves between the atria and ventricles closing.

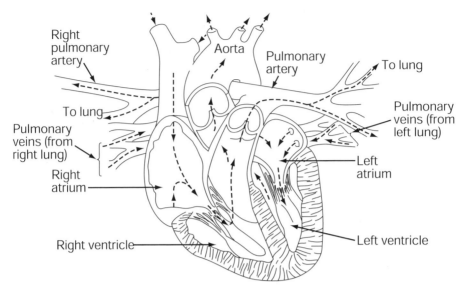

Pathway of Blood Through the Heart

The "dub" is the sound of the valves at the other end of the ventricles closing. After each beat, your heart pauses while blood fills the two atria. Then it beats again.

> ### ▓ TIP
>
> Note that the contractions on the left side of the heart are stronger than the contractions on the right side. This is because the left ventricle must propel the blood much farther than the right ventricle. This imbalance has led to the perception that the heart is on the left side of the body. In fact, the heart is in the center of the body. Therefore, when you put your hand on the left side of your chest as you sing the national anthem, you are covering your left lung, not your heart.

Control of the Heart

As you are aware, you cannot control your heart, at least not directly. In fact, the heart seems to have a mind of its own. It will continue to beat even after its connections to the brain and the rest of the body are severed. This is because your heart has an internal network of nerve cells that coordinate each beat. The heart contains areas of specialized tissue called **nodes.** The beat originates in a node in the right atrium called the **pacemaker.** The pacemaker sends a signal to the two atria that causes them to contract. It also sends a signal to a second node. From there, the signal spreads to both ventricles. This signal causes the ventricles to contract.

Occasionally, something goes wrong with the signals sent by the pacemaker. As a result, the atria no longer contract in a rhythmic, coordinated fashion. This condition is called atrial fibrillation or arrhythmia. Although bouts of arrhythmia in the atria may cause dizziness and shortness of breath and are certainly unnerving, they are usually not life-threatening. However, chronic arrhythmia can lead to other problems, such as stroke or heart damage. Ventricular fibrillation, in which the ventricles no longer beat in a coordinated, efficient manner, is far more serious. In most cases, this condition is fatal.

The pacemaker initiates and coordinates the beating of your heart. Signals from other parts of your body control the rate at which your heart beats. When you are at rest, your heart will beat 70 times per minute on average. When you exercise, the rate doubles or even triples. The rate is controlled both directly by the brain and by hormones synthesized in your glands.

Blood Vessels

Your circulatory system is composed of the following three types of blood vessels: arteries, capillaries, and veins.

ARTERIES

Blood is carried away from the heart by **arteries.** As you have already learned, oxygen-rich blood leaves the left ventricle and enters a giant artery called the aorta. Oxygen-poor blood leaves the right ventricle through the pulmonary artery. These giant arteries branch into smaller arteries, which branch into increasingly smaller arteries called **arterioles.** Blood that enters the arteries is under high pressure due to the contraction of the ventricles. So the walls of the arteries are thick, yet elastic. The walls of the arteries are also filled with smooth muscles. These muscles allow the arteries to narrow (constrict) or widen (dilate), and, therefore, regulate the amount of blood flowing to different tissues.

CAPILLARIES

The arterioles divide into vast networks or beds of tiny blood vessels called capillaries. You learned about capillaries earlier. Some capillaries are so narrow that only a single red blood cell can fit through at a time. Capillaries are the sites where oxygen, carbon dioxide, nutrients, and other molecules are exchanged between the blood and the cells. Capillary walls are only a single cell thick. They are also porous so chemicals can easily pass across them. You have already encountered the capillaries that surround the alveoli in the lungs. And you have learned about the capillaries inside the villi of the small intestine. Capillaries also extend to practically every cell in your body.

VEINS

The vessels that carry blood back to the heart are called **veins.** Capillaries join together to form small veins called **venules.** The venules come together to form increasingly larger veins. Veins have thinner walls than arteries, and they are flatter. By the time the blood reaches the veins, it is under a lot less pressure. So it needs help getting back to the heart. Smooth muscles in the vein walls help squeeze the blood through. The blood in your veins also gets a boost whenever you move your limbs around. Your arm and leg muscles actually massage the blood through. Many veins also contain one-way valves that prevent the blood from flowing backward.

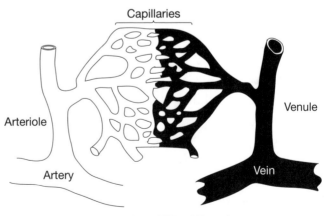

Branching of Blood Vessels

Lymphatic System

Your circulatory system is composed of more than just blood vessels. There is also a network of vessels called the **lymphatic system.** The lymphatic system drains excess fluids from around your cells. Unlike the blood vessels, the lymphatic vessels do not form a closed loop. Instead, fluid from around the cells diffuses into tiny collecting vessels. These vessels, which are the size of capillaries, merge into larger and larger vessels. All the lymphatic vessels eventually merge and form the **thoracic duct.** The thoracic duct empties the clear fluid, called **lymph,** into the superior vena cava just above the heart. Like veins, lymphatic vessels contain valves that prevent the lymph from flowing backward. The movement of body muscles kneads the lymph through.

On its way to the thoracic duct, the lymph passes through a series of way stations called **lymph nodes.** These nodes filter particles from the lymph. They also produce and house cells of the immune system. The cells destroy microorganisms, such as bacteria, that invade the lymphatic system. The tonsils at the back of your throat and your spleen are examples of large lymph nodes.

As you have already learned, lymphatic vessels in your villi channel lipids from your small intestine to the bloodstream.

Cardiovascular Diseases

Cardiovascular diseases (diseases of the heart and blood vessels) are by far the most common causes of death in the United States. A large proportion of these diseases is caused by blockages in the blood vessels. If a major artery around the brain becomes blocked, the pressure that builds up behind the blockage may burst. The blood that spills out will damage a piece of the brain. This condition is called a stroke.

Like all organs, your heart requires its own blood supply. The arteries that feed the heart are called **coronary arteries.** If one or more of these arteries becomes blocked, and the oxygen supply to the heart is shut off, a piece of the heart may die. This condition is called a heart attack. Heart attacks vary in severity depending on which part of the heart is affected.

The most critical heart attacks damage the heart's electrical circuits, such as the pacemaker or AV node.

The leading cause of heart attacks is the buildup of a hard plaque inside the arteries. This condition is called atherosclerosis. The buildup of plaque narrows the arteries and restricts the amount of blood that gets through. Larger particles, such as blood clots, may get lodged in the arteries and block the flow of blood altogether. Although many people may inherit a tendency to develop atherosclerosis, there are a number of actions you can take to reduce your risk.

Excess cholesterol in the blood can accumulate on the artery walls and lead to the formation of plaque. Excess saturated fats may also contribute to plaque formation. Therefore, it is important to have your blood tested for cholesterol and fat level on a regular basis. If the level is high, you will want to reduce the amount of saturated fats and cholesterol in your diet. Here things get more complicated, however, for not all cholesterol is bad. There are two types of cholesterol—high density lipoproteins (HDL) and low density lipoproteins (LDL). LDL, or "bad cholesterol," contributes to the formation of plaques. HDL, or "good cholesterol," may actually remove LDL from your blood. Therefore, reliable cholesterol tests measure the amount of LDL and HDL in the blood separately.

High blood pressure is also a risk factor for heart attacks. As you have already learned, blood leaves the left ventricle under tremendous pressure. Chronically high blood pressure is a condition called hypertension. With hypertension, the blood can wear down the artery walls and increase the chances that plaque and clots will form. In addition, high blood pressure forces the heart to work harder and may eventually wear the heart down. Fortunately, hypertension is easy to diagnose and treat. A blood pressure reading produces two numbers. The top number, called the **systolic pressure,** is the pressure of your blood when your heart contracts. The bottom number, or **diastolic pressure,** is the pressure of your blood between beats. Readings below 120/80 are considered normal. Smoking, a diet high in salt and fat, and being overweight can all contribute to hypertension. If reducing these risk factors is not enough, there are a number of medications that effectively reduce blood pressure.

It has been estimated that one fourth of all deaths from blockage of the coronary arteries is due to smoking. Smoking increases the risk of cardiovascular disease in several ways.

- Smoking decreases the amount of oxygen you take in—not only because it clogs or even destroys your alveoli, but because tobacco smoke contains carbon monoxide. Remember that carbon monoxide binds to the hemoglobin in the blood and prevents oxygen from binding. This decrease in oxygen puts extra strain on your heart.

- The nicotine in cigarette smoke causes glands on your kidneys to secrete a hormone that raises your blood pressure.

- Smoking accelerates the buildup of cholesterol inside your arteries.

Fortunately, the risk of a heart attack returns to normal two years after a person stops smoking. So it is never too late to quit smoking.

■ PRACTICE 50: The Circulatory System

Look at the list of terms below. Fill in each line with the letter of the term that correctly completes each statement.

a. veins   **c.** left atrium   **e.** atherosclerosis   **g.** arrhythmias

b. left ventricle   **d.** lymph nodes   **f.** aorta

1. Oxygen-rich blood enters the _____, gets pumped into the _____, then leaves the heart through a large blood vessel called the _____.

2. _____ are due to problems in the pacemaker and/or AV node.

3. Blood vessels that carry blood back to the heart are called _____.

4. Tonsils and the spleen are examples of large _____.

5. The buildup of plaque inside the arteries is called _____.

LESSON 17: Fighting Invaders

GOAL: To learn how your body defends itself against invaders

WORDS TO KNOW

allergies	histamine	mutate
antibodies	immune	pathogens
antigen	immune system	phagocytes
antiserums	interferons	platelets
autoimmune diseases	keratin	prion
B-cells	lymphocytes	T-cells
binding sites	macrophage	white blood cells

Pathogens

Many microorganisms would love to call your body home. And why not? Your body provides a warm, moist environment in which there is plenty of free food. Your body actually welcomes some of these organisms. You have already learned about the bacteria in your large intestine that break down food that you cannot digest and that synthesize vitamin K. But many organisms that try to take up residence in your body can harm or even kill their host. Fortunately, your body has many ingenious ways to fight off these invaders. In this lesson, you will learn about your body's defenses.

Pathogens are organisms that invade the bodies of larger organisms and cause disease. You will now take a look at some of the major types of pathogens and some of the diseases they cause.

Viruses

As you learned in Unit 2, a virus is a tiny particle that defies classification. They are no more than a strand of DNA or RNA enclosed in a protein shell. They do not meet the criteria of life that are listed at the beginning of

Lesson 1. Viruses do not grow, use energy, or carry out chemical reactions. They reproduce, but only with the help of the host organism. And, as you will see, viruses do adapt.

Still, these relatively simple particles are extremely good at invading and taking over the machinery of cells. Here is how a typical virus works.

1. The virus attaches itself to proteins on the cell membrane. These proteins act like name tags. They let cells recognize one another. Unfortunately, proteins also let viruses recognize the cells they are invading. This is why viruses typically only invade a certain type of tissue.

2. The cell takes in this virus particle and tries to dispose of it by engulfing it with a lysosome. Remember that lysosomes are organelles with powerful digestive enzymes. Then the virus springs its trap. The lysosome digests the protein coat, but not the nucleic acid. The nucleic acid is now free to do its dirty work.

3. The freed nucleic acid in the virus uses the cell's nucleic acids to replicate itself. The virus takes over the ribosomes and forces the cell to assemble viral proteins. The result is a cell literally bursting with new viruses.

4. The new viruses burst out of the cell, killing it. They then swarm to other cells where the cycle is repeated.

Viruses are the cause of some of the most common infectious diseases in the world. They are most often spread from person to person through the air, through direct contact, and through sexual contact. Some viruses are spread through animal bites, especially insect bites. Viral diseases include the common cold, influenza (the flu), hepatitis (liver infection), rabies, measles, polio, herpes, and HIV.

Bacteria

As you learned in Lesson 8, bacteria are small, relatively simple cells. Disease-causing bacteria harm their host in two ways. First, they compete for nutrients that the host needs and crowd out the host's cells. Second, they produce toxins that can harm or even kill the host. One type of bacterium, *Clostridium botulinum*, causes botulism. It produces one of the most powerful toxins in the world. These bacteria grow in canned food that has not been properly sterilized. A single, tiny bite of affected food can be fatal.

Bacteria invade your body in a number of ways. Like viruses, they can spread through the air. They also contaminate the food you eat. They can enter open wounds (animal bites are a common source). Or, they can be spread through sexual contact. Bacterial diseases include strep throat, food poisoning, tetanus, pneumonia, tuberculosis, bubonic plague, syphilis, and gonorrhea. The development of antibiotics has significantly reduced the impact of bacterial diseases. Antibiotics slow down the growth and multiplication of bacteria to give the body's immune system time to finish its job. But, as you will see later, the bacteria are fighting back.

Protists

Protists are single-celled organisms, some of which cause diseases. Protists reproduce inside red blood cells and destroy them. As you will learn, they are very good at evading the body's immune system.

Many protists are found in contaminated drinking water. In the United States, the protist *Giardia lamblia* has invaded many water sources, including fresh mountain streams. People infected with this protist usually develop severe stomach cramps and diarrhea. Fortunately, giardia is usually treatable. The most devastating protists are spread through insect bites, particularly mosquitoes. One mosquito-borne disease, malaria, is one of the most widespread and deadly diseases in the world.

Prions

Scientists were convinced that only organisms that contain either DNA or RNA—viruses, bacteria, and protists—could cause disease. Then, in 1986, a new disease struck cattle in England. The illness was called mad cow disease. It destroyed the animals' brains. The disease was always fatal.

Scientists ruled out a virus or other pathogens as the cause. The only thing that could be found in the brains of affected animals was a strange, misshapen protein in the dead cells. Slowly, scientists began to think that the protein—called a **prion**—was responsible for the illness. Not all scientists agree with this theory.

Then twelve people in England came down with a human prion disease that was very much like mad cow disease. It destroyed the brains of people with the disease. The disease in humans was called Creutzfeldt-Jakob disease (CJD). The people who came down with CJD had eaten meat or cheese known to have come from infected cattle. As a result, changes were made to the way that animals were fed. Before this, carcasses of dead animals were used to feed cattle and other animals. After the outbreak, this practice was stopped.

With better animal feeding practices, these diseases are probably controllable. However, some scientists think that other human illnesses might be caused by prions. More research is needed to find clear answers.

■ PRACTICE 51: Pathogens

Decide if each statement that follows is true (**T**) or false (**F**). Write the correct letter on each line.

_____ **1.** Viruses defy classification.

_____ **2.** Bacterial infections can be spread through animal bites.

_____ **3.** Viruses harm cells by carrying out chemical reactions.

_____ **4.** The most devastating protists are spread through human contact.

_____ **5.** Prions are misshapen proteins.

Physical and Chemical Defenses

Physical Barriers

Now that you know what your body is up against, you will learn how your body defends itself. The first and most obvious strategy is to keep the pathogens out in the first place. Your skin is an especially effective barrier. It is composed of a dense layer of dead cells. Cells underneath constantly divide and replace this top layer. A waterproof protein called **keratin** coats the top layer and prevents pathogens from penetrating. Keratin, the same protein that makes up your hair and fingernails, also resists the enzymes and toxins that bacteria release. Finally, your skin also secretes chemicals through the sweat glands that are toxic to potential invaders.

There are, however, natural openings in your body. Pathogens often enter the body through the respiratory tract, digestive tract, and reproductive tract. All three of these have passageways that are lined with mucous membranes. They secrete chemicals that kill many pathogens. As you have already learned, the mucous membranes in the respiratory tract secrete mucus. This mucus traps invading pathogens. Cilia sweep the mucus away. Most pathogens that enter the digestive tract succumb to stomach acids. Urine flowing through the ureter and urethra flushes out invading microorganisms. Sneezing, coughing, and vomiting forcefully also remove invading pathogens.

THINK ABOUT IT

Can you explain how reactions such as sneezing and coughing actually help spread pathogens—such as cold viruses—that infect the upper respiratory tract? Write your answer on a separate sheet of paper.

You also have help from other organisms. Friendly mites, fungi, and bacteria on your skin, and bacteria in your intestines, crowd out pathogens.

Inflammation

The physical barriers in your body successfully block most pathogens. Still, some get through. Your body then unleashes a number of chemicals and special cells called **white blood cells** to fight the pathogens. White blood cells are located both in your bloodstream and lymph nodes. As you will see, there are many different types of white blood cells. Each of them plays a different role in fighting pathogens.

As an example, see what happens when you cut yourself and bacteria invade the wound.

1. White blood cells release a chemical called **histamine.** Damaged cells in the skin also release histamine.

2. Histamine causes nearby blood vessels to dilate so that more blood can rush into the area. As a result, the area around the wound turns red, swells, and becomes hot.

3. Mast cells around the wound release chemicals that directly attack the invading bacteria. They also release chemicals that attract more white blood cells to the area.

4. White blood cells called **phagocytes** arrive. The phagocytes engulf the invading bacteria. Lysosomes inside the phagocytes digest the bacteria. Phagocytes are also present in your alveoli and lymph nodes. They also engulf other invading pathogens, toxins, debris such as dead cells, and even cancer cells.

5. In the meantime, cells in the blood called **platelets** initiate a complex series of chemical reactions that result in a clot. This clot plugs the damaged blood vessel and prevents more blood from leaving. The clot also keeps more bacteria from entering.

6. If the invader is a virus, infected cells secrete a group of proteins called **interferons.** These chemicals protect other cells by preventing the viral nucleic acids from synthesizing viral proteins.

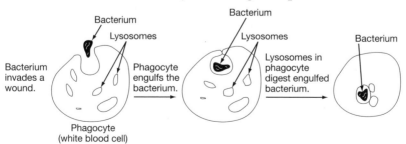

Phagocytes in Action

White blood cells and other cells in your body may also release a chemical that causes your body temperature to rise. This is why you often have a fever when you get sick. Many pathogens are sensitive to temperature and therefore will succumb more quickly. Fevers, however, are only helpful up to a point. If a fever is too high or lasts too long, it can do more harm than good.

THINK ABOUT IT

How can a fever harm your body? Write your answer on a separate sheet of paper.

■ PRACTICE 52: Physical and Chemical Defenses

Look at the list of terms below. Fill in each line with the letter of the term that correctly completes each statement.

a. keratin   **b.** interferons   **c.** histamine

1. A protein called _____ prevents pathogens from penetrating your skin.

2. White blood cells release a chemical called _____ that causes nearby blood vessels to dilate.

3. Proteins that interfere with viral reproduction are called _____.

The Immune System

You would think that with all of these defenses, no pathogens or toxins would ever get through and you would never get sick. Natural selection, however, works on pathogens in the same way it works on plants and animals. Some pathogens have evolved ways to get around the body's first two lines of defense. Some bacteria manage to resist, or even destroy, phagocytes. The bacteria that cause tuberculosis and leprosy actually escape the phagocytes by hiding inside other cells.

Fortunately, your body has a third line of defense. This line of defense is called the **immune system.** It involves a number of different types of white blood cells that interact in complex ways. It is incredibly precise and targets and chases down specific pathogens.

Unlike the body's other defenses, which respond immediately to invading pathogens, the immune system takes over a week to gear up. First, the immune system must recognize that there is a pathogen present. Second, it must identify exactly what pathogen it is. Finally, it must produce specific weapons capable of destroying that particular pathogen. You will now go through this process step by step.

Recognition

Like all cells, pathogens are studded with proteins that act as name tags. Each different type of bacterium, fungus, protist, virus, and even protein toxin has a unique name tag. When a pathogen enters the body, these name tags let the immune system know that it needs to respond. A substance that causes an immune response is called an **antigen.**

The immune response begins when a type of patrolling phagocyte, called a **macrophage,** encounters an invading pathogen or toxin and engulfs it. The macrophage, however, does more than just digest the invader. It takes the pathogen's or toxin's antigens and displays them. It is, in effect, alerting the rest of the immune system that there is a pathogen or toxin present and this is what its name is.

The next players in the immune response are white blood cells called **lymphocytes.** Lymphocytes are manufactured in the bone marrow and thymus. They are stored in the lymph nodes. There are two classes of lymphocytes—**B-cells** (manufactured in *b*one marrow), and **T-cells** (manufactured in the *t*hymus). Each individual B-cell and T-cell has a specific job. It must recognize and/or destroy a specific type of pathogen. As a result, your body contains millions of different lymphocytes. Each lymphocyte is capable of responding to a different invader.

The macrophage shows its captured antigens to any helper T-cell it encounters. When the helper T-cell that is specific for that particular antigen comes along, it will bind to the macrophage.

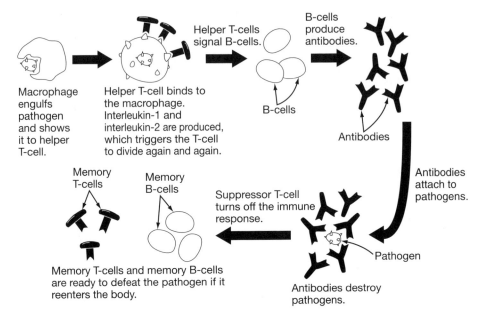

The Immune Response

Mobilization and Response

As soon as the helper T-cell and macrophage bind, the macrophage produces a protein that triggers the T-cell to divide again and again. The T-cell also produces a protein that triggers other T-cells that are specific to that antigen to divide.

Three types of T-cells are produced—killer T-cells, helper T-cells, and memory T-cells. As their name implies, the killer T-cells destroy any cells bearing the proper antigens. They also secrete chemicals that attract phagocytes to the area.

Helper T-cells have a different job. They find and bind to the other type of lymphocyte—the B-cell. Like T-cells, there is a different B-cell for each antigen. Once the helper T-cell binds to the correct B-cell, it secretes a protein that stimulates the B-cell to divide again and again. Some of these new B-cells become memory cells. These cells will "remember" the protein pattern of a bacterium. This will help prevent you from getting sick by the same bacterium again. The rest of the B-cells turn into what are called plasma cells and start producing huge numbers of Y-shaped proteins called **antibodies.** An individual B-cell may produce 2000 antibodies each second.

Antibodies are the keys that destroy pathogens. They are made up of four amino acid chains—two of them long and two of them short. The ends of the two prongs on the Y are the **binding sites.** The binding sites latch on to the antigens on the surface of pathogens. Once again, a single type of antibody can only bind to a single type of antigen.

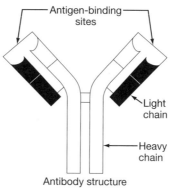

Antigen-binding sites

Light chain

Heavy chain

Antibody structure

Antibodies

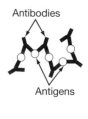

Antibodies

Antigens

Antibodies binding to antigens

Antibodies neutralize or destroy pathogens and toxins in several ways.

■ Toxins: Antibodies coat and neutralize toxins such as those produced by the tetanus bacterium.

■ Viruses: Antibodies coat viruses and prevent them from binding to host cells.

■ Bacteria: Some types of antibodies contain many active sites. They can bind to many bacteria at once. Therefore they clump the bacteria together. They also activate other bacteria-destroying chemicals.

The immobilized toxins and pathogens are now easy targets for roving phagocytes.

Recovery and Immunity

Once the pathogen or toxin has been purged from your system, another type of T-cell, called a suppressor T-cell, turns the immune response off. (Scientists still do not understand how this works.) Stopping the immune response is important because producing all those antibodies requires a huge amount of energy. In fact, the fatigue you feel when you are sick is due more to your immune response than to the actual pathogen.

After you have recovered from the invasion of a pathogen, it is unlikely that that pathogen will make you sick again. For example, people who get mumps, chicken pox, or measles will most likely not get these diseases again. In other words, you have become **immune,** or resistant, to these pathogens. Remember that some of the B-cells and T-cells produced during the immune response are memory cells. These cells stay in your bloodstream for decades. If they encounter the particular pathogen again, they immediately pump out antibodies and defeat the pathogen before it has a chance to get established.

The vaccines you received as a child induced an artificial immunity in your body. The vaccines are typically made from weakened or dead pathogens or toxins that still have their antibodies intact. Although they cannot hurt you, they do trigger an immune response. They also trigger the production of memory cells. Therefore, if you ever got infected by the real pathogen, your immune system would respond immediately. If you have already been afflicted by a disease such as tetanus or rabies, or if you have been bitten by a poisonous snake or a spider, a doctor may give you an injection of antiserum. **Antiserums** contain antibodies that other animals have manufactured. Although these antibodies help you fight the pathogen or toxin, they do not make you immune.

Problems with the Immune System

One of the most amazing things about the immune system is that it is able to recognize the cells of your body. Remember that all of your cells have antigens on their surfaces. Your immune system recognizes that these antigens are friendly. Occasionally, however, for reasons that scientists do not understand, a person's immune system will make a mistake and start attacking its own cells. These conditions, known as **autoimmune diseases,** are currently incurable and often life-threatening. Examples include rheumatoid arthritis (attacks joints), juvenile diabetes (attacks insulin-producing glands in the pancreas), multiple sclerosis (attacks the lining of nerve cells), and systemic lupus erythematosus (attacks connective tissue).

Allergies

Sometimes the immune system reacts to antigens that do not pose a danger to the body. These antigens may be present on pollen, mold, or proteins found in particular foods. Such overreactions are called **allergies.** Most people react by releasing histamines that trigger inflammation. People with hay fever know the symptoms—swollen sinuses and stopped-up nose, sneezing, and itchy eyes. Some reactions, such as allergic reactions to bee stings, foods, or medicines, can be extremely dangerous. They can cause the lining of the lungs to swell so that it is difficult to breathe. This condition is called asthma.

Pathogen Mutations and Adaptations

Just as some pathogens have evolved ways to get by phagocytes, others have evolved ways to avoid the immune system. For example, the viruses that cause colds and influenza **mutate,** or change, so that the immune system will not recognize them the next time they attack. That is why you can catch a cold several times a year. Each time you experience a cold, the virus has changed enough from the last time that your immune system must start from scratch.

Some protists, such as those that cause malaria and African sleeping sickness, have the unfortunate ability to change while they are inside the host. For example, people with the deadly African sleeping sickness, which is transmitted through the bite of tsetse flies in Africa, produce antibodies against the antigens on the surface of the protist. Just as the immune system is about to wipe them all out, a few of the protists activate a new set of genes. This produces a new set of antigens. The antibodies no longer work on these antigens. So the immune system must start all over again and produce new antibodies. In this way, the protist always stays one step ahead of the immune system.

Bacteria also adapt. Rather than adapting to the immune system, they adapt to the antibiotics that people use to kill them. In recent years, many dangerous bacteria, such as those that cause tuberculosis, have become resistant to antibiotics. As a result, scientists have had to scramble to find new antibiotics that are effective against these bacteria.

Finally, there is the example of HIV, the virus that causes AIDS. This deadly virus attacks helper T-cells and macrophages, crippling the immune system. Most people who die from AIDS succumb to secondary infections of pathogens that a healthy immune system would normally fight off.

■ PRACTICE 53: The Immune System

Look at the list of terms below. Fill in each line with the letter of the term that correctly completes each statement. (*Hint*: You may use some terms more than once.)

a. antibodies	**c.** antigens	**e.** macrophages
b. lymphocytes	**d.** autoimmune diseases	

1. _____ are white blood cells that initiate the immune response by capturing pathogens and displaying the _____.

2. B-cells and T-cells are examples of white blood cells called _____.

3. B-cells produce Y-shaped proteins called _____ that latch onto the _____ of invading pathogens or toxins.

4. _____ are conditions in which the immune system attacks the person's own cells.

LESSON 18: The Skin

WORDS TO KNOW

collagen	follicle	sebum
dermis	ground substance	skin
elastin	hair	subcutaneous layer
epidermis	mast cells	sweat
fibroblasts	melanin	sweat glands

Skin

Your **skin** is the organ that has the most contact with the outside world. In Lesson 17, you learned that your skin provides a defense against pathogens. Your skin must also provide information about the outside environment. What is the temperature? What is the nature and texture of the objects or other substances touching your body? Your skin also plays an important role in maintaining your body temperature. It also synthesizes vitamin D.

The skin is made up of three layers. The inner layer is called the subcutaneous layer. The **subcutaneous layer** contains mostly fat-storing cells. The fat is used both for energy and for insulation. Fat prevents heat from escaping from the body. Fat also cushions the structures beneath the skin. You will now take a closer look at the middle layer, or dermis, and the outer layer, or epidermis.

Dermis

The **dermis** is the thickest layer of the skin. It is composed mostly of a tough, fibrous protein called **collagen.** Collagen gives the skin its strength. Collagen also prevents the skin from tearing. A second protein found in the dermis is called elastin. As its name implies, **elastin** behaves like a rubber band; it helps the skin return to its normal shape after it has been stretched. A gel-like substance called **ground substance** helps glue together the cells and proteins in the dermis. Special cells in the dermis called **fibroblasts** secrete the collagen, elastin, and ground substance.

The dermis also contains white blood cells called phagocytes. As you learned in Lesson 17, phagocytes engulf pathogens and other debris. **Mast cells,** a specific type of phagocyte, help stimulate the inflammation response when the skin gets injured.

Winding through the collagen are networks of capillaries. Blood flowing through these capillaries provides oxygen and nutrients to the cells in the epidermis. Capillaries also play an important role in regulating your body temperature. If your body needs to shed heat, these blood vessels open up. Just as hot water flowing through a radiator releases heat, blood flowing near the surface of the skin gives off heat and cools the body down. If your body needs to conserve heat, these capillaries constrict, or tighten, to reduce heat loss.

The dermis also contains a variety of sensory nerves that detect pressure, temperature, and pain. In Lesson 19, you will learn how some of these sensory nerves work.

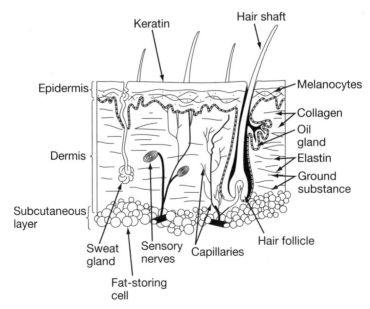

Skin Layers and Structures

Epidermis

The **epidermis**, or outer layer of skin, serves mostly as a protective layer. As you have already learned, the cells in the top layer of skin are dead. They are covered with a tough, waterproof protein called keratin. These dead cells, especially those on the hands and feet, are constantly getting rubbed off. Layers of living cells underneath constantly divide and replace the dead cells on top. Other living cells in the epidermis help stimulate the inflammation and immune responses.

The epidermis also contains cells that produce the pigment melanin. **Melanin** gives skin its color. The purpose of melanin is to protect the skin from harmful ultraviolet radiation from the sun. Too much exposure to ultraviolet radiation can cause a sunburn and may eventually lead to skin cancer.

Skin pigments, however, inhibit (prevent from happening) another important function of skin—the manufacture of vitamin D. Vitamin D enables the intestines to absorb the calcium needed to build bones and work muscles. People who do not get enough vitamin D can develop a disease called rickets. Rickets causes the bones to soften and become malformed. Cells in the skin synthesize vitamin D when exposed to certain types of ultraviolet light. Some anthropologists theorize that when Africans migrated north into Europe 75,000 years ago, they were unable to synthesize enough vitamin D because they were not absorbing sufficient sunlight through their dark skin. As a result, lighter skin gradually developed in these peoples.

Many structures bridge the dermis and epidermis. **Sweat glands** are one example. **Sweat** secreted by these glands contains chemical wastes that are excreted from the body. Sweat also helps cool the body down when it is overheated. Finally, friendly microorganisms on the surface of the skin feed on the sweat and secrete lactic acid. This acid environment discourages pathogens.

A **hair** comes from a cell called a **follicle** that is based in the dermis. Hair is composed mostly of the protein keratin. Unlike the hair of most mammals, human hair does not provide warmth or any other protection. Instead, hair serves a sensory function. That is, touching a hair stimulates nerves at the base of the follicle.

TIP

Touch the hairs on the top of your head without touching your scalp. You will be able to feel the sensation in your scalp.

Glands at the base of the hair follicles produce an oily substance called sebum. **Sebum** helps lubricate the skin and deters pathogens. Sometimes these glands become clogged. Bacteria trapped inside multiply and cause the region to swell. The result is a pimple.

■ PRACTICE 54: Skin

Look at the list of words below. Fill in each line with the letter of the word that correctly completes each of the following statements.

a. collagen   **c.** ultraviolet radiation   **e.** dermis

b. epidermis   **d.** keratin   **f.** subcutaneous layer

1. The three layers of skin cells, from bottom to top, are the _____, _____, and _____.

2. _____ is the protein found in the top layer of the epidermis and in hair.

3. The tough, fibrous protein that gives your skin strength is called _____.

4. The purpose of melanin is to protect the skin from _____.

LESSON 19: Bones

GOAL: To understand the function of the human skeleton

WORDS TO KNOW

appendicular skeleton	joints	spongy bone
axial skeleton	ligaments	stem cells
compact bone	marrow	sternum
cranium	osteocytes	synovial fluid
disk	pectoral girdle	synovial membrane
Haversian canal	pelvic girdle	vertebral column
Haversian systems	shaft	

Bones

To understand the function of your skeleton, think about what your body would be like if your skeleton were removed. Obviously, you would not be able to stand up. Your skeleton does more than just support your weight. It also provides a framework that gives your body its shape.

> **TIP**
>
> Your bones give your body shape the same way in which a mannequin gives shape to clothes that are displayed in a department store window. If you take away the mannequin, the clothes lie in a shapeless pile on the floor.

Your boneless body would also leave vital organs exposed. For example, your skull protects your brain. Your ribs and breastbone protect your heart and lungs. Your backbone protects your spine.

Finally, you would have a tough time moving your boneless body. As you will learn later in this lesson, muscles move your limbs by contracting and pulling on the bones, just as strings pull on a marionette. If your muscles have nothing to pull on when they contract, they are as useless as a pile of string.

The function of bones is not just structural. Bones manufacture both red and white blood cells. They also serve as a storage site for calcium.

The adult body contains 206 bones. Infants actually have 300 bones, but some fuse together as a child grows. The largest bone is the femur, which is in the upper leg. The smallest bone is the stapes, which is found in the inner ear. The stapes is only half a centimeter long. The skeleton consists of two major divisions—the axial skeleton and the appendicular skeleton.

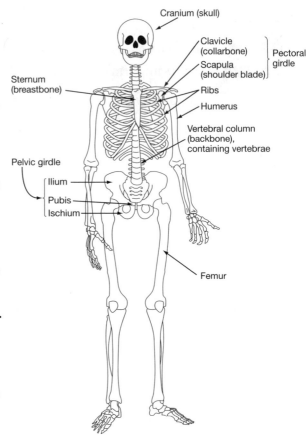

Human Skeleton

Axial Skeleton

The **axial skeleton** consists of your **cranium, vertebral column**, ribs, and **sternum.** As you know, your skull protects your brain. It is actually composed of several bones that are fused together.

The vertebral column extends from the base of your skull to the bottom of your back. It protects the spinal cord and supports the upper part of your body. The vertebral column is not a straight line. Instead, it is shaped like an S. Like a spring, it absorbs the shock from walking or jumping.

!

Many bones have common names as well as scientific names. Here are the common names and scientific names for some important bones.

Common Name	Scientific Name
backbone	vertebral column
breastbone	sternum
collarbone	clavicle
skull	cranium
shoulder blade	scapula
thigh bone	femur

The vertebral column contains 33 vertebrae. Each vertebra has a central opening called the spinal canal, through which the spinal cord passes. A soft but strong washer-shaped structure called a **disk** separates each vertebra. The disks are made out of a type of strong but flexible material called cartilage. Cartilage is composed of the protein collagen and various complex carbohydrates. A gel-like substance fills each disk. These disks provide cushioning and some flexibility to the vertebral column. The vertebrae toward the bottom of the vertebral column are fused together.

Because this flexible vertebral column is so complex and must bear so much stress, it is easily injured. Anyone who has pulled one of the many back muscles knows that a back injury can be very painful. One of the more common back injuries is a ruptured disk. Without the cushioning provided by the disk, the vertebrae rub together. The results are painful. Usually, the disks will heal after several weeks. Occasionally, however, surgery is required to repair the disk. More serious back injuries may harm the spinal cord. As you will learn, injury to the spinal cord may cause paralysis.

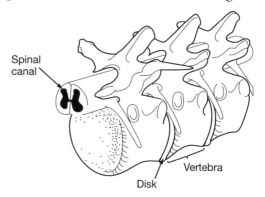

Spinal canal

Vertebra

Disk

Vertebrae

Appendicular Skeleton

The **appendicular skeleton** consists of the pectoral and pelvic girdles and the bones in the arms, legs, hands, and feet. The **pectoral girdle** is made up of the scapulae and clavicles. The bones of the pectoral girdle anchor the arm bones to the body. The pelvic girdle anchors the bones of the legs and feet to the body. The **pelvic girdle** is composed of three bones—the ilium, pubis, and ischium. Animals that walk on four legs have much larger and stronger pectoral girdles to support the weight. In humans, the pelvic girdle, or pelvis, supports all of the body's weight.

Joints

Joints are the junctions at which two bones meet. Strong, flexible cords called **ligaments** hold the bones together at the joints. Ligaments are mostly made out of collagen. Some joints, such as those between the bones of your cranium and between those in your pelvis, are immovable. The joints between your ribs and sternum are slightly more flexible. This flexibility enables your rib cage to expand when you inhale. The joints between each vertebra are also fairly flexible. You can see this for yourself by bending and twisting your upper body.

The most flexible joints are found in your limbs, neck, and hips. Yet these joints are flexible only in certain directions. Each type of joint is classified by its range of motion. Joints in your elbows, knees, fingers, and toes are called hinge joints. The hinge joint allows movement in two dimensions: one bone is moved by muscle and the other bone remains in a fixed position. Joints in your hips and shoulders are called ball-and-socket joints. In a ball-and-socket joint, the rounded end of one bone fits into a hollow depression in another bone. This allows movement in several directions. Joints in your wrists and ankles are called gliding joints. They allow for a sliding motion. Joints in your neck are called pivot joints. A pivot joint only allows rotation. You can turn your head from side to side because of the pivot joints in your neck.

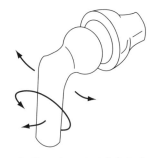

Ball-and-socket Joint of Upper Arm and Shoulder

Where else do you have pivot joints? Write your answer on a separate sheet of paper.

A smooth layer of cartilage covers the ends of your bones. This cartilage provides some cushioning and reduces the friction between the moving bones. Between the bones, there is a sac composed of a membrane called the **synovial membrane.** A greasy liquid called **synovial fluid** fills this sac and lubricates the joints. This prevents the bones from rubbing against each other and wearing down.

Over a lifetime of use, the cartilage at the end of the bones can wear down. As a result, flexing the joints becomes difficult and painful. This condition is called osteoarthritis. A more serious form of arthritis occurs when the body's immune system attacks the synovial membranes. This condition, called rheumatoid arthritis, causes pain and swelling in joints throughout the body.

Bone Structure

The material that makes up bone is both incredibly strong and surprisingly light. In fact, a comparable skeleton made out of steel would weigh five times more than your skeleton. A bone's strength comes from the minerals calcium and phosphorus. Bones also contain a lot of collagen. Collagen provides flexibility and enables bones to withstand stress. Without collagen, bones would shatter like glass if bent.

Bones are not dead. They contain cells that produce new bone. This accounts for the ability of broken bones to heal. Bones also contain cells that produce red and white blood cells.

Now look at the structure of the humerus, the large bone in your upper arm. The humerus contains two types of bone tissue: compact bone tissue and spongy bone tissue. **Compact bone** is found in the outer shell of the bone surrounding a central cavity. It is thickest in the middle area, or **shaft,** of the bone. If you look closely through a microscope, you will see that compact bone is composed of tightly stacked rods. These rods are called

Haversian systems. Each Haversian system contains layers of minerals and collagen. Individual cells called **osteocytes** are located in chambers embedded between these layers. Osteocytes maintain the compact bone by synthesizing collagen and assembling the minerals.

In the center of each Haversian system is a thin channel called a **Haversian canal.** Capillaries run through the Haversian canals. A network of tiny channels extends from the Haversian canal and carries nutrients and oxygen to each osteocyte.

Besides giving the bones strength, dense bone serves as a reservoir for calcium. Calcium is essential for the contraction of muscles. If there is not enough calcium in the blood, cells in the bone will actually break down the calcium minerals in the bone and release the calcium into the blood. This replenishes the calcium supply in your blood, but can seriously deplete the strength of your bones if your diet is low in calcium.

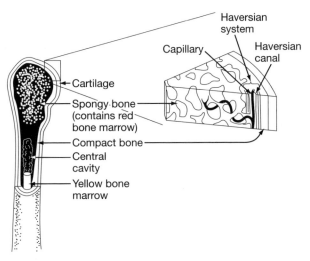

Cross Section of Humerus

Spongy bone is located at the enlarged ends of the humerus and on the inside of the shaft. Despite its name, spongy bone is not soft. It contains a latticework of hard bone and large pores, and, therefore, resembles a sponge. The arrangement of this latticework provides the spongy bone with the maximum amount of strength.

Tissue called **marrow** fills the pores in spongy bone. There are two types of marrow—red and yellow. Red marrow contains highly specialized cells called stem cells. **Stem cells** divide repeatedly and create red blood cells, white blood cells, and platelets (cells involved in clotting). Together, these stem cells produce two million new blood cells per second.

Treatments for cancer, including radiation and certain drugs (chemotherapy), can damage or destroy many of these stem cells. As a result, the patient may be unable to produce enough white blood cells to fight off infections. After receiving these treatments, the patient may require a bone marrow transplant. Doctors can first remove some marrow from the patient before the cancer treatment begins, and then inject it back into the patient afterward. If this is not possible, a doctor may use marrow donated by another person. This donor is almost always an immediate relative of the patient.

Bone marrow transplants may also be the only treatment option for people with leukemia. Leukemia is a type of cancer in which stem cells divide uncontrollably and produce too many white blood cells. Often, the only treatment for leukemia is to kill the marrow with radiation, then transplant marrow that a relative has donated.

In adults, red marrow is confined mostly to the ribs, sternum, pelvis, and vertebrae. Other bones, including the humerus, contain mostly yellow marrow. Cells in yellow marrow store dense fatty material. These cells can, however, turn into red marrow if the body starts losing a lot of blood.

■ PRACTICE 55: Bones

Decide if each statement that follows is true (**T**) or false (**F**). Write the correct letter on each line.

_____ 1. The region of the skeleton that contains the skull, vertebral column, and ribs is called the appendicular skeleton.

_____ 2. The pelvic girdle contains three bones.

_____ 3. The disks between the vertebrae are hard.

_____ 4. Channels in spongy bone contain capillaries called Haversian canals.

_____ 5. Tissue containing cells that divide into different types of blood cells is called red marrow.

LESSON 20: Muscles

GOAL: To understand the muscles in the human body and learn their functions

WORDS TO KNOW

actin	myosin heads
ADP (adenosine diphosphate)	sarcomere
cardiac muscle	sarcoplasmic reticula
fibers	skeletal muscles
inhibitors	smooth muscles
muscles	tendons
myosin	

Muscles

While your bones give structure to your body, your muscles maintain this structure. **Muscles** are masses of tissue that hold your bones in place and let you move. You use muscles when you stand. You use muscles when you sit. You use muscles to maintain your posture. You even use muscles when you curl up at night as you go to sleep.

And, of course, you use muscles to move. Not only do muscles move your arms and legs around, they move blood through your circulatory system, lymph (a plasmic fluid containing white blood cells) through your lymph system, and food through your digestive tract.

All muscles are composed of specialized cells called **fibers.** When stimulated by an impulse from a nerve, or occasionally by a hormone, these fibers contract, or shorten. All of the fibers in a single muscle contract at once and, therefore, cause the entire muscle to shorten. As you will see, the contraction of muscle fibers requires the use of the energy-rich molecule ATP.

In this section, you will learn about the three types of muscles in your body. Then you will learn how muscles work.

Smooth Muscles

Smooth muscles are also known as involuntary muscles. You cannot consciously control them. Smooth muscles lining your esophagus and small intestine push food through. Smooth muscles in your stomach churn the food and cause your stomach to growl. Smooth muscles lining your arteries control the blood flow to different tissues. For example, every time you are embarrassed, smooth muscles open the capillaries in your face and cause you to blush. Smooth muscles also cause your pupils to dilate and your hairs to stand on end. In asthma sufferers, smooth muscles around the bronchi contract, narrow the air passage, and make breathing more difficult.

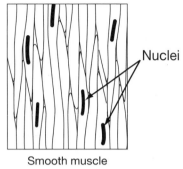

Smooth muscle

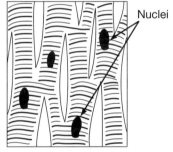

Cardiac muscle

Under the microscope, smooth muscles appear smooth, at least compared with the other two muscle types. Each muscle fiber is shaped like an oval with tapered ends. Each muscle fiber has a single nucleus. (As you will see, skeletal muscle fibers contain many nuclei.) Smooth muscle fibers are usually arranged in sheets or straps that wrap around structures like the esophagus or a blood vessel. When these straps contract, they squeeze the structure, forcing (for example) food or blood through. Smooth muscles tend

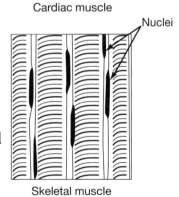

Skeletal muscle

Muscle Types

to contract more slowly than other types of muscles. Therefore, they require less energy. As a result, smooth muscles can work continuously without running short of oxygen and glucose.

Cardiac Muscles

Your heart is made out of cardiac muscle. **Cardiac muscle** has a remarkable ability to contract vigorously over and over again without growing tired. A rich supply of blood carries enough oxygen and glucose and sweeps wastes away fast enough to keep this muscle going.

Like smooth muscle fibers, cardiac muscle fibers have a single nucleus. The similarities end there. Cardiac muscle fibers are branched and look as if they have been woven together. The membranes at the ends of these branches contain many folds. These folds interlock with the folds in the adjacent fiber like pieces in a puzzle. This arrangement allows electrical signals to pass quickly from cell to cell so that they can contract in a coordinated manner. Cardiac muscle fibers also appear striated (striped). These stripes reflect the highly ordered arrangement of proteins in the cells. You will learn about the functions of these proteins later.

Skeletal Muscles

Skeletal muscles are voluntary. You can contract them whenever you want. You have about 640 skeletal muscles. They range in size from the giant muscles in your upper legs and buttocks to the tiny muscles that control your facial expressions and the movement of your eyes.

Skeletal muscles pull bones. Typically, a muscle is attached to two bones: a "base" bone, and the bone that the muscle is pulling. Collagen cords called **tendons** anchor the ends of the muscles to the bones. For example, one end of your biceps muscle is attached to the scapula (shoulder blade). The other end is attached to one of the bones in your forearm. When you contract that biceps muscle, your arm bends at the elbow.

Your biceps muscle, however, only pulls in one direction. It cannot push your forearm back. To straighten your arm, you must contract a second muscle called the triceps. Most skeletal muscles come in antagonistic, or opposing, pairs that pull the bone in opposite directions. When one muscle contracts, the muscle that pulls in the opposite direction must relax. It is important to remember, however, that muscles do not work in isolation. You use combinations of many muscles to move your arms or legs in different directions.

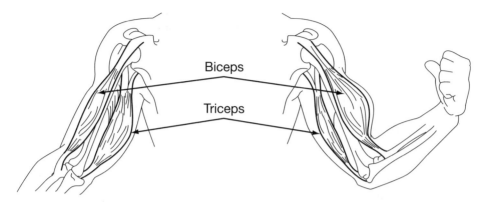

Triceps Contracted, Biceps Relaxed   **Biceps Contracted, Triceps Relaxed**

Skeletal muscle fibers are up to 30 centimeters long. They contain many nuclei, mitochondria, and structures called **sarcoplasmic reticula.** Sarcoplasmic reticula store calcium. As you know, calcium is vital to the contraction of muscles.

Skeletal muscles contain two proteins called **actin** and **myosin.** Both are long, ropelike proteins that are aligned side by side. Myosin, however, also has a series of extensions, or ratchets, called **myosin heads.** When the muscle is activated, these extensions reach out and attach to the adjacent actin fiber.

Now look at the precise arrangement of these proteins. Within each muscle fiber, there are bundles of actin and myosin proteins. Think of each bundle as a telephone cable and the actin and myosin inside as wires. Each of these cables has a sequence of vertical stripes that is clearly visible through a microscope. The sequence of stripes is white, pink, red, pink, white. The white stripe, called the I band, contains only actin fibers. Running down the center of each I band is a narrow Z line. The red stripe, or H zone, contains only myosin fibers. The pink stripes are where the myosin and actin fibers overlap. Together, the red and pink make up the A band. The area between two Z lines is called the **sarcomere.**

When a muscle is in its relaxed state, there are molecules called **inhibitors** that bind to the actin fibers. These inhibitors prevent the myosin heads from attaching to the actin.

A band
(red and pink)

| I band (white) | (pink) | H zone (red) | (pink) | I band (white) |

Z line

Z line

Myosin

Actin

Sarcomere

Skeletal Muscle Fiber Zones and Bands

When a muscle contracts, the actin and myosin fibers slide past one another. The pink areas, where the two proteins overlap, grow larger. The H zone and I bands narrow. The sarcomere is shorter. This sequence of events requires a lot of energy in the form of ATP (adenosine triphosphate). Now take a closer look at what happens when a muscle contracts.

You decide to bend your arm at the elbow. Your brain sends electrical signals through nerves to the fibers in your biceps muscle. The signal from the nerves causes the sarcoplasmic reticulum (singular of *reticula*) to release the calcium (Ca^{2+}) it is storing. The calcium binds to the actin and causes the actin to drop the inhibitors. An ATP molecule binds to the myosin head. An enzyme then breaks down the ATP molecule into **ADP (adenosine diphosphate)** and an additional phosphate molecule (P). This reaction releases a lot of energy. Now the myosin head can attach to the actin, forming the bridge. The myosin head is now in its high-energy configuration, as shown in the diagram below.

Suddenly, the ADP and phosphate molecule are released. The myosin head relaxes to its low-energy state. As it relaxes, the myosin head pulls the actin so that it slides past the myosin. As a result, the sarcomere shortens, and the muscle contracts.

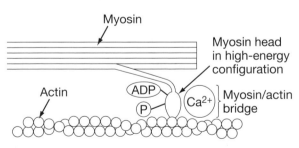

Myosin

Myosin head in high-energy configuration

Actin

ADP

P

Ca^{2+}

Myosin/actin bridge

The myosin head attaches to an actin binding site, with the help of calcium.

Muscle Contraction

As soon as the myosin head has pulled the actin along, it releases the actin. The sequence then repeats. A new ATP molecule attaches to the myosin head and provides the energy needed to put it into its high-energy configuration. The myosin head attaches to the actin, relaxes, and pulls the actin farther.

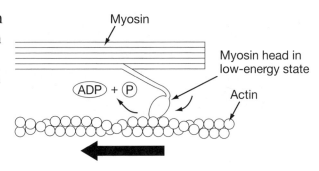

Myosin

Myosin head in low-energy state

ADP + P

Actin

With the release of ADP and P, the myosin head relaxes into a low-energy state and pulls the actin past the myosin.

Muscle Contraction, *continued*

■ PRACTICE 56: Muscles

Look at the list of words below. Fill in each line with the letter of the word that correctly completes each statement.

a. actin   **c.** calcium   **e.** skeletal muscles

b. smooth muscles   **d.** myosin

1. The muscles surrounding the digestive tract and blood vessels are

    _____.

2. The only types of muscles that are voluntary are the _____.

3. The two major proteins involved in muscle contraction are _____ and _____.

4. One of the major functions of the sarcoplasmic reticulum is to store

    _____.

LESSON 21: Nervous and Endocrine Systems

 GOAL: To learn about the two systems that enable different parts of the body to communicate with one another

WORDS TO KNOW

adrenal glands	epinephrine
adrenaline	frontal lobe
autonomic nervous system	glands
axons	growth hormone
blood-brain barrier	hemispheres
calcium gate	hindbrain
central nervous system	hormones
cerebellum	hypothalamus
cerebral cortex	incus
cerebrum	insulin
chemoreceptors	ion
cochlea	iris
cones	lens
cornea	limbic system
cortisol	malleus
dendrites	medulla
depolarization	meninges
ear canal	metabolism
effectors	motor cortex
endocrine system	myelin sheath *(continued)*

WORDS TO KNOW *(continued)*

nervous system	sclera
neurons	sensory receptors
neurotransmitters	somatic nervous system
nodes of Ranvier	stapes
norepinephrine	stimuli
occipital lobe	synaptic gap
optic nerve	synaptic knobs
pancreas	synaptic vesicles
parietal lobe	taste buds
pituitary gland	temporal lobe
polarization	thalamus
prefrontal area	thermoreceptors
pupil	thyroid
resting state	thyroid stimulating hormone (TSH)
retina	thyroxin
rods	tympanum
Schwann cells	vitreous humor

Neurons

A tree is about to fall on you. You must move out of the way or you are going to be hit. Doesn't it seem pretty simple? But think of all the things that must happen to get you to move out of the way in time. A remarkable amount of communication is involved. First, you must see the falling tree. But that is not enough. You must recognize that what you are seeing is a falling tree and that you are in danger. Then you have to decide what action to take to avoid it. Which muscles should you use? If the wrong fibers contract at the wrong time, you will not go anywhere. But in order for your muscles to work properly, your body must provide them with enough oxygen, glucose, and calcium.

Fortunately, your body has vast electrical and chemical systems that enable the various parts of the body to communicate with one another. These systems are the **nervous system** and the **endocrine system.**

Your nervous system is like the wiring inside a computer. Information in the form of electrical impulses travels at incredible speed—up to 120 meters per second—from cell to cell. This speed allows you to react quickly. For example, there is little lag time between the time you see that a tree is falling on you and the time that your muscles contract and get you out of the way.

Neural Pathway

Your nervous system has three main tasks.

1. Detection. Your nervous system must gather information. Sensory nerves in your eyes, ears, skin, nose, and tongue accomplish this task. Sensory nerves also monitor conditions inside your body. You have learned that sensory nerves detect increased acidity in your blood and signal you to breathe faster and harder. The cues that alert these sensory nerves—for example, the sights and sounds of a tree falling on you, or the level of carbonic acid in your blood—are called **stimuli.**

2. Integration. The information that your sensors detect travels to your brain for processing. For example, your brain takes the sights and sounds of the tree falling on you and interprets what is going on.

3. Response. The brain sends information that tells the cells what to do. For example, the brain will instruct certain muscle fibers to contract so that you can jump out of the way of the falling tree. The brain also sends signals to organs, such as your kidneys, lungs, and the organs that secrete hormones.

Scientists often refer to two different nervous systems—the somatic nervous system and the autonomic nervous system. The **somatic nervous system** controls sensations that you are aware of (sight, sound, pain) and the voluntary movement of muscles. The **autonomic nervous system** controls things that you are not aware of or cannot control. Examples include the constriction of arteries, the contraction of muscles surrounding the small intestine, and the release of hormones. The autonomic nervous system also supplies the brain with feedback from different regions of the body, such as if cells are getting enough energy or if body temperature is too high.

Neuron Structure

Nerves are composed of tightly wound bundles of cells called **neurons.** Neurons are like the wires in a telephone cable. There are three general categories of neurons—sensory neurons, interneurons, and motor neurons. As their name implies, sensory neurons detect stimuli such as light, sound, heat, or pressure. Sensory neurons relay this information to interneurons. The interneurons in turn relay information to other interneurons. Most of the neurons in the brain where integration takes place are interneurons. The motor neurons are the final links in the chain. Most motor neurons are linked to muscles. Stimuli from these motor neurons cause the muscle fibers to contract. Motor neurons also stimulate organs to release chemicals such as hormones. The tissues that motor neurons stimulate are called **effectors.**

Neurons are large cells. Some are almost a meter long. They consist of a cell body that contains the nucleus and all of the regular organelles. Extending from the cell body are two types of branches—dendrites and axons. **Dendrites** are the neuron's antennas. They receive information from stimuli or from other neurons. Dendrites are relatively short and highly branched, although the amount of branching varies depending on the type of neuron.

Whereas impulses enter the neuron through the dendrites, they leave through the axons. **Axons** are like cables. They transmit information from the cell body, either to the dendrites of other neurons, or to effectors such as muscles. Axons are usually far longer than dendrites and are less branched.

A fatty layer called the **myelin sheath** surrounds the axons of some types of neurons. Like the casing covering an electrical wire, the myelin sheath acts as an electrical insulator. The myelin sheath is composed of the membranes of cells called **Schwann cells.** These membranes wrap around the axon hundreds of times. A single Schwann cell does not cover the entire axon. Instead, the Schwann cells line up along the axon like sausages on a string. Between the individual Schwann cells are nodes called **nodes of Ranvier.** Impulses jump from node to node to allow for a fast transfer of nervous information.

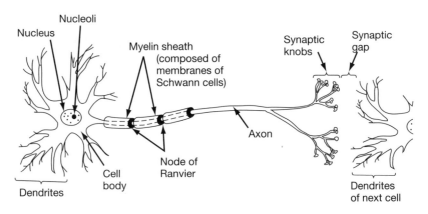

Neuron (Nerve Cell)

Multiple sclerosis is an autoimmune disease in which the immune system attacks the myelin sheaths on some neurons. As a result, the nerves are unable to fire properly. Severe cases of multiple sclerosis may lead to paralysis.

The structures at the tips of the axons are called **synaptic knobs.** These structures generate and transmit signals to the next neuron or to the effector. The axons of some neurons, particularly those in the spinal cord, are directly attached to the dendrites of the next neuron. In most neurons, however, the axons do not touch the dendrites of the neurons they are signaling. Instead, there is a space in between called the **synaptic gap.** You will see what happens in the synaptic gap shortly.

The region of the heart called the pacemaker contains motor neurons that generate the signals that cause the heart to beat. How do you think these motor neurons differ structurally from the typical neurons that have been described so far? Write your answer on a separate sheet of paper.

Transmission Within Neurons

So far, the nervous system has been compared to electrical wires. Just as information in the form of electrical impulses travels through the wires of a computer, information in the form of electrical impulses travels through your neurons. You will now see how this impulse travels from one end of the axon to the other. Then you will learn how this impulse is passed to the dendrite of neighboring neurons.

Major players in this process are sodium (Na^+) and potassium (K^+) ions. An **ion** is an atom that has either a positive charge or a negative charge. Sodium and potassium ions have a positive charge. The inside of the axon contains proteins with negative charges.

Another major player in this process is the membrane surrounding the axons. These membranes contain proteins that actively pump the sodium ions (Na^+) from the inside to the outside of the axon.

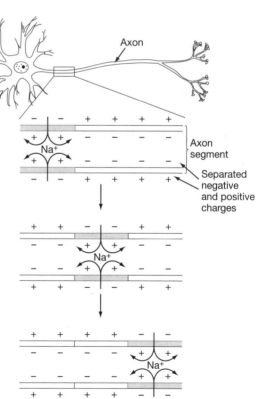

Depolarization Moving from Left to Right

When an impulse is not traveling along an axon, the neuron is said to be in a **resting state**. However, it is still working hard, pumping out the sodium ions. The result of this pumping is a huge buildup of positively charged sodium ions outside of the axon. Negatively charged proteins line the inside of the axon. Therefore, there is a positive charge outside the axon and a negative charge inside. This separation of positive and negative charges is called **polarization.**

Suddenly, there is a signal, either from a stimulus or from an adjacent neuron, causing the channels in the membrane to open. The sodium ions rush into the axon because they are attracted to the negative proteins. Thus, the inside of the cell becomes temporarily positive. This process is called **depolarization.**

This starts a domino effect. After one segment of the axon has been depolarized, a wave of depolarization sweeps down the axon from left to right. Once this wave of depolarization has reached the end of the axon, the sodium gates close, and the axon recharges. The axon is back to its resting state.

TIP

You could compare this process to a rowdy crowd of rock fans who are locked out of the stadium where their favorite band is about to perform. They are pressed against the gates, desperately trying to get in. The rock fans could be equated with the positive sodium ions and the rock band would be the negative proteins. Suddenly, one gate is opened, and the unruly crowd rushes in. A domino effect is created as other doors (moving left to right) are opened. This is similar to depolarization, because now more fans are inside than outside.

Transmission Between Neurons

You will now learn how impulses pass from one neuron to the next. Most neurons, including the interneurons in the brain, have a gap called a synaptic gap between the axon and the adjacent dendrite. The electrical impulse is translated into chemical messengers called **neurotransmitters** that travel across the synaptic gap. Here is how it works.

1. The synaptic knobs at the ends of the axons contain membrane-bound sacs called **synaptic vesicles.** The synaptic vesicles are filled with neurotransmitters. There are about 50 types of neurotransmitters, each of which is released by a different type of neuron. For example, motor neurons contain a neurotransmitter called acetyl-coline, which triggers muscle fibers to contract. Interneurons in the brain contain a large number of neurotransmitters.

2. When an impulse reaches the synaptic knobs, it triggers the opening of a **calcium gate** in the membrane. Calcium enters the axon through this gate and triggers the vesicles to release the neurotransmitters into the synaptic gap.

3. The neurotransmitters diffuse across the synaptic gap and bind to receptors on the neighboring dendrite. Once they bind, they cause sodium gates in the dendrite membrane to open, and a depolarization wave begins.

4. Enzymes in the synaptic gap break down the neurotransmitters immediately after they have bound to the receptors. If it were not for these enzymes, the neurotransmitters would continue to stimulate the neurons to fire. In fact, nerve gas and certain insecticides kill their victims by inhibiting these enzymes.

Not all neurotransmitters stimulate impulses in the adjacent neuron. Some actually inhibit the impulse. Neurons use these transmitters to slow down the firing of nerves.

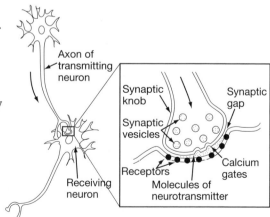

Synapse

■ PRACTICE 57: Neurons

Decide if each statement that follows is true (**T**) or false (**F**). Write the correct letter on each line.

_____ **1.** Sensory neurons trigger the contraction of muscle fibers.

_____ **2.** The branches of the neurons that receive signals from other neurons are called dendrites.

_____ **3.** Polarization separates positive charges from negative charges.

_____ **4.** The synaptic knob transmits signals to the next neuron.

The Senses

Sensory receptors translate stimuli—such as light, sound, odors, and pressure—into impulses that travel to the brain. Sensory receptors also monitor the body's temperature. They help to maintain your balance. Sensory receptors enable you to determine the exact locations of your hands and feet without looking. You will now learn about some of the major types of sensory nerves.

Touch

As you learned, your skin contains many types of sensory receptors. Your hands (especially the fingertips), feet, eyes, and lips contain the highest concentration of these receptors. Many of the receptors are stimulated by changes of pressure. The keratin in your scalp is structured to actually transmit an electrical signal to the central nervous system when your scalp is touched.

Different types of pressure receptors relay different types of information. Receptors near the surface of your skin detect light touches. Other receptors enable you to distinguish different textures, such as whether an object is hard, soft, fluffy, pointy, or smooth. Other more generalized receptors register pain. Pressure sensors in your arteries relay information about blood pressure.

Thermoreceptors detect temperature. Different receptors detect heat and cold.

Smell

Chemoreceptors are sensory nerves that detect specific chemicals. In humans, the chemoreceptors are concentrated in the nose and mouth. The chemoreceptors in the nose are called olfactory cells. These cells are located on a thumbnail-sized patch at the roof of your nasal cavity. Molecules floating in the air enter your nose when you sniff, dissolve in the mucus in your nose, and bind to the dendrites (antennas) of the olfactory cells. The impulses these molecules generate travel directly to an extension of the brain. There, the signals are processed.

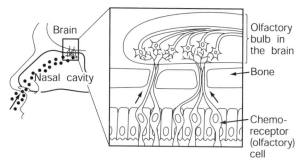

Human Nose

Taste

Taste buds are chemoreceptors that are located in grooves in your tongue. Chemicals from food dissolve in the saliva and bind to the ends of the dendrites. As discussed in Lesson 15, humans can only detect four types of tastes: sweet, sour, salty, and bitter.

IN REAL LIFE

Christina had visited the house of her in-laws on many occasions, but this time she had an especially good feeling after she entered. There was a familiar scent in the air. She realized that her father-in-law was cooking rhubarb pie. This smell triggered a flood of wonderful childhood memories for Christina. The part of the brain that processes smells is linked to the part that processes emotions. For that reason, certain smells are often linked with strong emotions.

Hearing

Auditory nerves are sensors that detect sound. The sensory nerves are located in the inner ear. Sound arrives in the ear in the form of pressure pulses or waves that cause the air molecules to vibrate. Now you can follow these vibrations as they move through the ear.

First, the sound waves enter a narrow chamber called the **ear canal.** Stretched across the end of this chamber is a thin, flexible membrane called the **tympanum,** or eardrum. The sound waves strike the eardrum and cause it to vibrate.

The eardrum in turn transfers these vibrations to three tiny bones in the middle ear called the **malleus** (hammer), **incus** (anvil), and **stapes** (stirrup). These three bones are attached by joints that resemble the elbow and knee joints. Of course, they are much smaller. The vibrations are transferred from one bone to the next.

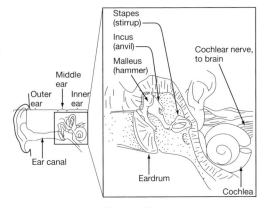

Human Ear

The stapes is attached to a coiled structure in the inner ear that resembles a tiny snail shell. This structure, called the **cochlea,** is filled with fluid. The vibration passes from the stapes to the fluid inside the cochlea, creating little waves. Stretching down the center of the cochlear tube is a membrane. Embedded in this membrane are tiny hairlike structures that are attached to neurons. The fluid vibrations cause these hairs to bend, triggering an impulse in these neurons. These neurons send a signal to the cochlear nerve, which in turn sends the impulse to the brain, where it gets processed.

TIP

Put your mouth within an inch of the top of a drum and shout. You will hear how the sound waves coming from your mouth cause the membrane stretched across the top of the drum to vibrate.

Sight

The eyeball is one of the most complex and fascinating sensory organs. You will now take a brief tour of the human eyeball.

A tough white membrane called the **sclera** covers most of the outside of the eyeball. Skeletal muscles attached to the sclera rotate the eyeball. Light enters the eye through a bulging disk on the front of the eyeball called the **cornea.** The purpose of the cornea is to focus the light entering the eye. The light then reaches a ring of smooth muscle called the **iris.** Pigments in the iris give eyes their color. In the center of the iris, there is an opening called the **pupil.** The smooth muscles of the iris regulate the amount of light that passes through by changing the size of the pupil. Behind the pupil is a flexible transparent **lens** that further focuses the light. A set of smooth muscles change the focus by bending the lens. This enables you to focus on objects that are close-up and on objects that are far away.

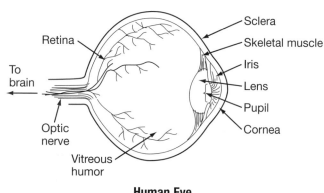

Human Eye

The light has now entered the inside of the eyeball, which is filled with a clear gel called the **vitreous humor.** The light travels to the back of the eyeball and strikes a stamp-sized patch called the **retina.** The retina is covered with patches of light receptors called rods and cones. **Rods** are the most sensitive to dim light. **Cones** relay information on color. There are three types of cones—red-sensitive, blue-sensitive, and green-sensitive. Cones do not respond well to dim light.

The sensors (rods and cones) in the retina contain pigments that convert the light they absorb into energy. The energy sets off a series of chemical reactions that trigger nerve impulses. These impulses travel through a bundle of neurons called the **optic nerve** to the brain. The brain then translates signals from the rods into black, white, and gray. It translates signals from the cones into color.

■ PRACTICE 58: The Senses

Look at the list of words below. Fill in each line with the letter of the word that correctly completes each statement.

a. cochlea   **c.** stapes (stirrup)   **e.** mouth   **g.** incus (anvil)

b. nose   **d.** malleus (hammer)   **f.** retina

1. Chemoreceptors can be found in your _____ and _____ .

2. The three bones in your middle ear are called the _____ , _____ , and _____ .

3. The _____ is the coiled structure in the inner ear that contains the sensory nerves.

4. Rods and cones are located on the _____ .

The Central Nervous System

So far, you have learned mostly about the nerves in your peripheral nervous system. These nerves include the sensory and motor neurons. Now you will concentrate on the part of the nervous system in which processing takes place. This region, called the **central nervous system,** includes the brain and spinal cord.

General Structure of the Brain

The human brain is capable of remarkable feats. It makes sure that your entire body functions properly. It is able to learn and apply information. The brain is also able to generate and articulate emotions that are unique to humans. Most impressively, it is self-aware. (That is why you are reading about the brain now.) Scientists have dissected the brain and developed detailed maps of its structure. They know the structures of all the neurons in the brain and the neurotransmitters that they produce. Yet true knowledge of how the brain really works—the patterns in which

100 billion neurons communicate with one another, the mechanism behind emotions—is still a mystery to researchers.

The brain is a delicate organ that weighs about 1.4 kilograms. Because it is so fragile and so important, the brain has plenty of protection. First there is the skull. Inside the skull are three protective membranes called **meninges.** Cerebrospinal fluid fills all the open spaces inside the skull and acts as a shock-absorber. The neurons of the brain are embedded in a protective matrix of cells called glial cells.

The brain requires huge amounts of glucose and oxygen to function, so it has a large blood supply. In fact, the brain burns 75 percent of the glucose the body takes in. The brain, however, is sensitive to toxic chemicals that might be present in the bloodstream. Therefore, the brain has an intensive screening process. In order for substances to enter the brain, they must cross what is known as the **blood-brain barrier.** The capillaries that run through the brain are impermeable to most substances. Chemicals that do escape the capillaries must pass through a selective set of star-shaped cells called astrocytes. Some toxic substances do manage to get through. One of the most common examples is alcohol.

The brain is divided into many regions that control specific functions. Researchers have learned a lot about which region of the brain controls each function by studying stroke and accident victims. Researchers match the part of the brain that has been damaged with the function that has been impaired. For example, people who have strokes in certain regions of the brain commonly have difficulty speaking. From this information, researchers have been able to learn which parts of the brain control speech.

Cerebrum

When you think of the brain, you probably imagine a large, wrinkly gray walnut. What you are picturing is actually the surface of the most dominant region of the brain in humans—the **cerebrum.** The wrinkled gray matter on top, called the **cerebral cortex,** is composed of tightly packed dendrites and cell bodies. Underneath the cortex are white mylenated axons that carry information to and from the cortex. The wrinkles or convolutions in the cortex increase its surface area. Therefore, its complexity is increased without increasing its volume.

The cerebrum is the center of intelligence. It takes information from sensory nerves, interprets it, then uses this information to direct the voluntary muscles. The cerebrum contains the language centers. It also contains the centers that make self-awareness possible.

The cerebrum is divided into two halves called **hemispheres.** The right hemisphere controls movement and interprets sensations on the left side of the body. The left hemisphere controls movement and interprets sensations on the right side of the body.

Each hemisphere of the cerebrum is divided into four lobes or sections—the occipital, temporal, frontal, and parietal. The **occipital lobe,** which is located at the back of the cerebrum, processes visual information.

The **temporal lobe** is located on the side of the brain below the temples. It processes sounds and smells, as well as some visual information. The **parietal lobe** is located between the frontal and occipital lobes. It receives signals from the neurons in the skin and from the neurons in the muscles that provide an awareness of the position of the body.

The **frontal lobe** both integrates the sensory information you receive and commands your voluntary muscles. The **prefrontal area** is at the front

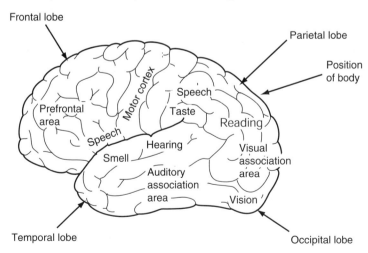

Left side (hemisphere)
Human Brain

of the frontal lobe. It sorts out all the sensory information your occipital and temporal lobes receive and places it into context. For example, the prefrontal area interprets the relative consequences of the sight of a tree falling toward you versus the sight of a pillow falling on you.

Farther up on the frontal lobe is a region called the **motor cortex.** It controls voluntary muscle movement. Different patches of the motor cortex control specific muscle groups. For example, there is a patch that controls the thumbs, a patch that controls the fingers, a patch that controls the shoulders, and so on.

None of these regions works in isolation. Look at the example of language. Every time you talk to a friend, you must use several parts of your cerebrum. The hearing center in the temporal lobe receives the sounds your friend speaks. Another region of the temporal lobe provides meaning to these sounds. The signal then gets relayed to the speech center, which translates what you want to say back into words. Finally, the information is sent to the part of the motor cortex that controls the muscles in the larynx, tongue, and lips.

Thalamus and Hypothalamus

The **thalamus,** which is located at the base of the cerebrum, is your brain's switchboard. The thalamus sorts all the information passing to and from the cerebrum. It then channels the information to the correct regions of the brain. For example, the thalamus makes sure that visual impulses go to the occipital lobe and that auditory impulses (sounds) go to the temporal lobe. The thalamus also is responsible for keeping your brain awake. It works a little like an alarm, sending signals that keep the brain alert.

The **hypothalamus** is anchored just below the thalamus. It regulates your autonomic nervous system. The hypothalamus monitors and adjusts your heart rate, blood pressure, body temperature, and appetite. It also stimulates hunger, thirst, and sex drive. In the next section, you will see how the hypothalamus regulates the release of hormones. The hypothalamus, along with several other nearby structures, controls your emotions and the expression of these emotions. Together, these structures form the **limbic system.**

Hindbrain

The **hindbrain** is the area of your brain just above the spinal cord. The lowest portion (the part directly connected to the spinal cord) is called the **medulla.** All signals passing between the brain and spinal cord pass through the medulla. The medulla directly controls autonomic functions, such as heart rate, breathing rate, and blood pressure. (Remember that the instructions for these functions originate in the hypothalamus.) The medulla also stimulates sneezing, coughing, swallowing, and vomiting.

The **cerebellum** is a bulbous structure in the back of the head just above the medulla. It organizes the signals from the motor cortex (the part of the cerebrum that controls the movement of voluntary muscles) so that your movements are organized and coordinated. The cerebellum also ensures that you keep your balance.

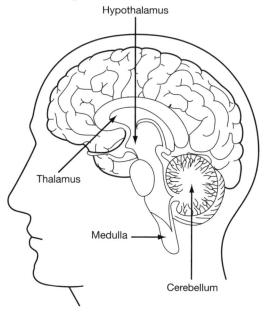

Parts of the Brain

■ PRACTICE 59: The Central Nervous System

Decide if each statement that follows is true (**T**) or false (**F**). Write the correct letter on each line.

_____ **1.** The three protective membranes surrounding the brain are called the meninges.

_____ **2.** The cerebrum is divided into four hemispheres.

_____ **3.** All sensory information is integrated in the prefrontal lobe.

_____ **4.** The hindbrain is a series of structures that control emotions.

The Endocrine System

You have already learned how hormones help regulate your heart rate and the amount of glucose and calcium in the blood. Now it is time to define exactly what a hormone is.

Hormones are chemical messengers (usually proteins) that are manufactured in organs called **glands.** They then travel through the bloodstream to target tissues or cells in other parts of the body. The hormones bind to these targets and trigger a response. Each hormone binds only to a specific target. Likewise, each target site has receptors that only accept a certain hormone. The system of glands and hormones is called the endocrine system.

Chemical messengers take a lot longer to reach their targets than impulses sent through the nervous system. Whereas your nervous system monitors conditions in your body and triggers quick actions, hormones trigger long-term changes such as growth and the development of sexual characteristics. As you will see, hormones also produce subtle changes that keep the body in balance.

Control of the Endocrine System

It is essential that your body control the number of hormones circulating in the body. It does so in three ways. First, your body has what is known as a negative feedback system. The presence of a high concentration of hormones in the bloodstream causes the glands to stop producing the hormones. When the hormone level falls, the gland begins producing hormones again.

Second, enzymes quickly break down hormones circulating in the blood in the same way that enzymes break down neurotransmitters. In this way, the body can turn off the hormonal response.

Finally, different hormones counteract each other. For example, the hormone insulin removes glucose from the bloodstream. Glucagon, another hormone, will turn off insulin as blood sugar levels decrease.

Pituitary Gland

Your nervous system controls the endocrine system. As you learned, the hypothalamus monitors the body and determines which hormones the body should produce and when. The hypothalamus controls hormone production through a marble-sized structure called the **pituitary gland.** This small gland is nestled in the brain just below the hypothalamus. The pituitary gland produces 10 different hormones. Most of these hormones do not directly influence the body. Instead, they switch other glands on and off. Say that the hypothalamus wants to stimulate your thyroid gland to produce the hormone thyroxin. (You will learn about the thyroid gland and thyroxin shortly.) The hypothalamus produces neurotransmitters that stimulate the pituitary gland to produce **thyroid stimulating hormone (TSH).** This hormone enters the bloodstream and binds with target cells on the thyroid.

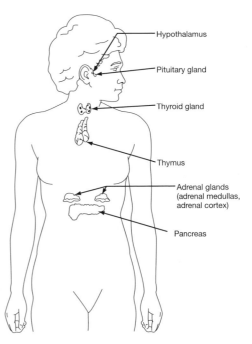

One of the hormones produced by the pituitary gland is called **growth hormone.** This hormone, as you probably guessed, triggers growth. It causes the target cells to take up more amino acids so that they can produce more proteins. Growth hormone causes the fat cells to release fat that can be used for energy, and causes the liver to break down glycogen into glucose.

Hypothalamus

Pituitary gland

Thyroid gland

Thymus

Adrenal glands (adrenal medullas, adrenal cortex)

Pancreas

The Endocrine System

Regulating Energy

Many hormones regulate **metabolism**—the rate at which your cells convert glucose to energy. Why is the rate of metabolism important? First, you need to produce enough energy to remain active, yet not so much energy that you become overly active or use up your energy reserves. There are also situations when you need a surge of energy. For example, you need extra energy to get out of the way of a falling tree or to recover from an injury. Second, the energy you produce keeps your body warm. Your body must maintain a constant temperature of about 98°F (37°C). Your hypothalamus monitors your body temperature and adjusts your metabolism accordingly.

The hormone **thyroxin** influences metabolism most directly. Thyroxin actually enters the target cells and speeds up respiration. The **thyroid,** a butterfly-shaped gland just below the larynx, produces thyroxin when stimulated by the pituitary gland.

Hormones also influence metabolism by controlling the amount of glucose available to the cells. Growth hormone is one example. Insulin and glucagon, both of which are synthesized in the **pancreas,** are two others. **Insulin** works by binding to the membranes of target cells throughout the body and triggering these membranes to actively transport the glucose into the cells.

Diabetes is a condition in which either the pancreas is unable to produce enough insulin (insulin-dependent diabetes) or the cells do not have enough insulin receptors (noninsulin-dependent diabetes). As a result, cells cannot take up enough glucose—a condition that can lead to severe complications. People with noninsulin-dependent diabetes often control it by carefully managing their diets. Insulin-dependent diabetes is far more dangerous. People with this condition usually require regular injections of insulin.

The **adrenal glands,** located on the kidneys, produce two hormones that provide you with a surge of energy. These hormones are **epinephrine** (also known as **adrenaline**) and **norepinephrine.** Both hormones cause your body to redirect blood away from organs such as the digestive tract and toward your skeletal muscles. In the meantime, your heart rate and blood pressure increase. Your liver loads extra glucose into the bloodstream. The adrenal glands also secrete a hormone called cortisol. **Cortisol** stimulates the body to convert amino acids and fats into glucose. Hormones from the pituitary gland stimulate the adrenal glands.

For months, Kari had felt tired and nauseated. She was constantly thirsty and had to urinate a lot. After a series of tests, a doctor told her she had noninsulin-dependent diabetes. Kari was not alone. Ten million Americans have been diagnosed with it. Untreated, diabetes can cause vision problems, heart disease, kidney failure, and infections in the fingers and toes. Overweight people are more likely to develop the disease. The doctor helped Kari develop a diet plan that helped her lose weight and control the disease.

Epinephrine, norepinephrine, and cortisol are triggered when you are in danger or are excited and need to respond quickly. Chronic stress can also trigger the release of these hormones. Continued production of them may lead to increased blood pressure, heart rate, and even a suppressed immune system, all of which can cause long-term health problems.

Your adrenal glands also produce two hormones that control the amount of salts the kidneys reabsorb. The more salts they reabsorb, the more water the body retains and the higher the blood pressure becomes, since adding more fluids increases the pressure inside your blood vessels.

■ PRACTICE 60: The Endocrine System

Look at the list of words below. Fill in each line with the letter of the word that correctly completes each statement.

a. adrenal glands   c. hypothalamus
b. pituitary gland   d. noninsulin-dependent diabetes

1. The _____ in the brain controls hormone production.

2. The _____ is located below the hypothalamus.

3. The _____ are located on the kidneys.

4. People who do not have enough insulin receptors have _____.

LESSON 22: Reproductive System

GOAL: To learn about the anatomy of the male and female reproductive systems, the development of sperm and eggs, and fertilization

WORDS TO KNOW

amniotic sac

blastocyst

blastoderm

chorion

corpus luteum

ectoderm

ejaculation

endoderm

endometrium

estrogen

fallopian tube

follicle

follicle stimulating hormone (FSH)

gastrulation

inhibin

luteinizing hormone (LH)

menstrual cycle

mesoderm

oogenesis

oogonia

ovaries

oviduct

ovulation

penis

placenta

primary oocytes

progesterone

prolactin

prostate gland

relaxin

scrotum

secondary sexual characteristics

semen

seminal vesicles

Sertoli cells

spermatids

spermatocytes

spermatogenesis   *(continued)*

spermatozoa	uterus
testes	vagina
testosterone	vas deferens
trimesters	

Reproductive System

For a brief time, you were a single cell. This cell formed when a male gamete (sperm) fused with a female gamete (egg). The sperm and egg are haploid cells. They contain only a single copy of each chromosome. The product of the fusion, called the zygote, contains chromosomes from both parents.

In this lesson, you will learn about the physiological processes by which the egg and sperm fuse together. You will learn about the anatomy of the male and female reproductive systems. You will study the formation of the sperm and eggs, and the complex set of hormones that control this process.

Male Reproductive System

The production of the haploid sperm, known as **spermatogenesis,** takes place in a pair of structures called **testes.** The testes hang outside the body in a sac called the **scrotum.** The testes hang outside the body because the developing sperm cannot survive the warm temperatures inside the body. If the testes become too cold, the scrotum contracts and brings the testes closer to the body. If the testes become too warm, the scrotum relaxes.

The testes are filled with long coiled tubes in which spermatogenesis takes place. A structure in each testis (singular of *testes*) stores the sperm. Cells surrounding the seminiferous tubules produce the male sex hormone, **testosterone.**

Spermatogenesis begins at puberty and is under strict hormonal control. The hypothalamus oversees it all. In males, the hypothalamus triggers the pituitary gland to release two hormones—**follicle stimulating hormone (FSH)** and **luteinizing hormone (LH).** Both hormones target the seminiferous tubules and trigger sperm production. Here is what happens.

Inside the seminiferous tubules are diploid cells called **spermatocytes.** Spermatocytes continually undergo mitosis. Remember that mitosis produces two identical diploid cells. One of the daughter cells from each mitotic division will then undergo meiosis. Remember that meiosis involves two divisions and results in four haploid cells. These cells are called **spermatids.** The other daughter cell continues to divide by mitosis.

The spermatids then transform themselves into cells called **spermatozoa,** or sperm. First, the cells lose most of their cytoplasm. Other cells called **Sertoli cells** provide the spermatozoa with nutrients and keep them alive. Then each spermatozoon grows a long protein tail called a flagellum. Each spermatozoon now consists of a head, where the nucleus and remaining organelles are located, and a long tail that propels it forward. At the tip of the head is an enzyme-laced cap called the acrosome. These enzymes will enable the sperm to penetrate the female egg. Once the spermatozoon has completed its development, it moves to the epididymis. Once enough sperm are produced, the seminiferous tubules secrete a hormone called **inhibin.** This hormone travels back to the pituitary gland and stops it from producing more FSH. As a result, sperm production slows down.

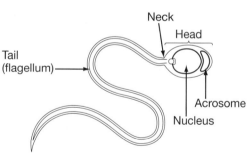

A Human Sperm Cell

In the meantime, LH triggers the tissue cells in the testes to produce testosterone. Testosterone is responsible for what are called male **secondary sexual characteristics.** These traits, which hit at full force during adolescence, include the growth of pubic hair and facial hair, the deepening of the voice, the further development of bones and muscles, and the enlargement of the penis and testes. The skin also begins to produce more oils, which often results in pimples. The hypothalamus monitors the amount of testosterone in the blood and adjusts the level accordingly.

Testosterone is also active in the male embryo. It is responsible for the basic development of the male reproductive system.

The process by which sperm is ejected is called **ejaculation.** During ejaculation, the sperm leave the epididymis and enter a pair of long tubes called the **vas deferens.** Smooth muscles surrounding the vas deferens push the sperm through. The two sperm-conducting tubes leave the scrotum, enter the body cavity, and merge just below the bladder. Finally, the vas deferens joins with the urethra. The urethra is the tube leading from the bladder to the outside of the body.

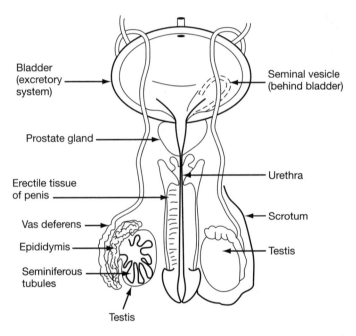

Male Reproductive System

Meanwhile, a pair of glands called the **seminal vesicles** and a larger gland called the **prostate gland** produce fluids that mix with the sperm. These fluids, called **semen,** provide the sperm with sugars and fatty acids—substances that fuel the sperm's long journey to the egg. The semen also neutralizes the acids that the sperm will encounter when they leave the penis and enter the female vagina.

The urethra then enters the penis. The **penis** is composed of three spongy regions of tissue. The end of the penis is filled with sensory nerves. When these nerves are stimulated, blood rushes into the spongy tissue, and the penis becomes erect. During ejaculation, smooth muscles around the seminal vesicles and prostate gland and skeletal muscles at the base of the penis contract. This propels the sperm out the tip of the penis. Each ejaculation releases between 300 million and 500 million sperm cells.

IN REAL LIFE

While Latrell was showering, he detected a small lump in one of his testes. He went to a doctor, who quickly determined that the lump was a tumor. Testicular cancer is the most common form of cancer in men between the ages of 15 and 35. Fortunately, Latrell had examined his testes regularly and caught the tumor early. Therefore, the chances that he would recover were excellent. If testicular cancer is not detected early, the cancer cells can spread to other parts of the body. If that happens, the chance of survival is poor.

■ PRACTICE 61: Male Reproductive System

Decide if each statement that follows is true (**T**) or false (**F**). Write the correct letter on each line.

_____ **1.** The hormones LH and FSH are produced in the adrenal gland.

_____ **2.** Spermatozoa are responsible for secondary sexual characteristics in males.

_____ **3.** The pituitary gland conducts sperm from the testes to the urethra.

_____ **4.** The glands that produce semen are the seminal vesicles and the prostate gland.

Female Reproductive System

The female reproductive system must do more than develop eggs. It must also carry and nourish the developing fetus for nine months before giving birth. Even after the child is born, the mother continues to nourish it. A complex interaction of hormones controls all phases of female reproduction.

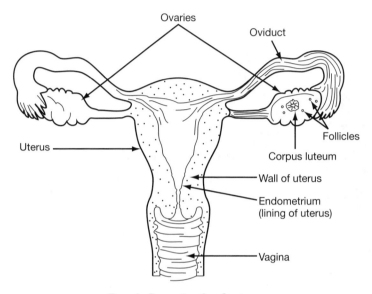

Female Reproductive System

Oogenesis

Eggs are produced in a pair of oval structures called the **ovaries.** The process is called **oogenesis.** Unlike males, who continuously manufacture millions of new sperm throughout their adult lives, females are born with all the gametes they are going to produce. Diploid cells called **oogonia** actually begin the process of meiosis in the developing fetus. Meiosis, however, stops after prophase I. These diploid cells, called **primary oocytes,** remain in this phase for years.

Starting at puberty, one primary oocyte at a time resumes meiosis and matures into an egg. This egg leaves the ovary. It then enters a tube called the **oviduct** or **fallopian tube.** The oviducts are not directly connected to the ovaries, so the eggs must cross a gap. Cilia lining the inside of the oviduct sweep the egg in, and with the help of muscle contractions, push the egg through the tube toward the uterus. The **uterus** is a hollow, pear-shaped structure. If the egg becomes fertilized, it will attach itself to the wall of the uterus and begin to develop into an embryo.

Journey of the Sperm

Fertilization takes place while the egg is still inside the oviduct. That means that the sperm have a long, perilous journey ahead of them. Of the approximately 400 million sperm that enter a woman, only about 100 reach the egg. The sperm are released into a muscular tube about 8 centimeters long called the **vagina,** or birth canal. The sperm must swim through mucus lining the vagina and up into the uterus. Muscle contractions in the vagina help the sperm along. The mucus in the vagina is acidic—a condition that wards off pathogens. Many sperm succumb to this acidic environment. The sperm must then cross the uterus and enter the correct oviduct. (Remember, there are two). Of the few sperm that reach the egg, only one can fuse with the egg.

Hormonal Control and the Menstrual Cycle

Just as hormones trigger sexual development and spermatogenesis in males, hormones control sexual development and the maturation of eggs in females. Once again, the hypothalamus controls the release of hormones. As with males, the hypothalamus stimulates the pituitary gland to produce luteinizing hormone (LH) and follicle stimulating hormone (FSH). LH stimulates the ovaries to produce a hormone called **estrogen.** During puberty, estrogen triggers the development of female secondary sexual characteristics. These include the development of breasts and nipples, the widening of the hips, and the growth of pubic hair.

Estrogen and a second hormone called **progesterone** also control a complex four-week cycle called the **menstrual cycle.** During the menstrual cycle, one of the primary oocytes matures into an egg and is released into the oviduct. This process is called **ovulation.** At the same time, the uterus develops a thick, blood-rich lining called the **endometrium.** The endometrium provides a fertilized egg with enough nutrients to begin developing. Here are the steps of the menstrual cycle in more detail.

1. The menstrual cycle begins when an unfertilized egg arrives in the uterus. The endometrium that has been building up in the uterus is no longer needed. Therefore, it breaks down and is shed through the vagina. This phase, called menstruation, lasts an average of three to five days.

2. While menstruation is occurring, the pituitary gland begins to release LH and FSH. The target is a structure in the ovary called the **follicle.** The ovaries contain many follicles, each of which houses a single primary oocyte. For reasons that are not understood, the hormones from the pituitary gland only act on one follicle at a time.

3. FSH causes the follicle to start growing and the primary oocyte to resume meiosis. Only one of the four daughter cells becomes an egg. The other three are not completely developed and form polar bonds. These will disintegrate. At the same time, LH induces the follicle to produce estrogen. The estrogen stimulates the development of a new endometrium in the uterus.

4. By about day 14, the follicle and egg have fully matured. The pituitary releases an extra-large dose of LH. This triggers the egg to burst from the follicle and enter the oviduct. Once the mature egg is gone, a new structure called the **corpus luteum**

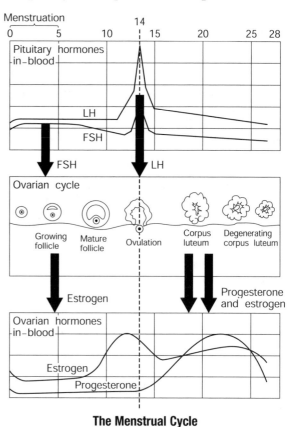

The Menstrual Cycle

develops inside the now collapsed follicle. This structure begins to produce estrogen and progesterone.

5. The progesterone serves two purposes. First, it contributes to the development of the endometrium. Second, it prevents other follicles and the primary oocytes inside from maturing.

6. Unless a sperm cell fertilizes the egg within a couple of days after it is released, the egg will die. High levels of estrogen and progesterone in the blood trigger the hypothalamus to shut off the production of LH and FSH. Without these two hormones, the corpus luteum disintegrates and stops producing progesterone and estrogen. As the level of these two hormones falls, the endometrium begins to break down. By day 28, progesterone levels are low, the endometrium is shed during menstruation, and a new follicle can begin to mature.

Pregnancy

If the egg is fertilized by a sperm, it will begin dividing even as it completes its journey to the uterus. When it reaches the uterus six days after fertilization, the embryo is a hollow ball of cells called a **blastocyst**. The blastocyst implants itself in the endometrium. Hormones that the embryo produces maintain the corpus luteum so that it can continue producing estrogen and progesterone. These hormones maintain the endometrium and prevent other eggs from becoming fertilized.

Inside the hollow blastocyst, there is a disk-shaped mass of cells called the **blastoderm.** Only the blastoderm will develop into the new baby. One of the most significant events in the development of the embryo is a process called **gastrulation.** About two weeks after fertilization, the cells in the blastoderm begin to differentiate. Then something amazing happens. A groove forms in the top of the disk. Cells on the outside then migrate through the groove to the inside of the disk and form a middle layer. (If anything goes wrong during this migration, the embryo will be unable to develop.) The result of this migration is three layers of cells—the ectoderm

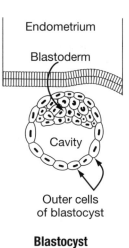

Endometrium

Blastoderm

Cavity

Outer cells of blastocyst

Blastocyst

(outer), mesoderm (middle), and endoderm (inner). Eventually, the **ectoderm** will develop into the skin and nervous systems. The **mesoderm** will develop into the skeletal, muscular, and circulatory systems. The **endoderm** will develop into the digestive and respiratory systems.

The other cells of the blastocyst form a series of structures that protect and nourish the embryo. One of these structures, called the amnion, develops into a fluid-filled sac called the **amniotic sac.** This sac cushions and supports the embryo. Another structure, called the **chorion,** combines with the endometrium to form an organ called the **placenta.** Nutrients and oxygen diffuse from the mother's blood into the placenta and travel to the

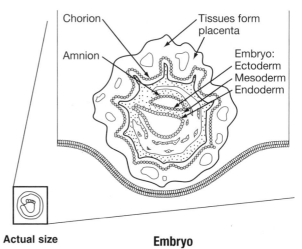

embryo through the umbilical cord. Wastes that the embryo produces diffuse back into the mother's blood and get processed by the mother's kidneys. The mother's blood and the embryo's blood never mix, and the placenta screens out many harmful substances. Viruses (such as the AIDS virus) and toxic substances (such as alcohol) can still get through, however.

Pregnancy lasts about nine months. It is traditionally divided into three three-month periods called **trimesters.** During the first trimester, the embryo develops from a ball of cells to something that actually looks like a human. From this point on, the developing human is called a fetus.

The major organs take shape during the first trimester. The central nervous system begins to appear shortly after gastrulation. At week 4, the heart and circulatory system become visible, and the heart starts pumping blood. By weeks 5 and 6, the arms and legs have formed. The digestive and respiratory systems have started to take shape. At week 8, the fetus is less than 3 centimeters long and weighs about 28 grams. The reproductive system has developed to the point where it is possible to determine if the fetus is male or female. By week 12, the regions of the brain have become distinct.

During the second and third trimesters, the fetus grows rapidly and the organs become functional. At week 16, the mother may feel the fetus kicking. At the third trimester (week 24), the lungs have developed to the point where the baby has a slight chance of surviving on its own if it were born prematurely, although it would require intensive hospital care.

At the end of nine months, the baby typically weighs between seven and ten pounds. When the baby is ready to be born, progesterone levels drop, and the pituitary secretes a hormone called oxytocin, which causes the muscles in the uterus to contract. Another hormone called **relaxin** loosens joints in the mother's pelvis so that the baby can pass out of the birth canal. The contractions become more frequent and push the baby down the birth canal, usually head first. Finally, a series of powerful contractions pushes the baby out into the world. The placenta, also called afterbirth, quickly follows.

After the baby is born, a pituitary hormone called **prolactin** triggers the mammary glands in the mother's breasts to produce milk. The milk provides the baby with nutrients. It also contains antibodies that help the baby fight off diseases.

■ PRACTICE 62: Female Reproductive System

Decide if each statement that follows is true (**T**) or false (**F**). Write the correct letter on each line.

_____ **1.** Oogenesis begins in the fetus, but stops at prophase I.

_____ **2.** The release of eggs into the oviduct is called menstruation.

_____ **3.** The hormone that triggers female secondary sexual characteristics is called estrogen.

_____ **4.** The nutritive tissue lining the uterus is called the endometrium.

_____ **5.** The hormone relaxin causes the uterus to contract.

UNIT 5 REVIEW

Circle the letter of the correct answer to each of the following questions.

1. In which part of your digestive tract does digestion occur without the aid of enzymes?
    a. mouth
    b. stomach
    c. small intestine
    d. large intestine

2. What is the role of the lymphatic system?
    a. It monitors and controls your heart rate.
    b. It monitors and controls your blood pressure.
    c. It provides your heart with oxygen.
    d. It drains excess fluids from around your cells.

3. Which of the following structures DOES NOT contain significant amounts of the protein collagen?
    a. dermis
    b. hair
    c. compact bone
    d. skeletal muscles

4. Most skeletal muscles come in antagonistic pairs. What does that mean?
    a. One muscle contains actin. The other contains myosin.
    b. One muscle pulls the bone in one direction. The other muscle pulls the bone in the opposite direction.
    c. One muscle is attached to a "base" bone. The other muscle is attached to a bone being pulled.
    d. One muscle is voluntary. The other muscle is involuntary.

5. What is the function of calcium in skeletal muscles?
    a. It prevents the myosin head from binding with actin.
    b. It enables the myosin head to attach to actin.
    c. It provides energy for muscle relaxation.
    d. It triggers the myosin head to push the actin.

6. What is the location of the sensory structures that translate things you see into nerve impulses?
   a. on the retina
   b. on the cornea
   c. in the cochlea
   d. in the olfactory bulb

7. The adrenal medulla produces the hormones epinephrine and norepinephrine. What is the main effect of these hormones?
   a. They cause bones to release calcium.
   b. They cause cells to take up glucose.
   c. They redirect blood to the skeletal muscles.
   d. They force the kidneys to retain salts.

Decide if each statement that follows is true (**T**) or false (**F**). Write the correct letter on each line.

_____ 8. In males, secondary sexual characteristics include the deepening of the voice, the growth of pubic and facial hair, and the development of bones and muscles.

_____ 9. Dropping levels of the hormone progesterone initiate childbirth.

_____ 10. The fetus obtains nutrients that are diffused from the mother's blood into the placenta.

UNIT 5 APPLICATION ACTIVITY 1
Iron It Out

The list of ingredients on the side of your cereal box contains important information about nutrients your body needs. Some nutrients that are added to cereals make a mixture, and these nutrients can be separated easily. One such nutrient is iron. In this activity, you will separate iron from a breakfast cereal.

Measure $1\frac{1}{2}$ cups of a breakfast cereal that contains 100 percent of the recommended daily requirement of iron. Place the cereal in a sealable plastic bag. Press the air out of the bag, and seal it. Crush the cereal into a fine powder, and pour it into a plastic container (such as a 2-pound margarine tub). Add enough water to completely cover the cereal. Using a bar magnet, stir the cereal-and-water mixture for approximately 10 minutes. Remove the magnet from the mixture, and allow the water to drain off from the magnet. Use a piece of tissue paper to brush off particles that are attached to the bar magnet onto a sheet of white paper. Observe the particles with a magnifying glass.

1. How do the particles appear?

_____

_____

2. How do you know the cereal is a mixture?

_____

_____

3. Why is iron an important nutrient?

_____

_____

_____

_____

_____

UNIT 5 APPLICATION ACTIVITY 2
Take a Breather

In this activity, you will see if your lungs work harder when you exercise.

1. Work with a partner. Pour 5 ml of limewater (which can be purchased from a biological supply company) into a test tube. Place a

straw in the test tube. Have your partner time you and count the breaths that you take as you gently exhale through the straw into the limewater. Inhale through your nose. DO NOT INHALE THROUGH THE STRAW. Continue inhaling through your nose and exhaling through your mouth until the limewater turns cloudy (which indicates carbon dioxide is present). Record the amount of time and number of breaths it took for the limewater to turn cloudy.

2. Use a clean test tube, limewater, and straw. Now run in place for two minutes. Right after you stop running, breathe through the straw into the limewater again. Have your partner time you and count the breaths that you take until the limewater turns cloudy. Again, record your data in the chart.

Caution: If you have asthma or any other respiratory illness, skip step 2 of this activity.

	You		Your Partner	
	Time	Number of Breaths	Time	Number of Breaths
At Rest				
After Exercise				

Reverse roles with your partner. Repeat steps 1 and 2.

1. Under what conditions does limewater turn cloudy faster?

_____

_____

2. What evidence do you have that illustrates that the lungs work harder while you are exercising?

_____

_____

3. What is the relationship between the amount of carbon dioxide in your breath before and after exercise?

_____

_____

4. Suppose you are planning to run in a race that takes place in an altitude that is much higher than you are used to. What effect will this have on your breathing? (_Hint_: Oxygen levels are lower at high altitudes.)

_____

_____

_____

_____

UNIT 5 APPLICATION ACTIVITY 3
Lip Saver

Do you often have dry, chapped lips? You can do something to help prevent your lips from drying out.

Cut two 4-cm-by-7-cm strips of white tissue paper. Apply petroleum jelly to the middle of one strip, rubbing it in gently with your finger. Leave a margin of 1 cm on each side of the tissue. Tape the tissue to a sheet of white paper towel. Tape the other strip of tissue paper next to the strip with petroleum jelly. This will be your control strip. Write _petroleum_ and _control_ under the appropriate pieces of tissue. Tape the paper towel to a piece of cardboard just a bit larger than the paper towel.

Place several drops of food coloring in a small cup of water. Put one or two drops of colored water in the middle of each tissue paper strip, and place the entire

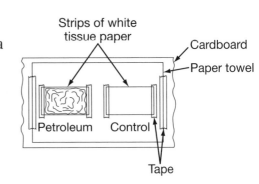

Strips of white tissue paper

Cardboard

Paper towel

Petroleum   Control

Tape

setup in a safe place for a day. After one day, remove the tissue strips and examine the paper towel.

1. What do you observe?

_____

_____

2. What effect did petroleum jelly have?

_____

_____

3. Why did you need a control?

_____

_____

4. How does this experiment apply to your own lips?

_____

_____

UNIT 5 APPLICATION ACTIVITY 4
Tensed Up

Muscles tense up, or contract, and then relax for every move you make. Most of the time you do not notice this muscle activity. You can make these movements visible with this activity.

Work with a partner. Have your partner hold a Popsicle stick out in front of him or her parallel to the top of a table or level desk. The person's arm and/or hand should not touch the table. Place a

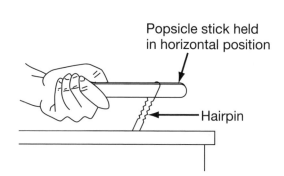

Popsicle stick held in horizontal position

Hairpin

hairpin over the Popsicle stick. Have your partner raise the stick just high enough from the table for the "legs" of the hairpin to touch the table and the "head" of the hairpin to rest on the edge of the Popsicle stick.

Have your partner hold the Popsicle stick as steady as possible for 20 seconds. Observe the hairpin. Repeat this last step for 20 seconds, but this time have your partner tighten his or her grip on the stick. Observe what happens. Repeat the entire exercise, switching places with your partner.

1. What happened to the hairpin for the first 20 seconds?

   _____

2. Why does this happen?

   _____

3. What happened to the hairpin when the Popsicle stick was held tighter for 20 seconds?

   _____

   _____

UNIT 5 APPLICATION ACTIVITY 5
Interactive Hormones

Using the words listed below, create a chart that shows how the endocrine glands, target organs, cells, and hormones interact. You may need to consult another source to find the information necessary to complete this activity.

hypothalamus	alsosterone	FSH
releasing hormones	kidneys	thyroid
inhibiting hormones	ACTH	mammary glands
pituitary	prolactin	androgens
TSH	body cells	LH
GH	hydrocortisone	adrenals
gonads	liver	thyroxin

1. Using a black pencil, draw a box around each endocrine gland. Then draw a triangle around each target that is not an endocrine gland and a circle around each hormone.

2. Using a red pencil, draw an arrow from each endocrine gland to the hormone or hormones it produces.

3. Using a green pencil, draw an arrow from each hormone to its target.

4. Some hormones stimulate their target glands to produce hormones, which the hypothalamus then detects. Using a blue pencil, draw an arrow from each of these target glands to the hypothalamus.

5. Two pituitary hormones secrete substances regulated by inhibiting as well as releasing hormones. Using a purple pencil, draw an arrow from these hormones to the hypothalamus.

1. What does your chart show about interactions of the endocrine system?

   _____

   _____

   _____

   _____

   _____

2. If a person has a low level of hydrocortisone, which glands might not be functioning properly?

   _____

   _____

   _____

UNIT 6

Ecology

LESSON 23: Ecosystems

GOAL: To learn about the field of ecology; to understand the processes that go on inside ecosystems

WORDS TO KNOW

carbon dioxide	extinct	precipitation
carnivore	food chain	primary consumers
community	food pyramid	producers
decomposers	food web	secondary consumers
ecologist	greenhouse effect	succession
ecology	habitat	tertiary consumers
ecosystem	herbivore	
evaporation	omnivore	

The Science of Ecology

Every animal and plant on Earth must interact with the climate, the soil, and other animals and plants to survive. The study of these interactions is called **ecology**. **Ecologists** look at how an organism adapts to its environment and to other organisms around it. The black cherry tree, for example, participates in a complex network of relationships that are invisible to most people.

Black cherry trees (*Prunus serotina*) grow in temperate climates where the summers are warm and wet. They prefer soils that are moist, but not too wet. They grow best in full sunlight, so they are usually found in forest openings, fields, and at the edges of woodlots.

Black cherries affect many organisms around them. Every spring, black cherries produce beautiful flowers that attract pollinators such as bees. In August, the trees produce delicious fruit. Birds and other animals rely upon this fruit as food. They eat the fruit and disperse the seeds. Birds and insects also make their homes in the trees.

Black cherries are also affected *by* other organisms. Mosses and lichens can grow on older trees. Some animals, such as deer, like to browse on the trees' leaves and twigs. To protect themselves, the twigs of black cherries are naturally laced with cyanide, a poison. But black cherries cannot protect themselves from another animal—tent caterpillars. During years when tent caterpillars are especially abundant, they can strip a black cherry tree of its leaves. Fortunately, wasps and birds—such as the black-billed cuckoo—eat tent caterpillars and keep the population in check.

Look at all of these interactions! A cherry tree interacts with the climate, the soil, animals, and other trees. An ecologist might study these interactions. For example, why do black cherry trees grow best in fields? Why do the trees not grow well on mountaintops? What makes certain black cherry trees produce more cherries than others? What would happen to a forest if all the black cherry trees suddenly disappeared? As you will see, questions like these are not always easy to answer.

Ecologists study these interactions at many levels.

Individual

An ecologist may look at individual cherry trees and how each has adapted to its environment. For example, an ecologist might look at how cherry trees disperse their seeds, why they grow best in certain soils, or how they discourage deer from eating their twigs.

Population

A population is a group of organisms of the same species living in one area. For example, a forest may contain a population of cherry trees. A population ecologist may be interested in whether the number of cherry trees is increasing or decreasing, and why.

Community

A **community** is made up of all the organisms that live in one area. A cherry tree is one element in a community. A forest community includes all the trees, herbs, insects, birds, mammals, fungi, and bacteria that live in the forest. A community ecologist studies how all the organisms within the community interact. He or she also may look at how the composition of a community changes over time.

Ecosystem

An **ecosystem** is defined both by the community of organisms present and by the physical environment. Physical factors include the amount of sunlight, water, and nutrients available. An ecosystem can be any size. It can be as big as a giant forest or as small as a mud puddle. In the rest of this lesson, you will study the processes that take place within ecosystems.

■ PRACTICE 63: The Science of Ecology

Circle the letter of the answer that correctly completes each of the following statements.

1. An ecosystem is _____.
   a. all the organisms that live in an area
   b. the fruit-bearing trees and the animals that eat the fruit
   c. the study of all animals, including birds and insects
   d. all the organisms in an area and their physical environment

2. The number of tent caterpillars in a forest at one time varies. Most years, there are very few. Every few years, there is a huge outbreak. These variations might be studied by _____.
   a. an ecologist who studies individual organisms
   b. a population ecologist
   c. a community ecologist
   d. an ecosystem ecologist

3. A forest community refers to _____.
   a. just a single species in the forest
   b. just plants in the forest
   c. all living organisms in the forest
   d. the physical environment of the forest

The Energy Cycle

Food Chain

Most organisms interact because they need to get energy. The sun is the source of all this energy. Once energy enters the ecosystem, it passes from organism to organism. This is known as the **food chain.** Here are the links of the food chain.

Producers

Producers are organisms that use the sun's energy to convert carbon dioxide into a simple sugar called glucose. In effect, producers store the sun's energy in the glucose. Producers include plants, algae, and simple-celled organisms called cyanobacteria.

Primary Consumers

Primary consumers get their energy by eating producers. Primary consumers include grazing animals such as cows and deer, insects that eat leaves, birds and mice that eat seeds or fruit, and fish that eat plankton. An animal that only eats plants is called a **herbivore,** or plant-eater.

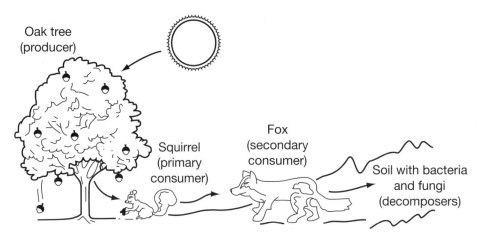

The Food Chain

Secondary Consumers

Secondary consumers get their energy by eating primary consumers. Animals that eat secondary consumers are **tertiary** (the third one in line) **consumers,** and so on. An animal that only eats other animals is called a **carnivore,** or meat-eater. An animal that eats both plants and other animals is called an **omnivore.**

Decomposers

The flow of energy does not stop with the top consumer. Once an organism dies, it is consumed by a host of organisms, including bacteria and fungi. These **decomposers** break down the dead organism and release nutrients into the soil.

Food Web

Ecosystems contain many food chains that can overlap in complex ways. The many pathways that energy takes through an ecosystem is called the **food web.**

Now look at an example. Grizzly bears are one of Alaska's most famous residents. The bears that live on the coast are the largest animals in the world that eat meat. Bears eat young moose and ground squirrels, both primary consumers. That would make the bears secondary consumers. Grizzlies also eat fish, especially salmon. Fish that eat insects and other fish are secondary consumers. That would make fish-eating grizzlies tertiary consumers. Grizzlies are also primary consumers, because they eat berries. So three different food chains end with the grizzly.

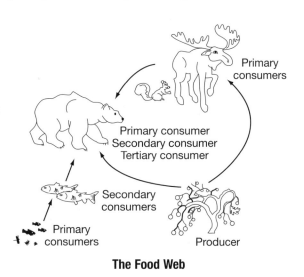

The Food Web

Many other plants and animals are involved in this food web. Birds eat plants, insects, and fish. Foxes eat fish, birds, ground squirrels, and even grizzly bears, if they stumble across a dead one. When you combine all these pathways that energy takes through an ecosystem, you have a web.

Food Pyramid

Now take a look at an 8-square-kilometer section of the African Serengeti, a huge grassland famous for its wildlife. If you took all the plants and put them on a scale, they would weigh 7500 tons. Lots of animals, including zebras, wildebeest, and gazelles, eat the plants. If you put all these primary consumers on a scale, they would weigh considerably less than the plants—only 61 tons. Lions eat these animals. However, this 8-square-kilometer area only supports a single lion. The lion weighs 450 pounds.

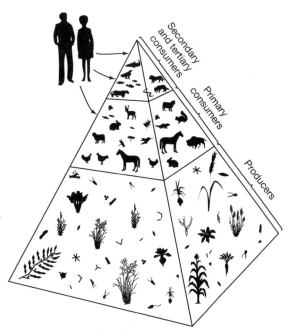

The Food Pyramid

This pattern is true everywhere you go. Producers greatly outnumber consumers. Primary consumers greatly outnumber secondary and tertiary consumers. This pattern is called the **food pyramid.**

To understand why this pattern exists, follow a unit of energy as it travels from the sun and works its way up through the food chain.

A lot can happen to energy when it reaches Earth. Some is absorbed by the air and by the ground. Some bounces back into space. A small part of it is absorbed by plants and is used to produce sugars. The plant only stores a small amount of the energy it takes in. Most of the energy goes toward growth, maintenance, and reproduction of the plant. So a zebra that eats the plant only takes in a fraction of the energy that the plant first absorbed. The zebra must eat a lot of plants to get enough energy. The zebra then uses most of the energy it takes in to move around, maintain its body temperature, and reproduce. Note how the original unit of energy keeps shrinking as it moves up through the food chain. A lion must eat many zebras to get enough energy. There are only enough zebras to support a small number of lions.

■ THINK ABOUT IT

Take your own inventory of producers and consumers in your area. Does the pattern hold true? Write your answer on a separate sheet of paper.

■ PRACTICE 64: The Energy Cycle

Circle the letter of the answer that correctly completes each of the following statements.

1. A bee that feeds on nectar from a flower is a _____.
    a. producer
    b. primary consumer
    c. secondary consumer
    d. tertiary consumer

2. It is probably NOT true that _____.
    a. lions outnumber zebras in Africa
    b. insects outnumber birds in Florida
    c. plants outnumber elk in Yellowstone National Park
    d. squirrels outnumber bears in the Northwest

3. Fungi and bacteria that break down the carcass of a dead bear are _____.
    a. decomposers
    b. producers
    c. tertiary consumers
    d. either a secondary or a tertiary consumer, depending on whether the bear was a primary or a secondary consumer

Nutrient Cycles

Organisms need more than energy to survive. They also need water, carbon, oxygen, and nutrients. Now examine how some of these substances cycle through an ecosystem.

The Water Cycle

All organisms need water. Fortunately, there is a lot of water on Earth. Oceans, lakes, rivers, and ponds cover three fourths of the planet. Water enters an ecosystem in the form of rain, snow, and other **precipitation.** Some of the precipitation soaks into the ground. Some runs off into oceans, lakes, and streams.

The sun's energy causes water to change from a liquid to a gas. This is called **evaporation.** Water evaporates from oceans, lakes, streams, moist soil, and the leaves of plants. The evaporated water eventually forms clouds. The clouds eventually cause precipitation to fall back to Earth.

You have learned how plants take up water from the ground. The water travels through the xylem from the roots to the leaves. It then evaporates from the leaves. Animals get their water directly from lakes and streams. Some get water from the plants and animals they eat.

Although there is a lot of water on Earth, it is not evenly distributed. Water that evaporates from one place may form rain in another part of the world. Many ecosystems have barely enough water to support the organisms that live there.

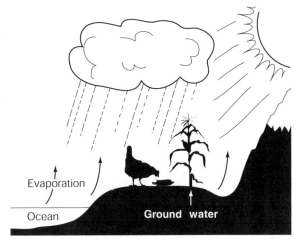

The Water Cycle

The Carbon Cycle

You have learned that carbon is one of the most important building blocks of life. Like water, carbon cycles between the air and the ground. In the air, carbon is in the form of a gas called **carbon dioxide.** Plants use the sun's energy to convert carbon dioxide into sugars. During this process, plants release oxygen into the air. Animals get their carbon by eating plants or other animals. Decomposers get their carbon by breaking down dead organisms.

All organisms, including plants, release carbon dioxide back into the atmosphere when they break down sugars for energy. This process is called respiration. Most organisms require oxygen to carry out the chemical reactions in respiration. Animals that live on land get their oxygen from the air.

Carbon dioxide also enters the atmosphere in ways other than respiration. Erupting volcanoes are a large source. The burning of forests and fossil fuels is another. Fossil fuels, which include coal, oil, and natural gas, are made of organisms that have been dead for many millions of years. Over the past 50 years, increased burning of fossil fuels has caused the amount of carbon dioxide in the air to increase. Most scientists worry that the buildup of carbon dioxide will cause Earth's climate to grow warmer. This process is known as the **greenhouse effect.** A warmer climate may melt enough of the ice caps around the North Pole and South Pole that the oceans may rise and flood coastal areas. A warmer climate may also drastically change weather patterns and increase the number of severe storms.

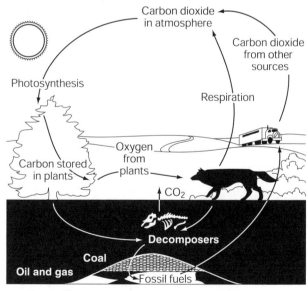

The Carbon Cycle

The Nitrogen Cycle

Organisms require many nutrients to carry out life processes. Nitrogen is one of the most important nutrients. It is used to build DNA and proteins.

Nitrogen is everywhere. About 80% of the atmosphere is made of nitrogen gas. Nitrogen is also in the soil. Plants take up nitrogen from the soil through their roots. However, the plants need help. They cannot use nitrogen from the air. Instead, the plants need bacteria in the soil to convert nitrogen from the air into a form that they can use. Legumes (such as beans, peas, clover, and alfalfa) have these bacteria growing on their roots.

Animals get their nitrogen by eating plants and other animals. When an organism dies, bacteria once again get to work. They convert the nitrogen in the dead organism into nitrogen gas or into the form that plants can take up.

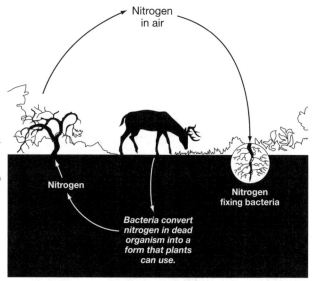

The Nitrogen Cycle

■ PRACTICE 65: Nutrient Cycles

Decide if each phrase below describes a water cycle (**W**), a carbon cycle (**C**), or a nitrogen cycle (**N**). Write the correct letter on each line. (*Hint*: There may be more than one correct answer for each phrase.)

_____ **1.** This substance cycles through the ground and the atmosphere.

_____ **2.** This substance must be altered by bacteria before it can be taken up by plants.

_____ **3.** This substance is increasing in the atmosphere due to the burning of fossil fuels.

_____ **4.** Energy from the sun is involved in this cycle.

_____ **5.** This is the only substance that is NOT absorbed through a plant's roots.

Changes in Ecosystems

Perhaps you have a favorite walk through the woods or in a park. If you have taken the walk often enough, you may know all the trees, or all the wet areas, or all the areas where birds are mostly likely to gather. It may seem as if nothing ever changes.

Ecosystems, however, do change. Some of these changes are small. The wind blows a tree over, letting more light into a forest. This light gives plants a new opportunity to grow. Or, change can occur over a much wider area. A beaver can build a dam and flood an entire forest. A fire can burn down the forest. Some changes occur over such a long period of time that people hardly notice them.

Natural Variations

Populations within communities rarely stay constant. One year, a storm or a disease may cause a population to decrease. For example, a severe winter can reduce a deer population. The next year, good weather, a good food supply, and other random factors may cause a population to increase.

Often, variations in the numbers of one type of organism can affect many other organisms. Here is an example.

During some years, oak trees produce an especially large crop of acorns. Many animals, such as mice, squirrels, and deer, feed on these acorns. When the acorns increase, these animals increase because they have so much to eat. As a result, the secondary consumers that prey on the acorn-eating animals also increase. Two years later, the oak trees hardly produce any acorns. The animals that depend on the acorns decrease. So, too, do the secondary consumers. The cycle begins anew when the oak trees once again produce a huge crop of acorns.

At the start of this lesson, you learned how tent caterpillar populations increase dramatically during some years. What other organisms might be affected by these caterpillar population booms? Write your answer on a separate sheet of paper.

Succession

Have you ever watched an abandoned pasture or vacant lot? For the first couple of years, grasses will remain. Soon, however, fast-growing trees and shrubs start to take over. These plants require a lot of sunlight to grow, so the open area provides perfect conditions. Soon these plants create too much shade for the grasses to survive. But they create perfect conditions for other types of trees. These new trees do not need a lot of sunlight to grow. Eventually, these slow-growing, shade-tolerant trees crowd out the faster-growing trees. As the plants change, so do the animals that live among them.

This progression from grasses to fast-growing trees and shrubs that require a lot of sunlight, to slow-growing, shade-tolerant trees is called **succession.** Succession happens everywhere in the natural world. It happens in a forest every time a storm knocks over a stand of trees or when a fire burns through an area. Many plants and animals depend on "openings" or opportunities created by storms or fires.

Succession can also take other forms. A lake slowly fills with sediment. After a number of years, a floating mat of sphagnum moss covers the lake. The lake is now a bog. Eventually, a forest grows on top of the bog.

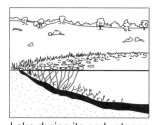
Lake during its early stages

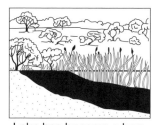
Lake has become a bog.

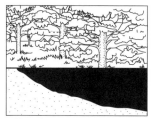
Bog becomes a forest.

Succession in Action

Long-Term Changes

Ecological conditions have changed many times during Earth's history. You can go back just 15,000 years. North America looked a lot different than it does today. An ice sheet over a kilometer thick covered the continent as far south as New York and Chicago. The forests were different. Trees found only in Canada today thrived in Georgia. The animals were also different. Woolly mammoths, lions bigger than those in Africa today, and saber-toothed tigers were common. Then the climate started to grow warmer. The huge ice sheets started to melt. Forests replaced the ice. In the south, warm-weather trees replaced the cold-weather trees. Large mammals such as the mammoths disappeared.

These changes happened over a long period of time. If you were alive 10,000 years ago, you would not be aware that these changes were happening. If you go forward in time, the climate will probably be different from that of today. Even a small rise in temperature can change weather patterns. Ecosystems are then forced to change, too.

Human-Caused Changes

Throughout human history, people have brought many changes to the environment. They have cleared forests; drained swamps; and plowed grasslands to create farms, build places to live, and gather resources such as wood and minerals. Many species have disappeared forever, or are **extinct.**

Loss of **habitat,** or living environment, is one cause of extinction. People have also hunted many animals to extinction. Many scientists think that the mammoths disappeared 11,000 years ago because of overhunting. Today, many large animals, including grizzly bears, tigers, rhinoceroses, elephants, and whales are at risk because of overhunting. Overfishing has reduced the number of fish such as cod and swordfish. Pollution has also had an effect. One pesticide, DDT, almost wiped out the bald eagles and peregrine falcons in the United States. DDT is now banned, and the number of eagles and falcons is increasing.

Even small changes in the environment may have unintended results.

Here are some examples.

- Actions that harm just one species of plant or animal may affect an entire ecosystem. For example, a species of predator (such as the wolf or the lion) helps keep the animals it eats under control. If this species of predator were to disappear (because of hunting or some other human behavior), the population of animals it eats would probably increase. These animals would then eat more plants and change the plant community.

THINK ABOUT IT

Go back to the example of the cherry tree at the beginning of the lesson. One of the animals mentioned is the black-billed cuckoo. The number of black-billed cuckoos is now declining, due to the loss of forests in Central America where the bird spends the winter. How might the disappearance of the black-billed cuckoo affect other plants and animals? Write your answer on a separate sheet of paper.

- Bringing a new plant or animal into an ecosystem can also be harmful. Often, these new species have no natural enemies, so they take over. The island of Guam in the South Pacific was once free of snakes. However, people accidentally brought snakes to the island. The snakes multiplied and ate most of the birds, including species of birds that live nowhere else. Many of these birds had fed on spiders, so as the number of birds decreased, the number of spiders increased.

There are many examples of new organisms changing ecosystems in the United States. Dutch elm disease and chestnut blight are caused by two species of fungi that were accidentally brought to this country. They have killed most of the elms and all of the chestnuts in the United States.

Angelina loved cats. She owned two cats that stayed outside most of the time. To her dismay, one of her cats came home with a bird it had killed. Soon, both cats started to bring home dead birds every day. (In fact, house cats kill millions of birds in the United States.) Angelina thought that in a while there would be no birds left. So she decided to keep her cats inside and spare the birds.

■ Adding nutrients such as nitrogen and phosphorus to lakes and rivers can change these ecosystems. These nutrients often come from fertilizers that people put on their fields or lawns. Rain washes the nutrients into the water. The addition of nitrogen and phosphorus to water may cause algae and bacteria to multiply. If these reach high enough numbers, they may use up the water's oxygen supply. Other organisms, such as fish, may suffocate as a result. These algae and bacteria may also be toxic to fish and to people.

Today, governments are trying to reverse some of the damage that people have done to the environment. They have created parks and reserves to protect ecosystems. They have banned the hunting of endangered animals and collecting of endangered plants. They have even tried to restore ecosystems that have been damaged. For example, some groups have reintroduced animals to habitats where they used to live. Scientists have also tried to get rid of plants and animals that are not supposed to be there.

These tasks, however, are not easy. To be successful, ecologists must understand the complex processes that occur within ecosystems. For example, they must understand the habitat requirements of the plants and animals they are trying to save. Are the requirements correct? Is there enough for the animals to eat? Is there enough space for them? How will they interact with other animals and plants? These types of questions pose the greatest challenge to ecologists today.

■ PRACTICE 66: Changes in Ecosystems

Circle the letter of the answer that correctly completes each of the following statements.

1. Succession may occur _____.
   a. before a forest fire
   b. before a storm knocks several trees down
   c. after a farmer abandons a field

2. Many companies that make laundry detergent have reduced the amount of phosphorus in their products. This is because _____.
   a. phosphorus that enters lakes and streams can cause harmful organisms to grow
   b. phosphorus is poisonous to most organisms
   c. phosphorus is a major cause of climate change

3. Mountain lions are now fairly common in some areas in the western part of the United States. Mountain lions mostly feed on elk. If hunters were to kill all the mountain lions, _____.
   a. the number of elk would likely increase
   b. the number of elk would likely decrease
   c. the number of elk would likely stay the same

4. In order to reverse some of the damage that people have done to the environment, governments have _____.
   a. added nitrogen to lakes and rivers
   b. created parks and reserves to protect ecosystems
   c. encouraged the hunting of endangered species

LESSON 24: Interactions

GOAL: To understand the ways in which organisms interact with one another; to understand how these interactions shape evolution

WORDS TO KNOW

camouflage	niche
commensalism	parasitism
competition	predation
herbivory	predator
interspecific competition	prey
intraspecific competition	specialize
mimicry	symbiosis
mutualism	

Types of Interaction

Now look once again at the many different types of interactions involving the cherry tree. It competes with plants for sunlight. Tent caterpillars eat the leaves. Black-billed cuckoos eat the tent caterpillars. Insects pollinate the flowers. Birds eat the cherries and distribute the seeds. In this lesson, you will examine these interactions more closely. You will see that how an organism handles these interactions can make the difference between life and death.

Competition

Before you go on, step out of the forest and into a chocolate shop. Every day at noon, a huge crowd of people rush in to buy truffles. Unfortunately, there are not enough truffles to go around, so customers are in **competition** for them. The fastest and strongest customers get most of the truffles and thrive. The others eventually die from a lack of chocolate.

Now consider an alternative. Instead of competing with one another for truffles, people decide to specialize. Some buy brownies. Others buy fudge. Others continue to buy truffles, but wait until 4 o'clock to come into the store. Now everybody is able to get all the chocolate they need.

Plants and animals do not compete for chocolate. They do, however, compete for energy, space, nutrients, and water. That is because ecosystems have a limited supply of these resources. Organisms that do not get enough of these resources do not survive and do not pass on their genes.

There are two types of competition.

Intraspecific Competition

Intraspecific competition refers to competition between individuals of the same species. Two cheetahs compete for gazelles. Two spruce trees compete for sunlight. The best competitor gets the most resources.

Interspecific Competition

Interspecific competition refers to competition between individuals of different species. For example, lions and cheetahs both hunt to survive. A species, however, can often avoid competing directly with another species. Like the chocolate shoppers, species specialize. They specialize in the type of environment they live in, the type of food they eat, even when and where they eat. For example, lions hunt larger animals such as zebras and wildebeest. Cheetahs hunt smaller animals such as gazelles. Lions mostly hunt at night. Cheetahs hunt mostly during the day.

This combination of specializations—what the species eats, where it lives, when it is active—is called a niche. Each species has its own unique niche.

Plant Competition

Plants must compete for space, water, and nutrients. They must even compete for the animals that pollinate their flowers. The most intense competition, however, is for light. Trees that grow taller and expose the most leaves to the sun usually "win."

Plants, however, are able to specialize and avoid competing with one another directly. In other words, plants occupy different niches. This gives them a better chance of survival.

To understand how plants specialize, take a walk through the woods. You will note that the forest contains many types of environments. Some areas are wetter than others. Some areas are warmer than others. The soils in one area may contain more nutrients than soils in another area.

You will also note different types of plants. Different species of plants specialize in different environments. Some plants grow best in swampy areas. Some grow best in dry, sandy soil. Some plants may even grow best on old, rotting logs. There are trees that need a great deal of sunlight and plenty of room for roots. Then there are smaller plants that are content to remain in the shadows.

Now look once again at succession. As you learned, some plants have adapted to take advantage of openings caused by storms or fires. For these plants, speed is of the essence. First, they must get their seeds into the openings quickly. Then they must grow quickly. If they are not fast, other plants will get there first and fill the openings.

These plants do not grow well in the shade of other trees. Many plants, however, specialize in areas in which there is little sunlight. These plants are in no hurry. Instead, they occupy the shade of other plants and wait for the plants above them to die or be knocked over. They will wait for many years if they have to do so. When the slightest opening occurs, these trees have a head start and can easily take over.

Animal Competition

Animals compete for food instead of sunlight. As you remember from the last lesson, the amount of energy available decreases as it moves up through the food chain.

Animals often have to fight one another for these resources. Fighting, however, uses a lot of energy. It can also be dangerous. Instead, animals assert their dominance in other ways. Many animals (such as lions, seals, and dragonflies) establish territories. The best territories contain plenty of food and shelter. Animals then defend these territories against intruders. Males with the best territory also may attract the most females.

Like plants, animals avoid direct competition with other species by specializing. They do so in two major ways.

- Different animals eat different foods. Some eat seeds. Some eat leaves. Some eat insects. Some eat small mammals. Some eat large mammals. Some kill their prey. Some eat animals that are already dead.

- Animals divide up territory. For example, look at birds. Different birds specialize in different habitats. Some live in fields. Others live in hardwood forests. Others live near the ocean. Even within forests, species divide up their territory. Some search for food on the ground. Some stay in shrubs. Some stay in the lower branches of trees, while others search for food at the tops of trees. Still others catch their food on the wing.

Effects of Competition

Now imagine a world in which resources are limitless. There would be far less variety. That is because plants and animals would no longer have to specialize in order to survive. The need to specialize is one of the driving forces of evolution.

Without limits, populations would grow indefinitely. Resources, however, are limited. Ecosystems can only support a certain number of organisms. If a population gets too large, it will run out of food and space.

People are some of the best competitors on Earth. People do not have to specialize, because they do not have to compete with other animals for food and space. As a result, their population has already reached 6 billion. By the year 2050, there may be as many as 9 billion people on Earth. How long can the population continue to increase before resources run out?

■ PRACTICE 67: Competition

Decide if each statement that follows is true (**T**) or false (**F**). Write the correct letter on each line.

_____ **1.** All organisms within an ecosystem occupy the same niche.

_____ **2.** Plants compete for nutrients and water only.

_____ **3.** Plants that specialize in growing in forest openings grow faster than plants that specialize in growing in the shade.

_____ **4.** Animals avoid competing with other species by eating different foods.

_____ **5.** Animals of the same species do not compete with one another.

Herbivory

You have learned how one type of interaction, specialization, drives evolution. Plants and animals must specialize in order to survive. Now turn to another important type of interaction—animals eating plants and animals eating other animals.

Herbivores are animals that eat plants. They do not kill the plants they eat, however. Instead, they may just eat a few of the leaves. The plants are able to regrow what the herbivores eat.

Herbivory (the act of eating a plant), however, can damage a plant. If a plant loses too many leaves, it cannot capture as much sunlight. Plants must use energy to recover. Therefore, they have to devote less energy to growing, producing flowers and seeds, and competing with other plants. As a result, they are less able to pass on their genes to the next generation. If enough herbivores attack the plant, it may die.

Plants have evolved ways to discourage herbivores. Some plants have mechanical protection. Cactuses, roses, and thistles have thorns that ward off herbivores. Some plants are covered with hairs that are hard for insects to penetrate.

Taro decided to take a shortcut through a field. He waded through some waist-high plants and suddenly felt a burning sensation on his legs. He scratched, but that made the burning much worse. It turned out he had brushed against nettles. The leaves of nettles are covered with hollow hairs. When Taro brushed the leaves, the hairs broke and squirted him with formic acid. Scratching just made the acid penetrate deeper into Taro's skin.

Another strategy is to make leaves less tempting to herbivores. Some plants have evolved tough leaves and stems that are hard to digest. These leaves or stems may contain a lot of cellulose, but few proteins and nutrients. Eating these tissues is a waste of time for herbivores, so they do not bother.

Plants also have chemical defenses. Remember how black cherry trees produce cyanide in their twigs to discourage deer? These chemicals can make a plant taste bad, can make it even more indigestible, or poison the herbivore. Many of the chemicals that plants produce may be familiar to you. They include nicotine, caffeine, and opium. Other chemicals that plants produce have medical uses.

With all of these impressive defenses, you may wonder how herbivores can survive by eating plants. The answer is that herbivores have evolved ways to get around these defenses. Now look at some examples.

- Many animals are able to strip away the inedible parts of the plant to get to the edible portions. Aphids, the scourge of many gardeners, actually poke their beaks through the cell walls and feed on sugars flowing through the phloem.

■ Most large herbivores, including cows, sheep, goats, deer, and antelopes, have a special type of digestive system that enables them to eat plants that are hard to digest. The grass that these animals eat first goes into a chamber called the rumen. The rumen is filled with bacteria that break down the indigestible material, such as cellulose. The animal then coughs up the food from the rumen and chews it again.

■ Many insects are not affected by the chemicals that plants produce. In fact, some insects are able to use the chemicals that plants produce to their advantage.

■ Plants that you eat have been bred to be less toxic, to taste better, and to be easier to digest. Unfortunately, these changes have made the plants easier for insects and other animals to eat as well.

Producing defenses against herbivores also has its costs. It takes energy to make chemicals and thorns. Plants that invest heavily in defending themselves have less energy to grow and produce seeds. But, as you will remember, herbivory can also be costly. Therefore, plants must strike a delicate balance between growing and defending themselves.

■ PRACTICE 68: Herbivory
Circle the letter of the answer that correctly completes each of the following statements.

1. Herbivores _____.
    a. eat plants and animals
    b. weaken the organisms they eat
    c. kill the organisms they eat
    d. do not harm the organisms they eat

2. Plants protect themselves from herbivores by _____.
   a. lowering the nutritional value of their leaves
   b. producing poisonous chemicals in their leaves
   c. growing thorns
   d. all of the above

3. Cows, sheep, and deer have a chamber called a rumen. It enables these herbivores to _____.
   a. detoxify chemicals
   b. get around structures such as thorns
   c. digest cellulose
   d. all of the above

Predation

Predation is the act of hunting or killing for food. A **predator** is an animal that kills other organisms for food. The food organism is called the **prey.** Most often people think of predators as animals that kill other animals. However, an animal that eats seeds is a predator, because a seed contains the beginnings of an entire plant.

Prey Adaptations

As you can imagine, it is important for animals to avoid being eaten. Unlike in herbivory, there are no second chances. Once an animal is eaten, it is dead. Therefore, animals have evolved many ways to baffle predators.

Size

Large animals are harder to kill than small animals. For example, elephants and grizzly bears do not have any natural predators. It also helps that elephants and grizzly bears are fierce.

Defenses

Animals have different ways of defending themselves. Crayfish and lobsters have large claws. Porcupines have quills covering their bodies. Clams and turtles retreat into shells. Many animals fight back with hooves, horns, antlers, and teeth.

Speed

Many animals use speed to escape predators. Deer and antelope can run very fast over short distances. Other animals use quickness to escape into trees or holes in the ground.

Camouflage

Not all animals can outrun a predator. Instead, they try to escape detection. One way is to use **camouflage** to blend into the background so that predators do not see them. For example, a light-colored moth might be the same color as the bark it lands on. The light-colored moths blend into the bark they are sitting on. Black moths, on the other hand, would be easily detected by a predator. A tree frog might be the same color as the leaves it hides in. Baby deer (fawns) are speckled so they blend into the light and shadows of the forest floor. Some insects even take on the shape of leaves or twigs. When they are sitting in a bush or a tree, these insects are hard to distinguish from the leaves around them.

Chemicals

Just as plants produce chemicals to protect themselves from herbivores, some animals produce chemicals to protect themselves against predators. Hornets, spiders, snakes, and jellyfish fight back with poison. Puffer fish and some tree frogs are poisonous to eat. Skunks spray a nasty liquid at attackers.

Some animals actually use poison from plants to ward off predators. The most famous example is the monarch butterfly. Monarch caterpillars are the only animals that eat milkweed—a plant that produces a powerful poison. The poison does not harm the caterpillar. Instead, it stays in the caterpillar's body, even after it turns into a butterfly. Animals that try to eat the butterfly get a nasty surprise. Usually they do not make the same mistake twice.

THINK ABOUT IT

Most poisonous animals are brightly colored. Why would this be to the animal's advantage? Write your answer on a separate sheet of paper.

Mimicry

Some animals fool predators through **mimicry,** or pretending to be something else. They pretend they are poisonous, when they are actually not. For example, there are flies that have black and yellow stripes just like bees. There are nonpoisonous snakes that have stripes like the poisonous coral snakes. There are butterflies that have the same colors and patterns as monarch butterflies. These animals all use forms of mimicry. Predators think they are poisonous, so they avoid them.

Behavior

Animals must constantly watch out for predators. Many animals look for food and water when predators are least likely to be around. Some species stay in large groups or herds. One advantage of being a member of a herd is that a predator would have a harder time sneaking up on any one animal. Another advantage has to do with odds. The more animals there are around you, the less chance there is that a predator will single you out.

Predator Adaptations

Just as herbivores have evolved ways to get around the defenses of plants, predators have evolved ways to get around the defenses of prey. Some predators can outrun their prey. Cheetahs are prime examples. Some predators, such as grizzly bears, use pure strength to overcome their prey. Wolves team up to bring down larger prey. Spiders and some snakes use poison.

Many predators use stealth to ambush or sneak up on their prey. Snakes must get very close to their prey before they strike. Leopards drop out of trees on top of their prey. These predators often need to be camouflaged to prevent prey from detecting them until it is too late.

Catching prey can be hard work. It is important that predators not use too much energy capturing prey. The more energy they use, the less benefit they get. Capturing prey is also dangerous. A well-aimed kick from an elk, for example, can injure an attacking wolf. If the injury is bad enough, the wolf might not be able to hunt again.

Predators, therefore, have to make good decisions. They need to choose carefully which prey to go after. Often, they will go after the weakest prey, which include the young and the sick, because they are the easiest to catch. Predators also must know when to give up if the chase is not going well.

Effects of Predation

One might think that predation would harm a population of animals. After all, predators kill other animals and reduce their numbers. In fact, predation can actually make a population healthier. To understand why, go back to what you learned about competition. Within ecosystems, there is a limited amount of food. If a population gets too big, food starts to run out. As a result, the animals in the population cannot get enough to eat and are much weaker. Weaker animals are more vulnerable to diseases. They are also less likely to survive a harsh winter. Predation prevents populations from getting too big. As a result, the animals that are not eaten are healthier.

■ PRACTICE 69: Predation

Circle the letter of the correct answer to each of the following questions.

1. Which of the following animals is NOT considered a predator?
   a. a goldfinch that eats seeds
   b. a snake that eats eggs
   c. a fish that eats plankton
   d. a mosquito that drinks blood

2. What is a mimic?
- **a.** a predator that uses poisons to kill its prey
- **b.** an animal that produces poisons to protect itself
- **c.** an animal that does not produce poisons, but looks like animals that do
- **d.** an animal whose colors help it blend into the background

3. Why is it important that a predator know when to give up when chasing prey?
- **a.** It should not waste energy.
- **b.** It should avoid risking injury.
- **c.** The prey may be poisonous.
- **d.** all of the above

Symbiosis

You have seen examples of close relationships between different species. Algae and fungi join together to form lichen. Parasites, such as tapeworms and flukes, live inside larger animals. Close relationships between two different species is called **symbiosis.** There are three types of symbiosis. They are based on how much each species benefits from the relationship.

Parasitism

Parasitism is a one-way relationship. The parasite benefits. The host suffers. Parasites rarely kill their hosts, but they do weaken them. An animal infested with parasites may have a harder time getting food. It may have a harder time competing with other animals. It also may be more susceptible to diseases and other stresses.

Commensalism

Commensalism is a relationship in which one species benefits while the second species is not affected at all. Perhaps you have seen pictures of birds perched on top of a rhinoceros. These birds eat the insects that land on the rhinoceros. Or perhaps you have seen pictures of small fish attached to sharks. These fish pick off scraps of food while the sharks are eating.

Mutualism

Mutualism is a relationship in which both species benefit. You have already seen many examples. Mycorrhizal fungi live on the roots of the trees. They get sugars from the roots. In exchange, they help the roots absorb nutrients. Birds that feed on fruit, such as cherries, help the tree by distributing the seeds.

In the tropics, there are trees called acacias that encourage ants to live on them. They do so by producing nectar to feed the ants. In return, the ants patrol the tree and drive off leaf-chewing insects. They also dispose of vines and other plants that grow on the tree.

In Africa, there is a bird called a honey guide that eats honey. However, it is unable to tear open beehives and get the honey. To solve this problem, the honey guide has formed a mutualistic relationship with a type of weasel called a honey badger. The honey guide finds a hive and leads the honey badger to it. The honey badger tears open the hive and eats its fill. After the honey badger eats its fill, the honey guide gets its turn.

■ PRACTICE 70: Symbiosis

Decide if each description below is an example of parasitism (**P**), commensalism (**C**), or mutualism (**M**). Write the correct letter on each line.

_____ **1.** A vine grows up a tree, puts a lot of stress on the branches, and blocks out the sun.

_____ **2.** A wasp lays its eggs inside the flower of a fig tree. The wasps that hatch carry pollen to other fig trees.

_____ **3.** Barnacles attach themselves to whales and filter food from the water. The whales do not seem to notice.

_____ **4.** A cowbird lays its eggs in the nest of another bird. The owner of the nest feeds the baby cowbirds. Meanwhile, its own chicks do not get enough food.

_____ **5.** A cleaner fish eats harmful parasites attached to larger fish.

LESSON 25: Biomes

GOAL: To understand the six major types of biomes in the world

WORDS TO KNOW

biome	epiphytes	taiga
deciduous forests	grassland	tropical rain forests
desert	permafrost	tundra

The Six Biomes

There are six major types of ecosystems: tropical rain forests, deserts, grasslands, deciduous forests, taiga, and tundra. Ecologists call each of these major types of ecosystems a **biome.** Biomes stretch over large areas. Each biome has a characteristic climate. Deserts, for example, are defined by hot, dry weather that lasts most of the year. That is true of deserts in North America, Africa, and Australia. The tundra, on the other hand, is defined by little rainfall; short, cool summers; and long, cold winters.

Each biome has a unique set of plants and animals that have adapted to these conditions. If you go to any desert in the world, you will see plants and animals with similar adaptations. These adaptations are completely different from those of tundra plants and animals.

Still, it is important to remember that not all deserts are the same. Even within a desert, there are subtle variations in climate and landscape. As a result, plants and animals also vary.

Tropical Rain Forests

Now start your tour of the biomes in the steamy rain forests of Central and South America. It has just rained, so the air is warm and muggy. Mist shrouds the treetops. The forest is filled with the rich smell of flowers and the cries of birds, frogs, and monkeys.

Rain forests occur where the climate is warm all year round and where it rains almost every day. The warm temperatures and plentiful rain make ideal conditions for plants. In fact, **tropical rain forests** contain more plant species than all other biomes combined. There are 30,000 species of flowering plants in South American rain forests alone. Most plants in tropical rain forests have woody stems. The growing season lasts all year long, so there are always flowers in bloom.

THINK ABOUT IT

Trees in tropical rain forests do not drop their leaves during the winter. Why do you think this is true? Write your answer on a separate sheet of paper.

Plants of the Rain Forest

One popular misconception about tropical rain forests is that you need a machete (a large knife) to hack your way through. In fact, walking through a tropical rain forest is easy. Bacteria, fungi, and insects keep the forest floor clean by consuming any leaves or dead branches that fall down. More importantly, the trees are so dense that very little sunlight reaches the forest floor. Plants on the forest floor cannot grow because there is not enough light to photosynthesize. Light only gets through when one of the larger trees fall. Many plants are adapted to quickly exploit these gaps.

To find most of the plants in a tropical rain forest, you actually have to climb up into a tree. That is because most plants grow in the tops of trees where there is plenty of sunlight. Plants that grow in trees instead of the soil are called **epiphytes.** Epiphytes do not directly harm the trees. They gather water from the humid air and nutrients from the surface of the branches. A tree, however, may become so burdened with epiphytes that it falls over.

Animals of the Rain Forest

As you can imagine, this rich plant growth supports many animals. There are perhaps 30 million species of insects in tropical rain forests. Many have yet to be discovered. Most animals live in the trees. Insects, birds, squirrels, monkeys, and bats feed on leaves, fruit, and flower nectar.

Spiders, birds, frogs, and lizards patrol the trees for insects. Snakes and hawks hunt for frogs, birds, and even monkeys.

Most flowering plants depend on animal pollinators. Insects are the most common pollinators, but bats and hummingbirds also pollinate plants. Flowers pollinated by bats produce a strong odor at night to attract the bats. Flowers pollinated by hummingbirds are usually red—a color that attracts the birds. The flowers are also tubular. Hummingbirds hover in front of the flowers and stick their long beaks into the tubes to feed on the nectar.

Insects and other invertebrates live on the forest floor, where they feed on leaves and branches that fall from the trees. In Central and South America, deer, piglike animals called tapirs, and long-legged rodents called agoutis feed on fallen fruit and on plants growing in the gaps. These animals are hunted by jaguars and smaller cats such as ocelots and margay. In southern Asia, elephants, tigers, and antelopes live in the rain forests.

Threats to the Rain Forest

Today, rain forests throughout the tropics are threatened. Human populations are expanding rapidly in countries where rain forests grow. Many of these people are poor and depend on farming to survive. They clear or burn large tracts of rain forest in order to plant crops. Clearing a rain forest can have many effects.

Rainforest soils support a huge number of plants, but they are surprisingly infertile. They lack important nutrients such as phosphorus, calcium, and magnesium. Nutrients become available when leaves, branches, fruit, and dead animals fall to the floor and decomposers break them down. In the rain forest, the nutrients stay in the soil a very short time. Trees absorb these nutrients quickly.

When people cut or burn the rain forest, they destroy the thin layer of soil that contains nutrients. The soil also heats up because trees no longer shade it. Decomposers that break down dead material cannot survive the higher temperatures. As a result, farmers can only use the soil to grow crops for a few years. Then they have to abandon the plot and clear a new section of rain forest. The soil becomes so badly damaged that the rain forest will not grow back.

Rain forests are disappearing at a fast rate. According to some estimates, an area twice the size of Maine is cleared every year. At this rate, all the rain forests will be gone in another few decades. The destruction of these forests is tragic for a number of reasons. The world is losing a huge number of species, some of which may be sources of medicines. Even the disappearance of one species of tree can spell doom to many plants and animals that depend on it.

The clearing of rain forests can also alter the climate. Rain-forest trees absorb water and release it slowly into the air. Without the trees, the water rushes into rivers, carrying nutrients with it. The swollen rivers cause floods. Because water is no longer released slowly into the air, clouds no longer form. The amount of rain decreases, and floods are followed by droughts. A rich, luxuriant forest is replaced by a wasteland.

TIP

Think of a rain forest as a sponge in a sink. The sponge absorbs the water dripping from the faucet. Some of the water evaporates from the sponge back into the air. If you take the sponge away, all the water runs down the drain.

■ PRACTICE 71: Tropical Rain Forests

Decide if each statement that follows is true (**T**) or false (**F**). Write the correct letter on each line.

_____ **1.** Most plants and animals live up in the trees in rain forests.

_____ **2.** Nutrients remain in the soil for a long time in the rain forest.

_____ **3.** Most flowering plants depend on animals to pollinate them and distribute their seeds.

_____ **4.** Rain-forest soils are ideal for farming.

_____ **5.** Rain forests are being cleared at an alarming rate.

Deserts

As you head north from Central America and travel through Mexico, you will notice that the climate starts to change. The sky gets clearer and the air gets drier. The vegetation grows thinner and more widely spaced. Soon the forests end completely, and you have entered the **desert.**

In deserts, water—not light—is the limiting resource. Deserts normally get less than 25 centimeters of rain per year. The Atacama Desert in western Peru and Chile averages less than 3 centimeters of rain per year. Compare that to the 250 centimeters of rain that tropical rain forests typically get per year. Usually the rain comes once a year in the form of heavy downpours. In the American southwest, rain usually comes in the form of intense thunderstorms.

Most deserts are extremely hot. Some average over 100 degrees each day. At night, however, temperatures can drop dramatically as the heat radiates into space. Not all deserts are hot. The Great Basin desert in the western United States is hot just a few weeks of the year. There are also deserts in cold climates such as Antarctica.

Plants of the Desert

Conditions are rough for plants and animals that live in the desert. They have to keep cool and conserve water. For plants, the competition for water is so fierce that you see plants clumped together. In fact, many desert plants release chemicals into the soil that prevent other plants from growing next to them. Now look at some of the other ways plants have adapted to the dry climate.

- Most plants grow long roots that penetrate deep into the ground. Others grow extensive roots along the surface of the soil that quickly absorb rainwater and dew.

- Remember that plants lose most of their water through their leaves. Most desert plants have small, thick, waterproof leaves. Some are covered with hairs to reduce water loss. Cactuses have gone even further. Photosynthesis takes place in the stems, not the leaves. The leaves themselves are reduced to thorns.

- Many plants, especially cactuses, are filled with fleshy material that stores water. These tissues are tempting to animals seeking water. Sharp spines help keep the animals away.

- Most desert plants only open their stomata at night. Through a special series of chemical reactions, they are able to store the carbon dioxide they take in until the daytime, when photosynthesis takes place.

- Many plants avoid the dry weather altogether. They produce seeds that can stay in the soil for a long time. When it rains, the seeds sprout, and the desert literally blooms. Within just a few days, the plants produce flowers and seeds, then die. The new seeds wait in the soil until the rains come the next year.

Animals of the Desert

Desert animals also must adapt to the lack of water. Most of the smaller animals get their water by eating plants and other animals. They also drink the dew that forms during the cold nights.

To keep cool, animals, from scorpions to snakes to rodents, hide in burrows during the day. Larger animals such as coyotes and javelinas (piglike animals) stay in the shade.

Many animals have physical adaptations for preventing water loss and keeping cool. Arthropods have waterproof exoskeletons. Reptiles have waterproof skin. Jackrabbits have long ears that act like radiators. When the rabbit gets too hot, blood flows to the ears and gives off heat. The large ears of African elephants serve the same purpose.

Camels have another remarkable adaptation. Instead of storing their fat under the skin like most mammals, they store it in their humps. Camels are able to lose heat quickly because the fat no longer insulates them. Camels are also able to break down their body fat to get water. These adaptations have made the camel extremely useful for people living in the desert.

■ PRACTICE 72: Deserts

Decide if each statement that follows is true (**T**) or false (**F**). Write the correct letter on each line.

_____ **1.** Most deserts have one brief rainy season.

_____ **2.** All deserts are hot all the time.

_____ **3.** Desert plants are often clumped together to compete for water.

_____ **4.** Desert animals rarely come out during the daytime.

_____ **5.** Long ears help jackrabbits retain heat.

Grasslands

Now head north through the deserts of Arizona and into California. If you then turn east and cross the Great Basin, then to the Rocky Mountains, you will enter a new type of biome. This area gets more rain than the deserts you just visited, but not much more. The soils are more fertile and support more plant life, but hardly a tree is in sight. You have entered a sea of grass—a **grassland.**

There are several different types of grasslands. Drier areas in Oklahoma and western Colorado feature short grasses. Tallgrass prairies occur farther east, where the climate is wetter. In tropical areas such as Africa, the savanna grasslands contain pockets of trees. There are even small grasslands along the east coast of the United States.

Plants of the Grasslands

Grasses are hardy plants. They can withstand dry conditions. Shallow, dense roots soak up all the water in the soil. Many grasses roll up their leaves to prevent water loss. Like desert plants, grasses also are able to keep their stomata closed during the day and take in carbon dioxide at night. Grasses are pollinated by the wind, so they do not rely on animals to distribute their pollen and seeds.

Grasses recover easily from herbivory. Grasses are connected by underground stems called rhizomes that quickly sprout new leaves. Therefore, grasslands can support a huge number of herbivores. The grasslands in Africa are some of the most famous examples. Huge herds of zebras and antelopes roam these grasslands. They, in turn, support predators such as lions and cheetahs.

Animals of the Grasslands

The herds that roamed the grasslands of North America once rivaled those in Africa. Early settlers described endless herds of bison, elk, and pronghorn. Wolves, mountain lions, and grizzly bears preyed on these large herbivores. Prairie dogs still live in vast underground tunnels. Badgers use powerful claws to dig them up, and black-footed ferrets go down the holes after them.

 **THINK ABOUT IT**

 Many grassland animals, such as pronghorns and cheetahs, are among the fastest animals in the world. Why is speed an important adaptation to life in grasslands? Write your answer on a separate sheet of paper.

Most of the large herbivores and all of the large predators, however, have been hunted to the brink of extinction.

Threats to Grasslands

Today, grasslands are some of the most endangered ecosystems in the United States. There are several reasons for this.

- The rich grassland soils are excellent for farming. As a result, most grasslands have been converted to farms.

- Farmers graze their cattle on grasslands. Unfortunately, cows tend to overgraze to the point where the grass cannot recover. When the grass dies, the roots no longer hold the soil together. Wind and rain then scatter the soil. In many parts of the world, overgrazing is actually turning grasslands into deserts.

- Many grasslands exist because fires periodically clear away the woody plants. Fires are especially important in maintaining grasslands along the east coast of the United States. Today, people try to put out every fire they see. Without these fires, many grasslands have turned to forest.

Protecting grasslands has only recently become a priority. States such as Oklahoma and Kansas now have grassland preserves. Yellowstone National Park now has a healthy herd of bison. Scientists even set periodic fires to maintain grasslands. But there will never again be the vast grasslands that once dominated the center of the country.

■ PRACTICE 73: Grasslands

Decide if each statement that follows is true (**T**) or false (**F**). Write the correct letter on each line.

_____ **1.** Grasses are well adapted to surviving dry climates.

_____ **2.** Grasses recover quickly from herbivory.

_____ **3.** Except for the savannas of Africa, grasslands have never supported much wildlife.

_____ **4.** One of the best ways to maintain grasslands is to put out fires.

Deciduous Forests and Taiga

It would take a long time to tour the many types of forests in North America. In southern California, where the summers are hot and dry and the winters are cool and wet, there are forests of broad-leafed evergreen shrubs. As you move north along the west coast, the climate gets cool and extremely wet. There you will find temperate rain forests filled with towering conifers such as redwoods. You will leave them and head east to the deciduous forests in the eastern half of the United States. Then you will head north into the vast taiga of Canada.

Deciduous Forests

Deciduous forests occur in areas with warm, wet summers and cold winters. Deciduous trees are trees that drop their leaves in the winter. They include beech, maple, ash, hickory, cherry, and many types of oak. As you remember, trees drop their leaves in the fall and winter to conserve water. The dropping of leaves has important effects on the forest.

- It returns important nutrients to the soil.

- The leaf litter provides food and shelter to a host of small animals. These include insects, spiders, centipedes, snails, and small rodents.

- In the spring, before the new leaves develop, enough light reaches the forest floor so that plants can grow.

Plants of the Deciduous Forest

There are three layers to a deciduous forest. The top layer contains trees. There are few, if any, epiphytes in deciduous forests. The middle layer includes smaller trees and shrubs such as dogwoods, rhododendrons, and holly. The bottom layer contains herbs, ferns, and mosses. Unlike tropical rain forests, sunlight reaches the forest floor when the leaves are off the trees. Most plants on the forest floor grow and bloom in the spring, before the trees regrow their leaves.

Animals of the Deciduous Forest

Deciduous forests support a variety of animals. Insects feed on the plants. Numerous birds feed on seeds and insects. When the insects disappear in the winter, many of the birds migrate south to the tropical forests. Forest mammals include mice, squirrels, skunks, porcupines, deer, and black bears. Predators include weasels, fishers, foxes, bobcats, and coyotes. Reptiles, such as snakes and turtles, and amphibians, such as frogs, also thrive on the forest floor.

Most of the deciduous forests in the United States have at one time been cleared for wood and to make space for farming. Unlike tropical rain forests, deciduous forests do grow back. In New England, forests have reclaimed abandoned farms. These new forests are often different from the older forests. Some contain fewer species, and therefore support fewer types of animals.

Taiga

As you head north, conifers start to replace the beeches, maples, and oaks. These needle-leafed evergreen trees are better suited to the cold weather and a shorter growing season. Eventually, you will reach the **taiga** or northern forests.

Plants of the Taiga

These forests, which cover most of Canada, Scandinavia, and Siberia, are dominated by spruce, fir, tamarack, birch, and poplar. Alder, willow, and blueberries make up the undershrub. Thick mats of moss and lichen cover the ground. Lakes and bogs are also common.

Animals of the Taiga

Cold weather slows everything down in the taiga. The soil is frozen much of the year. Leaf litter decomposes slowly, so the soils contain few nutrients. During the summer, however, the forests come alive. One of the first things you will notice as you walk through the taiga in June are the swarms of mosquitoes and black flies. Numerous birds fly up from the tropics to feast on these insects.

Taiga also contain a rich assortment of mammals. They include moose, black bear, snowshoe hares, martens, lynxes, and wolves.

■ PRACTICE 74: Deciduous Forests and Taiga

Decide if each statement that follows is true (**T**) or false (**F**). Write the correct letter on each line.

_____ **1.** The number of conifers decreases as you move north.

_____ **2.** Sunlight only reaches the forest floor during the summer.

_____ **3.** The soils in taigas are much poorer than the soils in deciduous forests.

_____ **4.** Deciduous forests do not recover after they are logged.

Tundra

As you head farther north, the trees begin to thin. Then they disappear altogether. You have entered the **tundra,** a cold, dry area where few plants grow. A mixture of grasses, mosses, lichens, and low shrubs, including willows, dwarf birch, and blueberries, cover the ground. During a brief period in the summer, spectacular wildflowers bloom, and the tundra is alive with yellows, pinks, and blues.

The climate on the tundra poses many challenges for plants and animals. The growing season may only last two or three months. During the rest of the year, it is too cold, and there is too little sunlight. Poor soil and little rainfall make life even harder for the plants. The soil is frozen most of the year. The top layer thaws during the summer, but the soil remains frozen deeper down. This frozen layer is called the **permafrost.** Plant roots cannot penetrate the permafrost. Because of these rough conditions, it can take years for damaged plants to recover. During the winter, snow covers the plants and insulates them from the wind and extreme cold.

Despite the low rainfall, the tundra can get quite swampy. That is because water cannot drain through the permafrost. Water also evaporates slowly due to the cold weather.

Plants of the Tundra

Surprisingly, many plants, including poppies, buttercups, and saxifrage, produce large, colorful flowers. Large flowers use a lot of energy, but they are essential to the plants' survival. The nectar they produce keeps insect pollinators alive. If the plants do not produce enough nectar, the pollinators die, and the plants cannot get pollinated.

Animals of the Tundra

Despite the harsh conditions, the tundra supports many animals. During the summer, huge herds of caribou migrate north from the taiga. Musk oxen stay around all year long. Arctic foxes prey on lemmings, ground squirrels, arctic hares, and birds such as ptarmigan. Grizzly bears feed on berries and the occasional caribou.

Other large predators include wolves and wolverines. During the summer, clouds of mosquitoes hatch and drive the caribou crazy. Many songbirds fly north to feed on these mosquitoes.

Animals survive the harsh winters mostly by avoiding them. Birds and caribou migrate south. Lemmings live in burrows that are insulated by the snow. Ptarmigans bury themselves in snowbanks. Grizzly bears hibernate in dens. During hibernation, their bodies literally shut down, and they use few energy reserves.

Musk oxen rely on their dense coats to keep warm. They move to areas where wind has swept away the snow and they can feed on lichens. They can also use their sharp hooves to chip away at the snow. Wolves pick off the stragglers.

THINK ABOUT IT

Many tundra mammals, such as the arctic fox, have rounded bodies and short, buttonlike ears. Why are these adaptations important for surviving cold weather? Write your answer on a separate sheet of paper.

You do not have to go to Canada to find tundra or even taiga. These ecosystems can be found at or near the tops of mountains. The higher up you go, the colder the climate becomes. So in many ways, climbing a mountain is similar to traveling thousands of miles north. In southern Arizona, you can go from desert to taiga. In South America, you can go from tropical rain forest to tundra. You can see all that just by climbing a 2500-meter mountain!

■ PRACTICE 75: Tundra

Decide if each statement on the next page is true (**T**) or false (**F**). Write the correct letter on each line.

_____ **1.** The tundra soil is often wet, even though there is little rainfall.

_____ **2.** Despite the harsh conditions, many tundra plants produce large flowers.

_____ **3.** Many tundra animals avoid the harsh winters by migrating south.

_____ **4.** Tundra is only found in the far north.

UNIT 6 REVIEW

Read the following passage. Then circle the letter of the answer that correctly completes each statement.

Wolves were once common in Yellowstone National Park. By the 1920s, however, people had killed all the wolves, and there were none left. In 1995, biologists released wolves back into Yellowstone. There are now about 100 wolves living in the area. Before the wolves were brought back, a huge fire burned through Yellowstone National Park. The fire cleared away many large trees. First herbs, then fast-growing trees and shrubs, took over.

1. Wolves mostly eat elk. They are, therefore, _____.
   a. producers
   b. primary consumers
   c. secondary consumers
   d. decomposers

2. The wolf population in Yellowstone may _____.
   a. eventually outnumber the elk population
   b. equal the elk population
   c. remain well below the elk population
   d. none of the above

3. Many animals depend on plants that grow immediately after fires. If all fires were suppressed in Yellowstone, these animals would likely _____.
   a. increase
   b. decrease
   c. stay the same
   d. become producers

4. After a fire, nitrogen from the charred plants returns to the soil. In the next step of the nitrogen cycle, _____.
   a. animals take up the nitrogen
   b. all of the nitrogen returns to the air
   c. plants take up the nitrogen
   d. bacteria convert the nitrogen into a different form

Circle the letter of the answer that correctly completes each of the following statements.

5. Plants and animals avoid competition by occupying separate niches. Examples include _____.
   a. two species of beetles that eat different types of plants
   b. a tree outgrowing a neighboring tree of the same species
   c. members of the same species of seabird nesting on separate parts of a cliff
   d. a lion and a hyena that fight over the same zebra

6. The bacteria that digest plant material in the rumen of cows are an example of _____.
   a. herbivory
   b. parasitism
   c. commensalism
   d. mutualism

7. Some plants produce chemicals that prevent neighboring plants from growing. This is an example of _____.
   a. competition
   b. herbivory
   c. predation
   d. parasitism

8. Some animals eat the leaves off of plants. This is an example of _____.
   a. mutualism
   b. commensalism
   c. herbivory
   d. predation

Circle the letter of the correct answer to each of the following questions.

9. Which biome is warm and wet all year round?
   a. tropical rain forests
   b. deserts
   c. deciduous forests
   d. arctic tundra

10. What adaptations do desert animals and tundra animals share?
    a. Both may burrow underground to escape weather extremes.
    b. Both migrate to avoid weather extremes.
    c. Both have large ears that act as radiators.
    d. Both hibernate during extreme conditions.

UNIT 6 APPLICATION ACTIVITY 1
Decaying Log Community

In a nearby field, stream, or forest, find a large, decaying log from a fallen tree. Examine it for organisms that appear to live near or in it. Do not forget to include any plants that are growing on the log or near it. Use a magnifying glass to help you identify small organisms not easily seen with only your eyes. Cut away some of the surface decay to investigate the organisms living deeper in the log.

On the lines below, record your findings by listing the organisms you found.

_____

_____

_____

On a separate sheet of paper, make sketches of the log and of the individual organisms living in, on, and around it.

On a separate sheet of paper, write a few paragraphs to describe the log community. For example, explain which plants and animals were most abundant; what ways plants and animals depend on the log to live; and what kinds of organisms cause the log to decay.

UNIT 6 APPLICATION ACTIVITY 2
Water Community Succession

Using a large jar with a lid (a pickle jar, peanut butter jar, or widemouthed applesauce jar will do), fill the jar about one fourth full with dried plant material taken from a forest floor or a pond. Add clean pond, brook, or bog water to fill the jar about three fourths full. Put the lid on the jar, and shake it thoroughly to mix the plants with the pond water.

Take a sample from the jar with a medicine dropper, and place the sample on a slide. Look at the slide under a microscope. Describe and illustrate what you see in a notebook.

Store the jar in a safe place that gets indirect sunlight. Observe a drop from the jar every day for one or two months. Record your daily observations in your notebook.

What evidence did you observe indicating succession had occurred?

_____

_____

Where did the organisms in the jar come from?

_____

_____

_____

_____

APPENDIXES

A. Biology Words

In biology, special terms are often used. Knowing word parts can help you figure out unfamiliar words. You can add up the word parts to find the meaning of the whole word. For example, if you came across the word *epidermis,* you might not know what it meant. But if you saw that it combined the word parts *epi,* which means "outer," and *derm,* which means "skin," you might guess that it means "outer layer of skin."

Here are some word parts that are often combined to make biology words.

Word Part	Meaning	Example
a-, an-	without	anaerobic
aero-	air	aerobic
ambi-, amphi-	both	amphibian
anti-	against	antibiotic
archae-	ancient	archaebacteria
arthr-	joint	arthropod
auto-	self	autoimmune
bi-	two	bivalve
bio-	life	biology
co-	with	codominant
derm-	skin	dermis
di-	twice	diploid
eco-	environment	ecology
endo-	inside	endoderm
epi-	outer	epidermis
exo-	outside	exoskeleton

Biology Words, *continued*

Word Part	Meaning	Example
geo-	earth	geology
homo-	same	homologous
hydro-	water	hydrologic
meter	measure	thermometer
micro-	tiny	microscopic
mono-	one	monocot
morph-	shape, form	metamorphosis
neur-	nerve	neural
-ology	study, science	biology
-ose	carbohydrate	glucose
ova-, ovi-	egg	ovary
per-	through	permeable
photo-	light	photosynthesis
phys-	nature	physical
plat-	flat	platyhelminthes
-pod	foot	gastropod
poly-	many	polygenic
pro-, proto-	first	protist
pseudo-	apparent	pseudopod
-scop	look	microscope
sperm	seed	gymnosperm
sub-	under	subcutaneous

Biology Words, *continued*

Word Part	Meaning	Example
sym-, syn-	together, with	symbiosis
terr-	earth	terrarium
therm-	heat	thermometer
trans-	across	transpiration
trop-	turn	phototropism
-vore	eater	carnivore
zoo-	animal	zoology

B. The Parts of a Cell

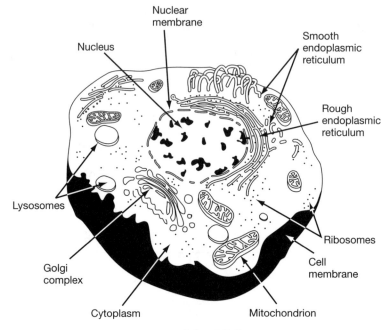

Nuclear membrane

Nucleus

Smooth endoplasmic reticulum

Rough endoplasmic reticulum

Lysosomes

Ribosomes

Golgi complex

Cell membrane

Cytoplasm

Mitochondrion

Animal Cell

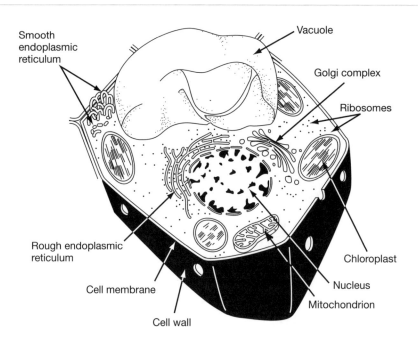

Smooth endoplasmic reticulum

Vacuole

Golgi complex

Ribosomes

Rough endoplasmic reticulum

Cell membrane

Cell wall

Chloroplast

Nucleus

Mitochondrion

Plant Cell

C. Classifying Living Things

The classification system used today includes six kingdoms: Animals, Plants, Archaebacteria, Eubacteria, Protists, and Fungi.

Animals

- Multicellular organisms that do not produce their own food but eat other organisms
- Include insects, fish, birds, mammals, mollusks, worms

Plants

- Organisms that have specialized cells, with cell walls
- Use chlorophyll and sunlight to make food by photosynthesis
- Include mosses, worts, lycopods, cone-bearing plants, flowering plants

Archaebacteria

- Single-celled organisms with no cell nucleus
- Most do not need oxygen

Eubacteria

- Single-celled organisms with no cell nucleus
- Some cause diseases such as Lyme disease
- Some, such as bacteria that turn milk into yogurt, are very useful

Protists

- Simple organisms with cell walls and nuclei
- Many are single-celled
- Some have many cells
- Include algae, protozoans, slime molds

Fungi

- Organisms that have cell walls, like plants, but do not photosynthesize
- Important decomposers
- Include mushrooms, molds, yeasts

The most common way to give the name of an organism is to list the name of the genus and the species. The name of the genus should be capitalized. The name of the species should be lowercase.

Kingdom

    Phylum/Division

        Class

            Order

                Family (Sub-Family)

                    Genus

                        Species (Subspecies)

D. The Parts of a Flowering Plant

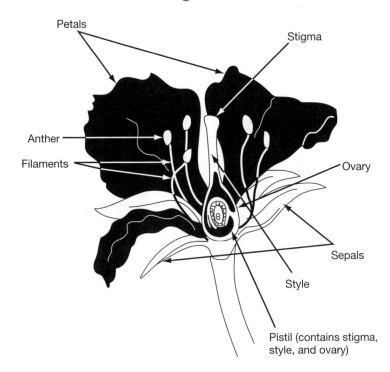

Petals

Stigma

Anther

Filaments

Ovary

Sepals

Style

Pistil (contains stigma, style, and ovary)

E. The Human Body

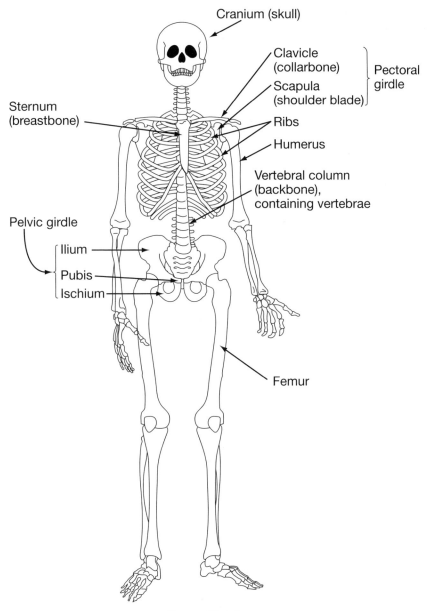

Cranium (skull)

Clavicle (collarbone)

Scapula (shoulder blade)

Pectoral girdle

Sternum (breastbone)

Ribs

Humerus

Vertebral column (backbone), containing vertebrae

Pelvic girdle

Ilium

Pubis

Ischium

Femur

Human Skeleton

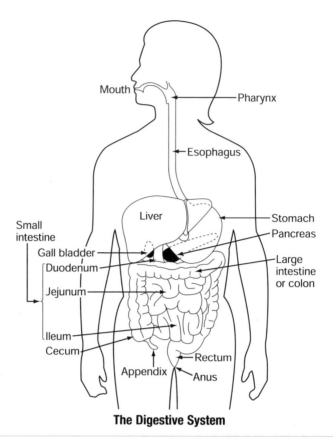

The Digestive System

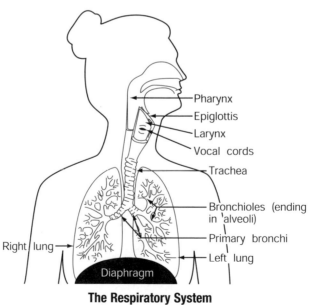

The Respiratory System

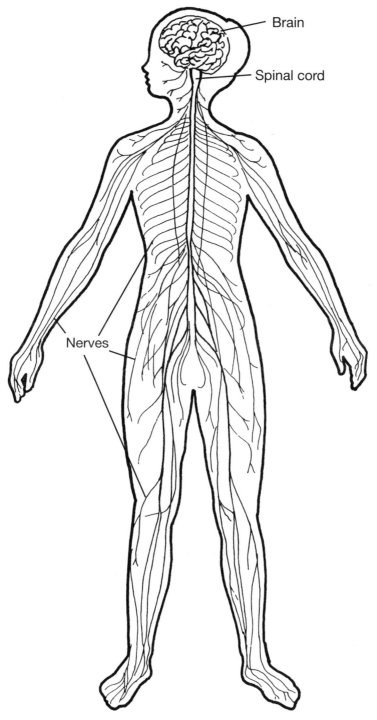

Brain

Spinal cord

Nerves

The Nervous System

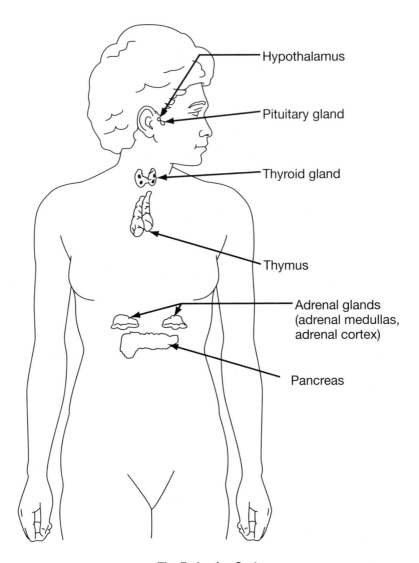

Hypothalamus

Pituitary gland

Thyroid gland

Thymus

Adrenal glands
(adrenal medullas,
adrenal cortex)

Pancreas

The Endocrine System

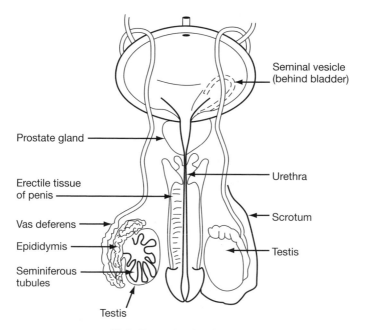

Male Reproductive System

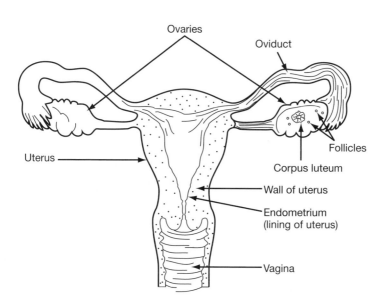

Female Reproductive System

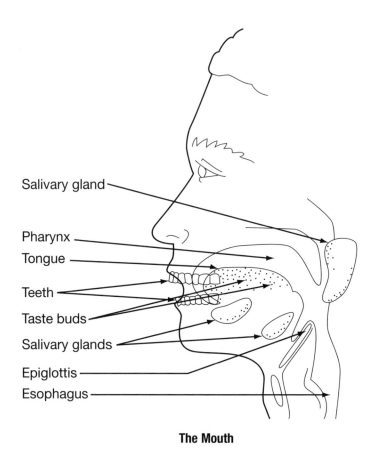

The Mouth

Salivary gland

Pharynx
Tongue

Teeth

Taste buds

Salivary glands

Epiglottis

Esophagus

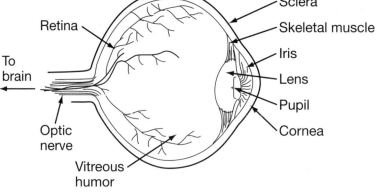

The Eye

Retina

To
brain

Optic
nerve

Vitreous
humor

Sclera

Skeletal muscle

Iris

Lens

Pupil

Cornea

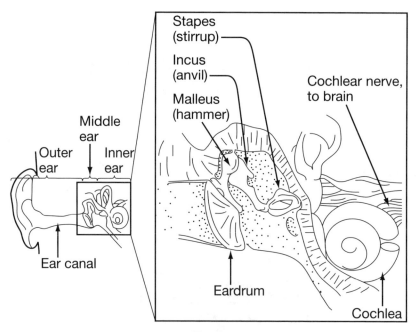

The Ear

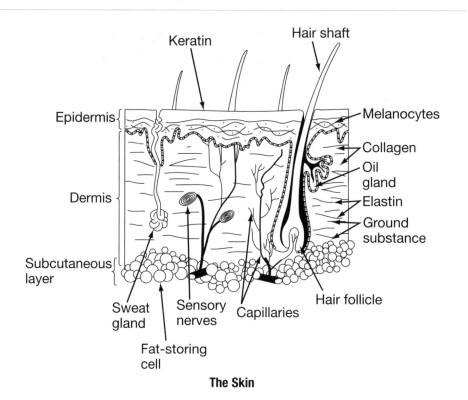

The Skin

F. Nutrition

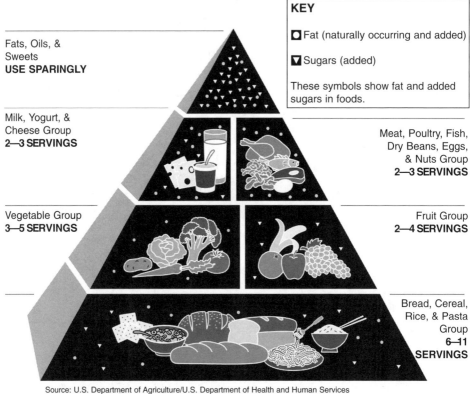

Food Guide Pyramid
A Guide to Daily Food Choices

KEY

◻ Fat (naturally occurring and added)

▼ Sugars (added)

These symbols show fat and added sugars in foods.

Fats, Oils, &
Sweets
USE SPARINGLY

Milk, Yogurt, &
Cheese Group
2—3 SERVINGS

Meat, Poultry, Fish,
Dry Beans, Eggs,
& Nuts Group
2—3 SERVINGS

Vegetable Group
3—5 SERVINGS

Fruit Group
2—4 SERVINGS

Bread, Cereal,
Rice, & Pasta
Group
**6—11
SERVINGS**

Source: U.S. Department of Agriculture/U.S. Department of Health and Human Services

G. The Six Major Biomes
Tropical Rain Forests
Distribution

- in the tropics, near the equator
- South America: Amazon; Africa; India; Southeast Asia; Australia

Climate

- warm all year round
- average rainfall 250 centimeters per year
- two seasons: rainy and dry

Plants

- more plant species than all other biomes combined
- trees 25–35 meters tall, mostly evergreen
- orchids, bromeliads, vines (lianas), ferns, mosses, palms

Animals

- antelopes
- bats
- birds
- deer
- elephants

- frogs
- insects
- jaguars
- lizards
- monkeys

- ocelots
- spiders
- snakes
- tapirs
- tigers

Threats

- deforestation

Deserts
Distribution

- hot and dry: Africa: Kalahari, Sahara, Namib; Australia: Great Sandy, Great Victoria, Simpson, Gibson, Tanami; North America: Mojave, Sonoran, Chihuahan, Great Basin; South America: Monte; South Asia: Thar; Southwest Asia: Arabian, Lut, Iranian

- semiarid: North America: Great Basin
- coastal: South America: Atacama
- cold: South America: Patagonian; Asia: Gobi, Turkestan; Antarctica: Antarctic

Climate

- very little rainfall
- climate can be hot and dry, semiarid, or cold

Plants

- cactus
- spiny bushes and shrubs (agave, mesquite, prickly pear, yucca)

Animals

- antelopes, deer, gazelles
- armadillos
- bats
- birds (eagles, hawks, ostriches, owls, penguins, roadrunners, vultures)
- camels
- coyotes
- elephants
- foxes
- hyenas
- insects (beetles, scorpions)
- jackals
- jackrabbits
- kangaroos
- rabbits and hares
- reptiles (lizards, snakes, tortoises)
- rodents (gerbils, mice, rats, squirrels)
- spiders
- toads
- wolves

Grasslands

Distribution

- in middle latitudes, in interiors of continents
- South America: Argentina, Uruguay; Asia: Siberia; Africa (Kenya, Uganda, South Africa, Tanzania); Australia; India; Europe: Hungary; North America: Oklahoma, western Colorado (prairie)

Climate

- either moist continental or dry subtropical
- two seasons: growing season, dormant season
- rainfall concentrated in one part of the year, followed by period of drought
- two main divisions: savanna, steppe

Plants

- grasses (buffalo grass, sagebrush, speargrass)
- small broad-leaved plants (asters, blazing stars, coneflowers, goldenrod, sunflowers, clover, indigo)
- occasional scattered trees (cottonwoods, oaks)

Animals

- antelopes
- badgers
- birds (blackbirds, grouse, hawks, larks, owls, quail, sparrows)
- bison
- cheetahs
- coyotes
- deer, elk, and gazelles
- elephants
- ferrets
- foxes
- giraffes

- hyenas
- insects (beetles, grasshoppers, termites)
- leopards
- lions
- moles
- mountain lions
- rabbits
- rodents (gophers, mice, prairie dogs, squirrels)
- snakes
- spiders
- wild horses
- wolves
- zebras

Threats

- overgrazing
- clearing for crops

Deciduous Forests

Distribution

- eastern North America, northeastern Asia, western and central Europe

Climate

- moderate climate
- warm, wet summers; cold winters

Plants

- broad-leaved trees that drop their leaves in winter (ash, basswood, beech, cherry, elm, hemlock, hickory, maple, oak, willow)
- spring-flowering herbs
- ferns
- mosses

Animals

- bears
- birds
- bobcats
- coyotes
- deer
- fishers
- foxes
- frogs
- insects
- mountain lions
- porcupines
- rabbits
- rodents
- skunks
- snakes
- turtles
- weasels
- wolves

Taiga

Distribution

- between 50–60 degrees N: Siberia, Scandinavia, Alaska, Canada

Climate

- short, moist, moderately warm summers; long, cold, dry winters
- temperatures very low

Plants

- cold-tolerant evergreen conifers (pine, fir, spruce, tamarack)
- shrubs (blueberries)
- ground cover (moss, lichen)

Animals

- badgers
- bats
- bears (black bear, brown bear)
- beavers
- birds (eagles, finches, geese, hawks, sparrows, woodpeckers)
- bobcats
- caribou
- deer
- foxes

- hares
- insects (ants, blackflies, mosquitoes)
- lynx
- moose
- rabbits
- rodents (chipmunks, mice, squirrels, voles)
- sheep
- shrews
- weasels (ermine, martens, minks, wolverines)
- wolves

Threats

- logging

Tundra

Distribution

- in far north of Greenland, Alaska, Canada, Europe, Russia
- high on mountain slopes, above the tree line

Climate

- little rainfall; short, cool summers; long, cold winters
- cold, desertlike
- two types of tundra: Arctic tundra, alpine tundra
- in Arctic tundra, top layer of soil thaws in summer but deeper layer remains frozen

Plants

- low shrubs (blueberries, sedges)
- liverworts, grasses, lichens, mosses
- wildflowers (poppies, buttercups, saxifrage)
- tussock grasses
- dwarf trees

Animals

- bears (grizzly, polar)
- birds (falcons, gulls, loons, ptarmigan, ravens, sandpipers, snow buntings, snow geese, snowy owls, terns, tundra swans)
- caribou
- elk
- fish (cod, flatfish, salmon, trout)
- foxes
- hares
- insects (butterflies, flies, grasshoppers, moths, mosquitoes)
- mountain goats
- musk oxen
- porcupines
- rodents (lemmings, squirrels, voles)
- sheep
- weasels (ermine, wolverines)
- wolves

GLOSSARY

abdomen (AB-duh-mun) the back part of the body of an arthropod, such as a spider or a crab

actin (AK-tun) long, ropelike protein found in skeletal muscles

active transport (AK-tiv   TRANS-pohrt) movement of materials through a cell membrane using energy

adaptation (a-dap-TAY-shun) a change in an organism that helps it survive in its environment

adenine (A-dun-een) one of the bases that make up the genetic code of DNA and RNA

ADP (AY-DEE-PEE) (abbreviation for *adenosine diphosphate*) compound formed when ATP is broken down within a cell; can be used by a cell for energy

adrenal glands (uh-DREE-nul   GLANDZ) glands located on the kidneys that produce the hormone adrenaline

adrenaline (uh-DRE-nul-un) hormone that increases heart rate and blood pressure; also called *epinephrine*

algae (AL-jee) plantlike protists that have chlorophyll and undergo photosynthesis; the singular form is *alga.*

PRONUNCIATION KEY

CAPITAL LETTERS show the stressed syllables.

a	as in mat	f	as in fit
ay	as in day, say	g	as in go
ch	as in chew	i	as in sit
e	as in bed	j	as in job, gem
ee	as in even, easy, need	k	as in cool, key

algal bloom (AL-gul BLOOM) a dramatic increase in the number of algae in a body of water

allele (uh-LEEL) a form of a gene that determines alternate forms of a trait

allergies (A-lur-jees) overreactions of the immune system to substances (such as pollen or mold) that do not pose a threat to the body

alveoli (al-VEE-uh-ly) tiny air sacs in the lungs; the singular form is *alveolus.*

amino acids (uh-MEE-noh A-suds) long strings of chemical compounds that are used to make proteins

amniotic sac (am-nee-O-tik SAK) a fluid-filled sac that protects and nourishes the growing fetus of a bird, a reptile, or a mammal

amoebocytes (uh-MEE-buh-syts) jellylike cells in a sponge that carry food to other cells

amphibian (am-FI-bee-un) a coldblooded vertebrate (animal with a backbone) that lives part of its life in the water and part of its life on land

anaerobic (a-nuh-ROH-bik) unable to survive when oxygen is present

anaphase (A-nuh-fayz) the third stage of mitosis in which the chromosomes split and move to opposite ends of the cell

---

PRONUNCIATION KEY

CAPITAL LETTERS show the stressed syllables.

ng	as in running	u	as in but, some
o	as in cot, father	uh	as in about, taken, lemon, pencil
oh	as in go, note	ur	as in term
oo	as in too	y	as in line, fly
sh	as in shy	zh	as in vision, measure
th	as in thin		

ancestor (AN-ses-tur) an earlier organism from which an individual or group has developed

annelids (A-nul-udz) worms with segmented bodies; they include marine worms, earthworms, and leeches.

antennae (an-TE-nee) slender, jointed sensory organs on the head of some arthropods, such as insects

anthers (AN-thurz) the parts at the tip of a plant's stamen that contain pollen

antibiotics (an-ti-by-O-tiks) medicines that kill disease-causing bacteria

antibodies (AN-ti-bo-deez) substances that act against specific pathogens

anticodons (an-ti-KOH-donz) group of three nucleotides that bind to codons on mRNA during protein synthesis

antigen (AN-ti-jun) a substance that causes the immune system to respond

antioxidants (an-tee-OK-suh-dunts) substances, such as vitamins C and E, that bind to and deactivate harmful chemicals in the body

antiserums (AN-tee-sir-ums) serums that contain antibodies against specific pathogens

anus (AY-nus) the opening at the end of the digestive system through which solid wastes are eliminated

---

PRONUNCIATION KEY

CAPITAL LETTERS show the stressed syllables.

a	as in mat	f	as in fit
ay	as in day, say	g	as in go
ch	as in chew	i	as in sit
e	as in bed	j	as in job, gem
ee	as in even, easy, need	k	as in cool, key

aorta (ay-OR-tuh) the main blood vessel that carries blood from the heart

appendicular skeleton (a-pun-DI-kyuh-lur   SKE-luh-tun) the bones of the upper and lower limbs, including the shoulders, collarbones, hips, arms, legs, and feet

appendix (uh-PEN-diks) a fingerlike structure in the large intestine that serves no function in the body

arachnids (uh-RAK-nuds) a large class of arthropods (invertebrates with jointed limbs) that includes spiders, scorpions, mites, and ticks

archaebacteria (ar-kee-bak-TIR-ee-uh) a kingdom of single-celled organisms with no cell nucleus; most live in very harsh environments.

arteries (AR-tuh-rees) blood vessels that carry blood from the heart to the rest of the body

arterioles (ar-TIR-ee-olz) small blood vessels that branch off from the arteries

arthropods (AR-thruh-podz) invertebrates (animals without backbones) that have segmented bodies and jointed limbs; includes insects, spiders, ticks, and crabs

astrocytes (AS-truh-syts) star-shaped cells in the central nervous system

atmospheric pressure (at-muh-SFIR-ik   PRE-shur) the normal pressure created by gas molecules (such as oxygen and carbon dioxide) in the air

---

PRONUNCIATION KEY

CAPITAL LETTERS show the stressed syllables.

ng	as in running	u	as in but, some
o	as in cot, father	uh	as in about, taken, lemon, pencil
oh	as in go, note	ur	as in term
oo	as in too	y	as in line, fly
sh	as in shy	zh	as in vision, measure
th	as in thin		

atoms (A-tumz) the smallest parts of an element that have all the chemical properties of the element

ATP (AY-TEE-PEE) (abbreviation for *adenosine triphosphate*) a compound, found in living cells, that can store and release energy

atrium (AY-tree-um) a chamber of a mammal's heart that receives blood from the veins; the plural form is *atria.*

autoimmune diseases (aw-toh-im-YOON   di-ZEEZ-ez) diseases in which the immune system mistakenly attacks the body's own cells

autonomic nervous system (aw-tuh-NO-mik   NER-vus   SIS-tum) the part of the nervous system that controls things we are not aware of or cannot control, such as the release of hormones

autosome (AW-tuh-sohm) a chromosome that determines all body features

axial skeleton (AK-see-ul   SKE-luh-tun) the part of the skeleton that includes the skull, spinal column, ribs, and breastbone

axons (AK-sonz) fibers on nerve cells that carry nerve impulses away from the cell

bacilli (buh-SI-lee) rod-shaped bacteria; the singular form is *bacillus.*

bacteria (bak-TIR-ee-uh) single-celled organisms that have no cell nucleus; the singular form is *bacterium.*

PRONUNCIATION KEY

CAPITAL LETTERS show the stressed syllables.

a	as in m**a**t	f	as in **f**it
ay	as in d**ay**, s**ay**	g	as in **g**o
ch	as in **ch**ew	i	as in sit
e	as in b**e**d	j	as in **j**ob, **g**em
ee	as in **e**ven, **ea**sy, n**ee**d	k	as in **c**ool, **k**ey

B-cells (BEE-selz) lymphocytes manufactured in bone marrow that recognize and/or destroy a specific type of pathogen

behavioral adaptation (bi-HAY-vyuh-rul   a-dap-TAY-shun) a change in the way an organism acts, or behaves

bile (BYL) a liquid produced in the liver that aids in the digestion of fats

binary fission (BY-nuh-ree   FI-shun) reproduction by splitting in two to produce two identical cells

binding sites (BYND-ing   SYTS) places on the ends of amino acid chains that latch on to the antigens on the surface of pathogens

biome (BY-ohm) any one of six major ecosystems that has a characteristic climate and kinds of organisms

bivalves (BY-valvz) mollusks, such as clams and scallops, that have two hinged shells

bladder (BLA-dur) the part of the body that stores urine

blastocyst (BLAS-tuh-sist) an embryo when it is a hollow ball of cells

blastoderm (BLAS-tuh-durm) a disk-shaped mass of cells inside the blastocyst that is the part that will turn into the baby

blood-brain barrier (BLUD-BRAYN   BAR-ee-ur) the intensive screening process substances must go through to enter the brain

---

PRONUNCIATION KEY

CAPITAL LETTERS show the stressed syllables.

ng	as in running	u	as in but, some
o	as in cot, father	uh	as in about, taken, lemon, pencil
oh	as in go, note	ur	as in term
oo	as in too	y	as in line, fly
sh	as in shy	zh	as in vision, measure
th	as in thin		

bony fish (BOH-nee FISH) fish with skeletons made of bones

Bowman's capsule (BOH-munz   CAP-sul) a structure at the end of a nephron that contains a knot of blood vessels

bronchi (BRON-ky) tubes that lead from the trachea to the lungs; the singular form is *bronchus.*

bronchioles (BRON-kee-ohlz) small tubes that branch from the secondary bronchi

bud (BUD) a tightly packed bundle at the end of a twig on a tree in the spring that opens up into a leaf

calcium gate (KAL-see-um   GAYT) point at which calcium enters the axon

cambium (KAM-bee-um) a layer of growth tissue inside a tree trunk

camouflage (KA-muh-flozh) a method that animals use to protect themselves from predators in which they blend into the background of their environment

capillaries (KA-puh-ler-eez) tiny blood vessels that connect arteries to veins

carapace (KAR-uh-pays) the protective shield that covers the body of a crustacean

carbohydrates (kar-boh-HY-drayts) starches and sugars

PRONUNCIATION KEY

CAPITAL LETTERS show the stressed syllables.

a	as in m**a**t	f	as in **f**it
ay	as in d**ay**, s**ay**	g	as in **g**o
ch	as in **ch**ew	i	as in s**i**t
e	as in b**e**d	j	as in **j**ob, **g**em
ee	as in **e**ven, **ea**sy, n**ee**d	k	as in **c**ool, **k**ey

carbon (KAR-bun) element that forms the basis for living tissue

carbon dioxide (KAR-bun   dy-OK-syd) the form of carbon when it is in the air

carbonic acid (kar-BO-nik   A-sud) an acid formed when the carbon dioxide released during respiration reacts with water

cardiac muscle (KAR-dee-ak   MUH-sul) the muscle that makes up the heart

carnivore (KAR-nuh-vohr) an animal that eats other animals

cartilage (KAR-tul-ij) a strong connective tissue that is lighter and more flexible than bone

cartilaginous fish (kar-tuh-LA-juh-nus   FISH) fish that have skeletons made of cartilage

cecum (SEE-kum) the first part of the large intestine

cell wall (SEL   WOL) a rigid barrier that surrounds the cells of organisms such as plants, algae, and fungi

cells (SELZ) the basic units of all living things

cellulose (SEL-yoo-lohs) carbohydrates woven together to make up the cell wall in plants, algae, and fungi

---

PRONUNCIATION KEY

CAPITAL LETTERS show the stressed syllables.

ng	as in running	u	as in but, some
o	as in cot, father	uh	as in about, taken, lemon, pencil
oh	as in go, note	ur	as in term
oo	as in too	y	as in line, fly
sh	as in shy	zh	as in vision, measure
th	as in thin		

central nervous system (SEN-trul NER-vus SIS-tum) the part of the nervous system where processing takes place; includes the brain and the spinal cord

centriole (SEN-tree-ohl) a structure at each pole of a cell

cephalopods (SE-fuh-luh-pods) mollusks with no outer shell; includes squid and octopuses

cephalothorax (se-fuh-luh-THOHR-aks) the front section of the body where the head and thorax are combined in some anthropods, such as spiders and crustaceans

cerebellum (ser-uh-BE-lum) the part of the brain that controls coordination and balance

cerebral cortex (suh-REE-brul KOR-teks) the wrinkled gray matter on top of the cerebrum, which is composed of tightly packed dendrites and cell bodies

cerebrum (suh-REE-brum) the part of the brain that controls most voluntary thought and actions

chelicerae (ki-LI-suh-ree) clawlike mouthparts of some arthropods, such as spiders

chelicerates (ki-LI-suh-rayts) class of arthropods that includes arachnids

---

PRONUNCIATION KEY

CAPITAL LETTERS show the stressed syllables.

a	as in mat	f	as in fit
ay	as in day, say	g	as in go
ch	as in chew	i	as in sit
e	as in bed	j	as in job, gem
ee	as in even, easy, need	k	as in cool, key

chemoreceptors (kee-moh-ri-SEP-turz) sensory nerves that detect specific chemicals

chitin (KY-tun) a hard but flexible substance found in the exoskeleton of arthropods; in the cell walls of fungi; and in the fingernails, claws, and hair of mammals

chlorophyll (KLOHR-uh-fil) a plant substance, usually green, that absorbs light energy for use in photosynthesis

chloroplasts (KLOHR-uh-plasts) the part of a plant where photosynthesis is carried out

choanocytes (KOH-a-nuh-syts) group of cells lining the inside cavity of a sponge

chordates (KOR-dayts) organisms that, at some stage of development, have gill slits, a central nerve cord, and a flexible rod of cells forming a support along the back

chorion (KOHR-ee-on) a structure that combines with the endometrium to form the placenta

chromatid (KROH-muh-tud) each copy of the chromosome that results from the prophase of mitosis

chromatin (KROH-muh-tun) the combination of histones and DNA

PRONUNCIATION KEY

CAPITAL LETTERS show the stressed syllables.

ng	as in running	u	as in but, some
o	as in cot, father	uh	as in about, taken, lemon, pencil
oh	as in go, note	ur	as in term
oo	as in too	y	as in line, fly
sh	as in shy	zh	as in vision, measure
th	as in thin		

chromosomes (KROH-muh-sohmz) bundles of coiled DNA inside the nucleus

chyme (KYM) partly digested food that passes from the stomach to the small intestine

cilia (SI-lee-uh) tiny, hairlike projections; the singular form is *cilium.*

class (KLAS) group of related orders of organisms; division of a phylum

classification (kla-suh-fuh-KAY-shun) a system of grouping organisms based on similar features

classify (kla-suh-FY) to group together

closed circulatory system (KLOHZD   SUR-kyuh-luh-tohr-ee   SIS-tum) a system that pumps blood through veins in an endless loop

cnidarian (ny-DAR-ee-un) invertebrate with a hollow body and tentacles with stinging cells; occurs in two forms, polyp and medusa; includes jellyfish, anemones, and corals

cocci (KO-kee) round or oval eubacteria; the singular form is *coccus.*

cochlea (KOH-klee-uh) a coiled structure in the inner ear that receives sound waves

codominance (koh-DO-muh-nuns) in heredity, when two genes are present for a trait and neither one is either dominant or recessive

---

PRONUNCIATION KEY

CAPITAL LETTERS show the stressed syllables.

a	as in m**a**t	f	as in **f**it
ay	as in d**ay**, s**ay**	g	as in **g**o
ch	as in **ch**ew	i	as in s**i**t
e	as in b**e**d	j	as in **j**ob, **g**em
ee	as in **e**ven, **ea**sy, n**ee**d	k	as in **c**ool, **k**ey

codons (KOH-dons) three-letter sequences in the mRNA molecule

coeloms (SEE-lums) fluid-filled hollow spaces in an animal's body that contain the digestive organs

coenzymes (koh-EN-zymz) vitamins that activate enzymes by binding to them and changing their shape

coldblooded (KOHLD-BLUH-dud) unable to control body temperature from inside, but taking on the temperature of the outside air or water

collagen (KO-luh-jun) a tough, fibrous protein that makes up most of the dermis and gives skin its strength

collecting duct (kuh-LEK-ting   DUKT) a duct that runs through the medulla to the ureter through which water may passively flow

colon (KOH-lun) part of the large intestine

commensalism (kuh-MEN-suh-li-zum) a relationship in which one species benefits while the second species does not benefit, but is not harmed

community (kuh-MYOO-nuh-tee) made up of all the organisms that live in one area

compact bone (kum-PAKT   BOHN) the hardest part of a bone

competition (kom-puh-TI-shun) the struggle between organisms for resources such as food, water, and light

---

PRONUNCIATION KEY

CAPITAL LETTERS show the stressed syllables.

ng	as in running	u	as in but, some
o	as in cot, father	uh	as in about, taken, lemon, pencil
oh	as in go, note	ur	as in term
oo	as in too	y	as in line, fly
sh	as in shy	zh	as in vision, measure
th	as in thin		

cones (KOHNZ) parts of the eye that detect color

conifers (KO-nuh-furz) cone-bearing trees, such as pines or firs

cornea (KOR-nee-uh) the clear, curved covering through which light enters the eye

coronary arteries (KOR-uh-ner-ee   AR-tuh-rees) arteries that provide blood for the heart

corpus luteum (KOR-pus   LOO-tee-um) a hormone-producing structure that forms in the ovary after a mature egg is released

cortex (KOR-teks) structure on the kidney that contains filtering structures

cortisol (KOR-tuh-sol) a hormone that stimulates the body to convert amino acids and fats into glucose

cranium (KRAY-nee-um) the skull; part of the axial skeleton

crossing over (KROS-ing   OH-vur) the exchange of DNA in prophase I

crustaceans (krus-TAY-shuns) mostly water-dwelling arthropods that have a hard outer covering; includes lobsters, crabs, and shrimp

cytoplasm (SY-tuh-pla-zum) a jellylike material in most cells that surrounds the nucleus

cytosine (SY-tuh-seen) one of the bases that make up the genetic code of DNA and RNA

PRONUNCIATION KEY

CAPITAL LETTERS show the stressed syllables.

a	as in m**a**t	f	as in **f**it
ay	as in d**ay**, s**ay**	g	as in **g**o
ch	as in **ch**ew	i	as in s**i**t
e	as in b**e**d	j	as in **j**ob, **g**em
ee	as in **e**ven, **ea**sy, n**ee**d	k	as in **c**ool, **k**ey

dark phase (DARK FAYZ) second phase of photosynthesis, during which light is not needed

daughter cells (DO-tur SELZ) cells produced by division of the parent cell that are identical copies of the parent

deciduous forests (di-SI-juh-wus FOR-usts) ecosystem found in areas with warm, wet summers and cold winters in which trees drop their leaves in winter

decomposers (dee-kum-POH-zurz) organisms, such as bacteria and fungi, that break down dead organic matter

dendrites (DEN-dryts) short, branching extensions of nerve cells that receive information from stimuli or from other nerve cells

deoxyribose (dee-ok-si-RY-bohs) a five-carbon sugar found in DNA

depolarization (dee-poh-luh-ruh-ZAY-shun) process by which the inside of a cell becomes more positively charged than the outside of the cell

dermis (DUR-mus) a thick layer of skin under the epidermis

desert (DE-zurt) a biome that usually receives less than 25 centimeters of rain each year

diaphragm (DY-uh-fram) a sheet of muscles under the lungs that aids in breathing

---

PRONUNCIATION KEY

CAPITAL LETTERS show the stressed syllables.

ng	as in running	u	as in but, some
o	as in cot, father	uh	as in about, taken, lemon, pencil
oh	as in go, note	ur	as in term
oo	as in too	y	as in line, fly
sh	as in shy	zh	as in vision, measure
th	as in thin		

diastolic pressure (dy-uh-STO-lik   PRE-shur) the pressure of the blood in the veins between heartbeats; the second number in a blood pressure reading, such as 120/80

dicot (DY-kot) a plant whose seeds have two seed leaves

diffusion (di-FYOO-zhun) the movement of molecules from an area of higher concentration to an area of lower concentration

digestive tract (di-JES-tiv   TRAKT) the system that breaks food down into nutrients that the body can use

diploid cells (DY-ployd   SELZ) cells that contain two sets of chromosomes, with one set from each parent

disk (DISK) a small, circular cushion between the bones of the spine

division (duh-VI-zhun) the second-highest level of classification for plants, between kingdom and class

DNA (DEE-EN-AY) the molecules in a cell that contain genetic information that determines the structure and function of the cell; abbreviation for *deoxyribonucleic acid*

DNA polymerase (DEE-EN-AY   PO-luh-muh-rays) an enzyme that unwinds the double helix of DNA molecules during mitosis

dominant (DO-muh-nunt) a gene or trait that always shows itself

---

PRONUNCIATION KEY

CAPITAL LETTERS show the stressed syllables.

a	as in mat	f	as in fit
ay	as in day, say	g	as in go
ch	as in chew	i	as in sit
e	as in bed	j	as in job, gem
ee	as in even, easy, need	k	as in cool, key

double helix (DU-bul HEE-liks) the twisted, ladderlike shape of two DNA strands wrapped around each other

duodenum (doo-uh-DEE-num) the first section of the small intestine

ear canal (IR kuh-NAL) a narrow chamber of the ear through which sound waves enter

ecologist (i-KO-luh-jist) a person who studies how living things interact

ecology (i-KO-luh-jee) the study of interactions among living things

ecosystem (EE-koh-sis-tum) the plants, animals, and nonliving things that make up a community and its environment, and the relationships between these living and nonliving things

ectoderm (EK-tuh-durm) the outer layer of cells in an embryo that will develop into the skin and nervous system

effectors (i-FEK-turz) tissues that become active in response to nerve impulses

egg (EG) the female reproductive cell

ejaculation (i-ja-kyuh-LAY-shun) the discharge of sperm from the male penis

elastin (i-LAS-tun) a protein that helps skin go back to its normal shape after it has been stretched

---

PRONUNCIATION KEY

CAPITAL LETTERS show the stressed syllables.

ng as in runni**ng**	u as in b**u**t, some
o as in c**o**t, f**a**ther	uh as in **a**bout, tak**e**n, lem**o**n, penc**i**l
oh as in g**o**, n**o**te	ur as in t**er**m
oo as in t**oo**	y as in l**i**ne, fl**y**
sh as in **sh**y	zh as in vi**s**ion, mea**s**ure
th as in **th**in	

element (E-luh-munt) one of the fundamental substances, such as oxygen and carbon, that can be combined to make up all matter; each element contains atoms of only one kind.

embryo (EM-bree-oh) the early stage of growth of a plant or an animal after an egg is fertilized

endocrine system (EN-duh-krun   SIS-tum) the system of glands and hormones that helps regulate other body systems, such as heart rate and glucose levels in the blood

endoderm (EN-duh-durm) the inner layer of cells in an embryo that will develop into the digestive and respiratory systems

endometrium (en-doh-MEE-tree-um) the thick, blood-rich lining of the uterus during ovulation

endoplasmic reticulum (ER) (en-duh-PLAZ-mik   ri-TI-kyuh-lum) (EE-AR) a network of folded membranes within the cell that manufactures and stores many chemicals

energy (E-nur-jee) the ability to do work

enzymes (EN-zymz) proteins produced by living cells that can speed up or slow down biological reactions such as the digestion of food

epidermis (e-puh-DUR-mus) the outermost layer of skin

---

epiglottis (e-puh-GLO-tus) a flap of tissue that keeps food and liquids from entering the windpipe

epinephrine (e-puh-NE-frun) a hormone produced by the adrenal glands that provides you with a surge of energy

epiphytes (E-puh-fyts) plants that grow in trees instead of soil

esophagus (i-SO-fuh-guhs) the tube that moves food from the mouth to the stomach

essential amino acids (i-SEN-shul   uh-MEE-noh   A-suds) amino acids that are necessary for growth but that cannot be made in the body and so must be obtained from food

estrogen (ES-truh-jun) a female sex hormone that triggers the development of secondary sex characteristics, such as the development of breasts and the widening of the hips

eubacteria (yoo-bak-TIR-ee-uh) single-celled organisms with no cell nucleus that are more complex than archaebacteria

eukaryote (yoo-KAR-ee-oht) a cell that has a nucleus

evaporation (i-va-puh-RAY-shun) changing from a liquid to a gas

evolution (e-vuh-LOO-shun) the gradual change in organisms over time

---

PRONUNCIATION KEY

CAPITAL LETTERS show the stressed syllables.

ng as in runni**ng**	u as in b**u**t, s**o**me
o as in c**o**t, f**a**ther	uh as in **a**bout, tak**e**n, lem**o**n, penc**i**l
oh as in g**o**, n**o**te	ur as in t**er**m
oo as in t**oo**	y as in l**i**ne, fl**y**
sh as in **sh**y	zh as in vi**s**ion, mea**s**ure
th as in **th**in	

exoskeleton (ek-soh-SKE-luh-tun) a hard outer covering found around the body of some invertebrates such as insects

extinct (ik-STINKT) no longer existing

fallopian tube (fuh-LOH-pee-un TOOB) a tube in mammals through which the egg travels from an ovary to the uterus

family (FAM-lee) in classification, a grouping of related genera; a subdivision of order

fat-soluble (FAT-SOL-yuh-bul) needing fats to be digested, absorbed, and carried through the body

feces (FEE-seez) solid waste material left over at the end of the digestive process, which is expelled from the body

ferns (FURNZ) vascular plants, with leaflike fronds, that reproduce by spores

fertilization (fur-tul-uh-ZAY-shun) the joining of male and female reproductive cells

fetus (FEE-tus) a developing young mammal in the uterus

fibers (FY-burs) specialized cells that make up muscles

fibroblasts (FY-bruh-blasts) cells found in connective tissue that secrete collagen and elastin

---

PRONUNCIATION KEY

CAPITAL LETTERS show the stressed syllables.

a	as in mat	f	as in fit
ay	as in day, say	g	as in go
ch	as in chew	i	as in sit
e	as in bed	j	as in job, gem
ee	as in even, easy, need	k	as in cool, key

Glossary • Biology

fibrous root system (FY-brus ROOT SIS-tum) a root system made up of many stringy roots that cling to the soil

filaments (FI-luh-munts) 1. the threadlike chains of cells that make up fungi; 2. the thin parts of a plant's stamen that support the pollen-containing anthers

first order consumer (FIRST OR-dur kon-SOO-mur) animal that eats only plants

fitness (FIT-nus) an individual's ability to reproduce and pass on its genes

flagella (fluh-JE-luh) whiplike structures that move simple organisms around; the singular form is *flagellum.*

follicle (FA-li-kul) a small sac or pore, such as those in the skin from which hairs grow, and those in the ovary where eggs develop

follicle stimulating hormone (FSH) (FA-li-kul STIM-yuh-lay-ting HOR-mohn) (EF-ES-AYCH) a hormone released by the pituitary gland that triggers ovulation in females and sperm production in males

food chain (FOOD CHAYN) a series of organisms in which each organism uses the next one as a food source

---

PRONUNCIATION KEY

CAPITAL LETTERS show the stressed syllables.

ng as in runni**ng**	u as in b**u**t, s**o**me
o as in c**o**t, f**a**ther	uh as in **a**bout, tak**e**n, lem**o**n, penc**i**l
oh as in g**o**, n**o**te	ur as in t**er**m
oo as in t**oo**	y as in l**i**ne, fl**y**
sh as in **sh**y	zh as in vi**s**ion, mea**s**ure
th as in **th**in	

food pyramid (FOOD PIR-uh-mid) 1. guideline prepared by the USDA that shows the number of servings of different kinds of foods you should get every day; 2. a pyramid-shaped diagram that shows food relationships among organisms in an ecosystem; the chief predator appears at the top of the pyramid and each level preys on the level below, with plants on the bottom level.

food web (FOOD WEB) all the possible feeding relationships in an ecosystem

fossil record (FO-sul RE-kurd) the traces of ancient organisms that are preserved in earth and rock and that help scientists understand when different organisms were alive, where they lived, and what they looked like

fronds (FRONDZ) large, feathery leaves

frontal lobe (FRUN-tul LOHB) the part of the cerebrum at the front of the head, responsible for speech, movement, emotional control, and thinking processes such as problem solving and decision making

fungi (FUN-jy) organisms that have cell walls and do not produce chlorophyll; examples: mushrooms, molds, yeast; the singular form is *fungus.*

gallbladder (GOL-bla-dur) a small organ that stores bile

gametes (GA-meets) sex cells

PRONUNCIATION KEY

CAPITAL LETTERS show the stressed syllables.

a	as in mat	f	as in fit
ay	as in day, say	g	as in go
ch	as in chew	i	as in sit
e	as in bed	j	as in job, gem
ee	as in even, easy, need	k	as in cool, key

gastropods (GAS-truh-podz) mollusks with a muscular foot and either a single shell or no shell at all; include snails and slugs

gastrulation (gas-truh-LAY-shun) process in the development of the embryo during which cells in the blastoderm develop differences and form layers

gene (JEEN) a factor that controls inherited traits

gene pool (JEEN POOL) the sum of all the genes in a population

genotype (JEE-nuh-typ) the genetic makeup of an individual organism

genus (JEE-nus) in classification, a group of related species; subdivision of family

geotropism (JEE-uh-troh-pi-zum) the tendency for plant roots to move downward in response to gravity

germinate (JUR-muh-nayt) start to grow

gill slits (GIL SLITS) structures in water-dwelling organisms that filter food and oxygen from the water

gills (GILZ) organs that filter food and oxygen from water

glands (GLANDZ) organs that make chemical substances such as sweat and bile that are used or released by the body

---

PRONUNCIATION KEY

CAPITAL LETTERS show the stressed syllables.

ng	as in running	u	as in but, some
o	as in cot, father	uh	as in about, taken, lemon, pencil
oh	as in go, note	ur	as in term
oo	as in too	y	as in line, fly
sh	as in shy	zh	as in vision, measure
th	as in thin		

glial cells (GLEE-ul SELZ) cells that support and protect nerve cells in the brain

glomerulus (gluh-MER-uh-lus) a knot of blood vessels inside the Bowman's capsules of the kidney

glucagon (GLOO-kuh-gon) one of two hormones that control sugar levels in the blood

glucose (GLOO-kohs) a sugar that is an important source of energy in plants and animals

glycogen (GLY-kuh-jun) the form in which glucose is stored in the liver and muscles

Golgi complex (GOL-jee KOM-pleks) a series of flattened sacs within a cell where materials are modified and distributed to other parts of the cell

gram-negative (GRAM-NE-guh-tiv) refers to bacteria that do not react to a certain dye

gram-positive (GRAM-PO-zuh-tiv) refers to bacteria that react to a certain dye by turning purple

grassland (GRAS-land) an ecosystem in which grasses are the most common plant and few trees or shrubs are found

---

PRONUNCIATION KEY

CAPITAL LETTERS show the stressed syllables.

a	as in mat	f	as in fit
ay	as in day, say	g	as in go
ch	as in chew	i	as in sit
e	as in bed	j	as in job, gem
ee	as in even, easy, need	k	as in cool, key

greenhouse effect (GREEN-haus i-FEKT) the warming effect on Earth's atmosphere created when carbon dioxide and other gases trap heat in the atmosphere

ground substance (GROWND SUB-stunts) a gel-like substance that fills the spaces between cells and proteins in the skin

growth hormone (GROHTH HOR-mohn) a chemical in plants or animals that regulates growth

guanine (GWO-neen) one of the bases that make up the genetic code of DNA and RNA

gymnosperms (JIM-nuh-spurmz) plants that produce uncovered seeds such as pine cones

habitat (HA-buh-tat) the type of place where an organism usually lives

hair (HAYR) a slender, threadlike growth made up mostly of keratin

haploid cells (HA-ploid SELZ) cells with only one set of chromosomes; usually sex cells

Haversian canal (huh-VUR-zhun kuh-NAL) thin canal within bone tissue that carries nutrients and oxygen

Haversian systems (huh-VUR-zhun SIS-tums) in compact bone, tightly stacked rods that contain layers of minerals and collagen

---

PRONUNCIATION KEY

CAPITAL LETTERS show the stressed syllables.

ng as in runni**ng**	u as in b**u**t, s**o**me
o as in c**o**t, f**a**ther	uh as in **a**bout, tak**e**n, lem**o**n, penc**i**l
oh as in g**o**, n**o**te	ur as in t**er**m
oo as in t**oo**	y as in l**i**ne, fl**y**
sh as in **sh**y	zh as in vi**s**ion, mea**s**ure
th as in **th**in	

heart (HART) the organ that pumps to move blood through the circulatory system

hemisphere (HE-muh-sfir) one of the two halves of the cerebrum

hemocoels (HEE-muh-seelz) in arthropods and mollusks, the spaces between the organs that blood flows through

hemoglobin (HEE-muh-gloh-bun) the part of red blood cells that can carry oxygen

herbivore (UR-buh-vohr) an animal that eats plants

herbivory (ur-BI-vuh-ree) eating plants

heredity (her-ED-i-tee) the passing on of characteristics from parent to offspring

heterozygous (he-tuh-roh-ZY-gus) having two different forms of a gene for the same trait, one from each parent

hindbrain (HYND-brayn) the part of the brain behind the spinal cord that includes the cerebellum and the medulla

histamine (HIS-tuh-meen) a chemical released by white blood cells and damaged skin cells that causes blood vessels to dilate

histones (HIS-tohns) proteins that help package DNA into chromosomes

---

PRONUNCIATION KEY

CAPITAL LETTERS show the stressed syllables.

a	as in m**a**t	f	as in **f**it
ay	as in d**ay**, s**ay**	g	as in **g**o
ch	as in **ch**ew	i	as in s**i**t
e	as in b**e**d	j	as in **j**ob, **g**em
ee	as in **e**ven, **ea**sy, n**ee**d	k	as in **c**ool, **k**ey

homologous (hoh-MO-luh-gus) similar in appearance and structure, but not necessarily having the same function

homozygous (hoh-muh-ZY-gus) having two like genes for the same trait

hormones (HOR-mohnz) chemical messengers that are produced in one part of an organism and affect another part

horsetails (HORS-taylz) ancient vascular plants that look like reeds with evenly spaced joints along the stem

hydrochloric acid (hy-druh-KLOHR-ik   A-sud) a powerful acid (molecular formula HCl) secreted in the stomach that starts the chemical digestion process

hydrotropism (hy-DRO-truh-pi-zum) plant movement in response to water

hypha (HY-fuh) a long, threadlike chain of cells that is the basic structure of the fungus; the plural form is *hyphae.*

hypothalamus (hy-poh-THA-luh-mus) area of the brain above the pituitary gland that secretes hormones and regulates heart rate, blood pressure, body temperature, and appetite

ileum (I-lee-um) part of the small intestine

immune (i-MYOON) resistant to, not affected by

PRONUNCIATION KEY

CAPITAL LETTERS show the stressed syllables.

ng as in running	u as in but, some
o as in cot, father	uh as in about, taken, lemon, pencil
oh as in go, note	ur as in term
oo as in too	y as in line, fly
sh as in shy	zh as in vision, measure
th as in thin	

immune system (i-MYOON SIS-tum) the system that protects the body against foreign substances and things that might cause disease

impermeable (im-PUR-mee-uh-bul) unable to be penetrated

incus (IN-kus) one of the tiny bones in the middle ear; also called the *anvil*

inhibin (in-HI-bun) a hormone that stops the production of follicle-stimulating hormone, or FSH

inhibitors (in-HI-buh-turz) molecules that prevent chemical reactions in a muscle that is in a relaxed state

insects (IN-sekts) small, six-legged invertebrates whose bodies are divided into three distinct parts

insulin (IN-suh-lun) a chemical produced in the pancreas that controls blood sugar levels

interferons (in-tuh-FIR-onz) proteins secreted when cells are infected by a virus that protect other cells from the virus

interphase (IN-tur-fayz) growth period of a cell during which the chromosomes are duplicated

interspecific competition (in-tur-spi-SI-fik kom-puh-TI-shun) competition between individuals of different species

---

Glossary • Biology

intraspecific competition (in-truh-spi-SI-fik   kom-puh-TI-shun) competition between individuals of the same species

invertebrate (in-VUR-tuh-brut) an animal that has no backbone

ion (Y-un) an atom that has either a positive charge or a negative charge

iris (Y-rus) the colored part of the eye that controls the size of the pupil

jawless fish (JO-lus   FISH) a group of fish that do not have true jaws; they usually eat by suction.

jejunum (ji-JOO-num) a section of the small intestine

joints (JOINTS) places in the body where two or more bones meet; for example, knees, elbows, hips

keratin (KER-uh-tun) a protein that makes up human hair and fingernails and the top layer of human skin

kidneys (KID-neez) organs that remove impurities from the blood

kingdom (KING-dum) in classification, the most general of the seven levels

large intestine (LARJ   in-TES-tun) the lower part of the digestive system, which receives a soupy mix of digested food from the small intestine, absorbs most of the fluids, and passes the remaining material out of the body through the anus

---

PRONUNCIATION KEY

CAPITAL LETTERS show the stressed syllables.

ng	as in running	u	as in but, some
o	as in cot, father	uh	as in about, taken, lemon, pencil
oh	as in go, note	ur	as in term
oo	as in too	y	as in line, fly
sh	as in shy	zh	as in vision, measure
th	as in thin		

larvae (LAR-vee) organisms at an immature stage of development in which they look different from the adult form; the singular form is *larva.*

larynx (LAR-inks) the boxlike entrance to the windpipe that contains the vocal cords

leaves (LEEVZ) the parts of plants that grow from a stem or twig and make food by photosynthesis; the singular form is *leaf.*

legumes (LE-gyooms) plants, such as alfalfa and soybeans, that have bacteria in their roots that convert nitrogen to a form the plant can use, thus adding nitrogen to the soil

lens (LENZ) the transparent, flexible part of the eye that focuses light entering the eye

lichen (LY-kun) a symbiotic relationship between an alga and a fungus

ligaments (LI-guh-munts) strong, flexible cords made of collagen that hold bones together at joints

light phase (LYT   FAYZ) the stage of photosynthesis that is driven by energy from the sun

limbic system (LIM-bik   SIS-tum) structures in the brain that control emotions

lipase (LY-pays) an enzyme produced by the pancreas that breaks fats down as part of the digestive process

---

PRONUNCIATION KEY

CAPITAL LETTERS show the stressed syllables.

a	as in m**a**t	f	as in **f**it
ay	as in d**ay**, s**ay**	g	as in **g**o
ch	as in **ch**ew	i	as in s**i**t
e	as in b**e**d	j	as in **j**ob, **g**em
ee	as in **e**ven, **ea**sy, n**ee**d	k	as in **c**ool, **k**ey

lipids (LI-puds) fats and oils

liver (LI-vur) a large organ that converts sugar to glycogen; removes and stores excess cholesterol; and produces bile, which is used to digest fat

loop of Henle (LOOP UV HEN-lee) U-shaped section in the kidney that helps adjust the concentration of water in urine

luteinizing hormone (LH) (LOO-tee-uh-ny-zing HOR-mohn) a hormone that stimulates ovulation in females and sperm production in males

lycopod (LY-cuh-pod) primitive evergreen mosslike plant that uses spores to reproduce

lymph (LIMF) a clear fluid that contains white blood cells and circulates through the body, removing bacteria and certain proteins from tissues and transporting fat from the small intestines

lymph nodes (LIMF NOHDZ) nodes that filter particles from lymph and produce and house cells of the immune system

lymphatic system (lim-FA-tik SIS-tum) a network of vessels that returns fluid lost by the blood to the circulatory system

lymphocytes (LIM-fuh-syts) disease-fighting white blood cells

lysosomes (LY-suh-sohmz) enzyme-containing cell parts that help digest food and break down old cell parts

---

PRONUNCIATION KEY

CAPITAL LETTERS show the stressed syllables.

ng	as in running	u	as in but, some
o	as in cot, father	uh	as in about, taken, lemon, pencil
oh	as in go, note	ur	as in term
oo	as in too	y	as in line, fly
sh	as in shy	zh	as in vision, measure
th	as in thin		

M phase (EM FAYZ) stage of the cell cycle when cell division takes place; the M stands for mitosis.

macrophage (MA-kruh-fayj) phagocyte cell of the immune system that destroys pathogens and toxins and displays their antigens

malleus (MA-lee-us) tiny, outermost bone in the middle ear, also known as the *hammer*

maltose (MOL-tohs) a sugar formed when digestive enzymes begin to break down starch

mammal (MA-mul) a warmblooded, highly developed vertebrate that has body hair and produces milk to feed its young

mammary glands (MA-muh-ree GLANDZ) glands in female mammals that produce milk

mantle (MAN-tul) the thin sheet of tissue in mollusks that surrounds the internal organs and usually creates a shell

marrow (MAR-oh) the soft tissue inside bones; yellow marrow is high in fat and red marrow makes blood cells.

marsupial (mar-SOO-pee-ul) a mammal that gives birth to undeveloped embryos, which are then carried in an exterior pouch until they are ready to survive on their own

---

PRONUNCIATION KEY

CAPITAL LETTERS show the stressed syllables.

a	as in mat	f	as in fit
ay	as in day, say	g	as in go
ch	as in chew	i	as in sit
e	as in bed	j	as in job, gem
ee	as in even, easy, need	k	as in cool, key

mast cells (MAST SELZ) phagocytes that help stimulate the immune response when the skin gets injured

medulla (muh-DUH-luh) part of the brain that controls involuntary functions

medusa (mi-DOO-suh) the umbrella-shaped, free-swimming stage of some cnidarians

meiosis (mee-OH-sus) cell division process that creates sex cells

meiotic interphase (mee-O-tik IN-tur-fayz) the period between meiosis I and meiosis II in the cell division process

melanin (ME-luh-nun) pigment that gives skin its color and protects the skin from harmful ultraviolet radiation from the sun

membrane (MEM-brayn) a thin, flexible sheet or layer

meninges (muh-NIN-jeez) three protective membranes inside the skull

menstrual cycle (MEN-stroo-ul SY-kul) the four-week cycle during which an oocyte matures into an egg and travels to the uterus, and the blood-rich endometrium is then shed

mesoderm (ME-zuh-durm) the middle layer of cells in an embryo that will develop into the skeletal, muscular, and circulatory systems

---

PRONUNCIATION KEY

CAPITAL LETTERS show the stressed syllables.

ng	as in running	u	as in but, some
o	as in cot, father	uh	as in about, taken, lemon, pencil
oh	as in go, note	ur	as in term
oo	as in too	y	as in line, fly
sh	as in shy	zh	as in vision, measure
th	as in thin		

mesoglea (me-zuh-GLEE-uh) fluidlike substance in a cnidarian that acts like a skeleton, giving the animal its shape

messenger RNA (mRNA) and (ME-sun-jur   AR-EN-AY) type of RNA involved in protein synthesis

metabolism (mu-TA-buh-li-zum) the rate at which cells produce chemical changes in substances, creating energy

metamorphosis (me-tuh-MOR-fuh-sus) a change in body type or structure during life, as with a caterpillar becoming a butterfly

metaphase (ME-tuh-fayz) second stage of mitosis or meiosis in which spindles arrange the chromosomes in the middle of the cell

microscopic (my-kruh-SKO-pik) able to be seen only when magnified by a microscope

mimicry (MI-mi-kree) resemblance of one living thing to another or to natural objects that gives an advantage, such as protection from predators

mitochondria (my-tuh-KON-dree-uh) round or rod-shaped structures in a cell in which food molecules are broken down to produce energy; the singular form is *mitochondrion.*

mitosis (my-TOH-sus) cell division process during which chromosomes are equally distributed to the two daughter cells

---

PRONUNCIATION KEY

CAPITAL LETTERS show the stressed syllables.

a	as in mat	f	as in fit
ay	as in day, say	g	as in go
ch	as in chew	i	as in sit
e	as in bed	j	as in job, gem
ee	as in even, easy, need	k	as in cool, key

molecules (MO-li-kyoolz) a group of two or more atoms held together by a bond

mollusks (MO-lusks) soft-bodied invertebrates that usually have a shell

molting (MOL-ting) process in which a creature sheds its outer covering, hair, shell, feathers, or horns, which are then replaced with new growth

monocot (MO-nuh-kot) a flowering plant with one seed leaf in each seed

motor cortex (MOH-tur   KOR-teks) region of the brain's frontal lobe that controls voluntary muscle movement

mucous membrane (MYOO-kus   MEM-brayn) tissue that lines the inside of the nasal passages

mucus (MYOO-kus) slippery substance produced by mucous membranes to moisten and protect body areas; also produced by snails and slugs to slide along on top of

muscles (MUH-sulz) tissues that are attached to the bones and aid in movement, assist organs in their work, or are part of the heart

muscular foot (MUHS-kyuh-lur   FUT) strong appendage used by many mollusks to move, to grip surfaces, and to dig into the ground

mutagens (MYOO-tuh-junz) agents that cause mutations

mutate (MYOO-tayt) to go through mutation

PRONUNCIATION KEY

CAPITAL LETTERS show the stressed syllables.

ng	as in running	u	as in but, some
o	as in cot, father	uh	as in about, taken, lemon, pencil
oh	as in go, note	ur	as in term
oo	as in too	y	as in line, fly
sh	as in shy	zh	as in vision, measure
th	as in thin		

mutation (myoo-TAY-shun) a physical change in a chromosome or a chemical change in a gene that is inherited

mutualism (MYOO-chuh-wuh-li-zum) relationship between different kinds of organisms in which both organisms benefit

mycelium (my-SEE-lee-um) in fungi, an interwoven mat made up of branching hyphae

myelin sheath (MY-uh-lun   SHEETH) a fatty layer that surrounds some nerve fibers

myosin (MY-uh-sun) long, ropelike proteins in muscles

myosin heads (MY-uh-sun   HEDZ) a series of extensions, or ratchets, on strands of myosin

natural selection (NA-chuh-rul   suh-LEK-shun) changes in populations that occur when organisms with favorable variations for a particular environment survive and pass on those variations

nectar (NEK-tur) sweet liquid produced by flowers to entice insects, birds, and bats to pollinate them

nematodes (NE-muh-tohdz) invertebrate phylum that includes all roundworms

nephrons (NE-fronz) tiny structures in the kidneys that filter wastes from the blood

---

PRONUNCIATION KEY

CAPITAL LETTERS show the stressed syllables.

a	as in m**a**t	f	as in **f**it
ay	as in d**ay**, s**ay**	g	as in **g**o
ch	as in **ch**ew	i	as in s**i**t
e	as in b**e**d	j	as in **j**ob, **g**em
ee	as in **e**ven, **ea**sy, n**ee**d	k	as in **c**ool, **k**ey

nervous system (NER-vus SIS-tum) body system that includes the brain, spinal cord, and all peripheral nerves

neurons (NOO-ronz) tightly wound bundles of cells that make up nerves

neurotransmitters (nur-oh-trans-MI-turs) substances that transmit nerve impulses across a synaptic gap

niche (neesh) the part an organism plays in an ecological community

nitrogen-containing base (NY-truh-jun-kun-TAYN-ing BAYS) DNA base that is composed of one or two rings of nitrogen and carbon

nodes (NOHDZ) a distinct mass of one kind of tissue enclosed in tissue of a different kind

nodes of Ranvier (NOHDZ UV RON-vee-ay) nodes of nerve fibers; impulses jump from node to node to allow for a fast transfer of nervous information

nondisjunction (non-dis-JUNK-shun) failure of chromosomes to separate properly

nonvascular plants (non-VAS-kyuh-lur PLANTS) plants that cannot store and transport water

norepinephrine (NOR-e-puh-NE-frun) a neurotransmitter, and an energy-producing hormone in the adrenal glands

---

PRONUNCIATION KEY

CAPITAL LETTERS show the stressed syllables.

ng	as in running	u	as in but, some
o	as in cot, father	uh	as in about, taken, lemon, pencil
oh	as in go, note	ur	as in term
oo	as in too	y	as in line, fly
sh	as in shy	zh	as in vision, measure
th	as in thin		

notochord (NOH-tuh-kord) a strong but flexible rod of cells found under the nerve cord; in vertebrates, the structure from which the backbone develops

nuclear envelope (NOO-klee-ur   EN-vuh-lohp) the membrane that surrounds the nucleus

nucleic acids (nu-KLEE-ik   A-sudz) complex organic acids that form nucleotide chains; the major ones are DNA and RNA, and contain an organism's basic genetic information

nucleoid (NOO-klee-oid) a region of cytoplasm where the cell's DNA is found

nucleoli (noo-KLEE-uh-ly) organelles within the nucleus where ribosomal RNA is produced; the singular form is *nucleolus.*

nucleotides (NOO-klee-uh-tydz) long chains of compounds that are the basic structural units of nucleic acids

nucleus (NOO-klee-us) the part of a cell that controls many of the functions of the cell and contains the organism's DNA

occipital lobe (ok-SI-puh-tul   LOHB) section at the back of the brain that processes visual information

offspring (OF-spring) new organisms produced by living things

omnivore (OM-ni-vohr) a consumer that eats both plants and animals

---

PRONUNCIATION KEY

CAPITAL LETTERS show the stressed syllables.

a	as in mat	f	as in fit
ay	as in day, say	g	as in go
ch	as in chew	i	as in sit
e	as in bed	j	as in job, gem
ee	as in even, easy, need	k	as in cool, key

oogenesis (oh-uh-JE-nuh-sus) the process by which eggs are formed and mature

oogonia (oh-uh-GOH-nee-uh) diploid cells that begin the process of meiosis in the developing fetus

optic nerve (OP-tik NURV) bundle of neurons that carries visual information from the retina of the eye to the brain

order (OR-dur) in classification, a group of related families

organ (OR-gan) group of specialized tissues that perform an activity together

organelles (or-guh-NELZ) small structures inside cells that have specialized functions

organic molecules (or-GA-nik MO-li-kyoolz) large molecules made up mostly of carbon atoms that are unique to living things and make life possible

organism (OR-guh-ni-zum) a living thing

osmosis (oz-MOH-sus) movement of water across a semipermeable membrane from a high concentration to a low concentration

osteocytes (OS-tee-uh-syts) cells that maintain compact bones by synthesizing collagen and assembling minerals

---

PRONUNCIATION KEY

CAPITAL LETTERS show the stressed syllables.

ng	as in running	u	as in but, some
o	as in cot, father	uh	as in about, taken, lemon, pencil
oh	as in go, note	ur	as in term
oo	as in too	y	as in line, fly
sh	as in shy	zh	as in vision, measure
th	as in thin		

ovaries (OH-vuh-rees) female reproductive organs

oviduct (OH-vuh-dukt) tube through which the egg cell travels from an ovary to the uterus in mammals

ovulation (ov-yuh-LAY-shun) the release of a mature egg cell from an ovary

pacemaker (PAYS-may-kur) a node in the right atrium of the heart that sends signals that establish and maintain a steady heartbeat

pancreas (PAN-kree-us) a large gland that produces digestive enzymes and the hormones insulin and glucagon

parasites (PAR-uh-syts) organisms that live in, on, or with other organisms, usually gaining benefits while causing harm to the hosts

parasitism (PAR-uh-suh-ti-zum) a close association between two organisms in which a parasite benefits while harming the host

parietal lobe (puh-RY-uh-tul   LOHB) section of the brain that processes nerve impulses related to body sensations; it helps maintain balance.

partial pressure (PAR-shul   PRE-shur) the pressure exerted by each individual gas in a mixture of gases

passive transport (PA-siv   trans-POHRT) the movement of molecules across a cell membrane without use of energy by the cell

pathogens (PA-thuh-junz) organisms that invade the bodies of larger organisms and cause disease

---

PRONUNCIATION KEY

CAPITAL LETTERS show the stressed syllables.

a	as in mat	f	as in fit
ay	as in day, say	g	as in go
ch	as in chew	i	as in sit
e	as in bed	j	as in job, gem
ee	as in even, easy, need	k	as in cool, key

pectoral girdle (PEK-tuh-rul GUR-dul) the arch of bones or cartilage that supports the forelimbs of a vertebrate

pedipalps (PE-duh-palps) second pair of mouthparts on an arachnid

pelvic girdle (PEL-vik GUR-dul) the arch of bones or cartilage that supports the hind limbs of a vertebrate

penis (PEE-nus) the male sex organ through which sperm flow

pepsin (PEP-sun) a protein-cutting enzyme produced in the stomach

peripheral nervous system (per-I-fur-al NER-vus SIS-tum) all nerves in the human body except the brain and spinal cord

peristalsis (per-uh-STOL-sus) waves of involuntary, coordinated muscle contractions during the process of digestion

permeable (PUR-mee-uh-bul) able to allow fluids and particles to pass through

petals (PE-tulz) leaflike flower parts, often brightly colored or perfumed

phagocytes (FA-guh-syts) cells such as white blood cells that engulf and consume foreign materials such as invading bacteria and debris

pharynx (FAR-inks) a muscular tube in vertebrates that extends from the back of the mouth and nasal cavity to the esophagus; air and food pass through it.

PRONUNCIATION KEY

CAPITAL LETTERS show the stressed syllables.

ng	as in running	u	as in but, some
o	as in cot, father	uh	as in about, taken, lemon, pencil
oh	as in go, note	ur	as in term
oo	as in too	y	as in line, fly
sh	as in shy	zh	as in vision, measure
th	as in thin		

phenotype (FEE-nuh-typ) a trait that you can see on an individual organism

phloem (FLOH-em) tissue in the roots, stems, and leaves of higher plants that carries dissolved food through tubes from those parts to other parts of the plant

phosphate (FOS-fayt) an organic compound made up of a phosphorus atom surrounded by three oxygen atoms

photosynthesis (foh-toh-SIN-thuh-sus) a process in which plants and some other organisms use energy from the sun to convert water and carbon dioxide to food

phototropism (foh-TO-truh-pi-zum) plant movement in response to light

phylum (FY-lum) a level of classification below kingdom; the broadest group within each kingdom

physical adaptation (FI-zi-kul   a-dap-TAY-shun) a physical change in an organism that helps it survive in a particular environment

pistil (PIS-tul) female part of a flower

pituitary gland (puh-TOO-uh-ter-ee   GLAND) gland in the human brain that secretes growth hormones and reproductive hormones

placenta (pluh-SEN-tuh) organ developed during pregnancy that supplies the fetus or embryo with food, water, and oxygen

PRONUNCIATION KEY

CAPITAL LETTERS show the stressed syllables.

a	as in mat	f	as in fit
ay	as in day, say	g	as in go
ch	as in chew	i	as in sit
e	as in bed	j	as in job, gem
ee	as in even, easy, need	k	as in cool, key

placental (pluh-SEN-tul) a mammal that is fully developed at birth

plasmodium (plaz-MOH-dee-um) a community of slime molds

platelets (PLAYT-luts) tiny disks in mammals' blood that helps blood to clot

platyhelminthes (pla-ti-HEL-min-theez) invertebrate phylum that includes flatworms such as tapeworms

polarization (poh-luh-ruh-ZAY-shun) the process by which the inside of a cell becomes more negatively charged than the outside of the cell

pollen (PO-lun) microspores in a seed plant that appear as a fine yellow dust and contain the male reproductive cells of the plant

pollination (po-luh-NAY-shun) the transfer of pollen from the anther to the stigma

polygenic traits (po-lee-JEE-nik   TRAYTS) traits that are determined by more than one gene

polyp (PO-lup) an invertebrate that has a hollow, tubelike body

population (po-pyuh-LAY-shun) a group of organisms of the same species living in one area

pores (POHRS) tiny openings in animals or plants, especially those that allow matter to pass through a membrane

---

PRONUNCIATION KEY

CAPITAL LETTERS show the stressed syllables.

ng as in runni**ng**	u as in b**u**t, s**o**me
o as in c**o**t, f**a**ther	uh as in **a**bout, tak**e**n, lem**o**n, penc**i**l
oh as in g**o**, n**o**te	ur as in t**er**m
oo as in t**oo**	y as in l**i**ne, fl**y**
sh as in **sh**y	zh as in vi**s**ion, mea**s**ure
th as in **th**in	

poriferan (poh-RIF-ur-un) invertebrate phylum containing sponges

precipitation (pri-si-puh-TAY-shun) water that falls to earth as rain, snow, sleet, hail, or mist

predation (pri-DAY-shun) the act of hunting or killing for food

predator (PRE-duh-tur) an animal that hunts and kills another organism for food

prefrontal area (pree-FRUN-tul   AR-ee-uh) area at the front of the brain's frontal lobe that sorts out all the sensory information your occipital and temporal lobes receive and places it into context

prey (PRAY) an organism that is hunted and killed by another organism for food

primary consumers (PRY-mer-ee   kun-SOO-murz) organisms that get their energy by eating producers

primary oocytes (PRY-mer-ee   OH-uh-syts) immature eggs that remain in prophase I for years

producers (pruh-DOO-surz) organisms that use the sun's energy to convert carbon dioxide into a simple sugar called glucose

progesterone (proh-JES-tuh-rohn) a female sex hormone that stimulates changes in the uterus so it will accept a fertilized egg and nourish the developing embryo

PRONUNCIATION KEY

CAPITAL LETTERS show the stressed syllables.

a	as in m**a**t	f	as in **f**it
ay	as in d**ay**, s**ay**	g	as in **g**o
ch	as in **ch**ew	i	as in s**i**t
e	as in b**e**d	j	as in **j**ob, **g**em
ee	as in **e**ven, **ea**sy, n**ee**d	k	as in **c**ool, **k**ey

prokaryote (proh-KAR-ee-oht) a cell that does not have a nucleus

prolactin (proh-LAK-tun) a pituitary hormone that triggers the mammary glands in the mother's breasts to produce milk

prophase (PROH-fayz) the first stage of mitosis, in which the nucleus begins to change greatly; also the first stage of meiosis, in which chromosomes become visible under a microscope

prostate gland (PROS-tayt GLAND) doughnut-shaped gland in males that produces semen, the fluid that transports sperm

prothallus (proh-THA-lus) the gametophyte generation in ferns and other spore-bearing plants

protist (PROH-tist) simple organism with cell walls and nuclei; many are single-celled, but some have many cells.

protozoans (proh-tuh-ZOH-unz) protists that behave very much like animals in many ways

pseudocoelom (soo-duh-SEE-lum) cavity, or hollow place, in roundworms outside the digestive tract, filled with fluid that helps cushion the digestive tract and also acts as a skeleton

pseudopod (SOO-doh-pod) temporary cytoplasm "feet" used by amoebas for movement and catching prey

---

PRONUNCIATION KEY

CAPITAL LETTERS show the stressed syllables.

ng	as in running	u	as in but, some
o	as in cot, father	uh	as in about, taken, lemon, pencil
oh	as in go, note	ur	as in term
oo	as in too	y	as in line, fly
sh	as in shy	zh	as in vision, measure
th	as in thin		

puberty (PYOO-bur-tee) the period during which young mammals become sexually mature

pulmonary (PUL-muh-ner-ee) relating to the lungs

pulmonary artery (PUL-muh-ner-ee   AR-tuh-ree) artery that brings venous blood (oxygen-depleted blood from the veins) from the heart to the lungs

pulmonary veins (PUL-muh-ner-ee   VAYNZ) veins that return oxygen-rich blood from the lungs to the heart

Punnett square (PUH-nut   SKWAYR) a chart used to calculate possible gene combinations

pupa (PYOO-puh) the stage of metamorphosis from which the larva emerges as an adult

pupil (PYOO-pul) the opening in the iris of the eye that lets light in

purebred (PUR-bred) organisms with ancestry that does not contain hybrids

recessive (ree-SES-iv) a gene that is not expressed in the offspring

rain forest (RAYN   FOR-ust) a tropical, wet biome

rectum (REK-tum) final segment of the digestive system; passes feces out of the body through the anus

---

PRONUNCIATION KEY

CAPITAL LETTERS show the stressed syllables.

a	as in mat	f	as in fit
ay	as in day, say	g	as in go
ch	as in chew	i	as in sit
e	as in bed	j	as in job, gem
ee	as in even, easy, need	k	as in cool, key

red blood cells (RED BLUD SELZ) reddish cells of the blood that contain hemoglobin and deliver oxygen from the lungs to the body's tissues

relaxin (ri-LAK-sun) sex hormone that loosens joints in the mother's pelvis so that the baby can pass out of the birth canal

renal artery (REE-nul AR-tuh-ree) large blood vessel that brings blood in need of filtering to a kidney

renal pelvis (REE-nul PEL-vus) hollow area in the center of a kidney where urine is temporarily stored

renal vein (REE-nul VAYN) vein through which cleansed blood leaves a kidney

reproduction (ree-pruh-DUK-shun) the way in which organisms produce offspring

reptile (REP-tyl) coldblooded, air-breathing vertebrate that lays amniotic eggs

resource partitioning (REE-sohrs par-TI-shun-ing) the situation when organisms live in the same geographic area and consume slightly different foods or use resources in slightly different ways

respiration (res-puh-RAY-shun) the process of taking in oxygen and releasing carbon dioxide

---

PRONUNCIATION KEY

CAPITAL LETTERS show the stressed syllables.

ng	as in running	u	as in but, some
o	as in cot, father	uh	as in about, taken, lemon, pencil
oh	as in go, note	ur	as in term
oo	as in too	y	as in line, fly
sh	as in shy	zh	as in vision, measure
th	as in thin		

resting state (RES-ting STAYT) the state of a neuron when an impulse is not traveling along an axon

retina (RE-tun-uh) a stamp-sized patch at the back of the eyeball that detects light

rhizomes (RY-zohmz) underground stems of some plants

ribonucleic acid (RNA) (ry-boh-nu-KLEE-ik A-sud) (AR-EN-AY) any of various nucleic acids that contain ribose and are associated with protein synthesis

ribose (RY-bohs) a five-carbon sugar found in RNA nucleotides

ribosomal RNA (rRNA) (ry-buh-SOH-mul AR-EN-AY) RNA that is a fundamental element of the structure of ribosomes

ribosomes (RY-buh-sohmz) tiny structures that make proteins for the cells

RNA polymerase (AR-EN-AY PO-luh-muh-rays) an enzyme active in the synthesis of RNA

rods (RODS) light receptors in the retina that are most sensitive to dim light

roots (ROOTS) 1. underground organs in plants that absorb water and nutrients and transport them to the stem of the plant; 2. the part of the tooth that contains nerves and blood vessels

---

PRONUNCIATION KEY

CAPITAL LETTERS show the stressed syllables.

a	as in mat	f	as in fit
ay	as in day, say	g	as in go
ch	as in chew	i	as in sit
e	as in bed	j	as in job, gem
ee	as in even, easy, need	k	as in cool, key

saliva (suh-LY-vuh) moisture in the mouth that begins the digestive process

salivary glands (SA-luh-ver-ee GLANDZ) three glands in the mouth that produce saliva

sarcomere (SAR-kuh-mir) a part of the muscle fiber between stripes of actin fibers

sarcoplasmic reticula (sar-kuh-PLAZ-mik ri-TI-kyuh-luh) a structure within muscle fibers that stores calcium

schwann cells (SHWON SELZ) fatty membranes that make up the sheath around some nerve cells, protecting the cells and acting as electric insulators

sclera (SKLER-uh) a tough white membrane that covers most of the eyeball

scrotum (SKROH-tum) a sac that hangs outside the male body and contains the testes

sebum (SEE-bum) an oily substance produced by hair follicles that lubricates the skin

secondary consumers (SE-kun-der-ee kun-SOO-murz) organisms that get their energy by eating primary consumers; meat eaters

secondary sexual characteristics (SE-kun-der-ee SEK-shuh-wul kar-ik-tuh-RIS-tiks) characteristics caused by an influx of sex hormones, such as growth of facial hair in males and breast development in females

PRONUNCIATION KEY

CAPITAL LETTERS show the stressed syllables.

ng as in running	u as in but, some
o as in cot, father	uh as in about, taken, lemon, pencil
oh as in go, note	ur as in term
oo as in too	y as in line, fly
sh as in shy	zh as in vision, measure
th as in thin	

secrete (si-KREET) to produce a substance within a cell, a gland, or an organ and release it

semen (SEE-mun) sperm-containing fluid produced by males

seminal vesicles (SE-muh-nul VE-si-kulz) two glands in males that produce semen

semipermeable (se-mee-PUR-mee-uh-bul) able to allow some fluids and particles to pass through, but not others

sense organs (SENS OR-gunz) organs used to detect changes in the outside world, such as an insect's antennae and a human's eyes and ears

sensory neurons (SENS-ree NOO-ronz) neurons that detect stimuli such as light, sound, heat, or pressure

sensory receptors (SENS-ree ri-SEP-turz) organs and nerves that translate a stimulus into an electric impulse that can be used by the brain to interpret the stimulus

sepals (SEE-pulz) a circle of green petals at the base of a flower

sertoli cells (sur-TOH-lee SELZ) cells that provide the spermatozoa with nutrients

serum proteins (SIR-um PROH-teenz) an assembly of amino acids that compose the liquid part of the blood

---

PRONUNCIATION KEY

CAPITAL LETTERS show the stressed syllables.

a	as in mat	f	as in fit
ay	as in day, say	g	as in go
ch	as in chew	i	as in sit
e	as in bed	j	as in job, gem
ee	as in even, easy, need	k	as in cool, key

sex cells (SEKS SELZ) gametes, or cells that can be used in reproduction; in humans, the sperm and the egg

sex-linked (SEKS-LINKD) any trait located on the X chromosome; usually carried by the female and expressed in the male; recessive

sexual reproduction (SEK-shuh-wul ree-pruh-DUK-shun) reproduction that involves two organisms of the same species, each contributing genetic information to the offspring

shaft (SHAFT) the middle area of long bones such as the humerus, which forms a hollow ring that contains spongy bone tissue such as marrow

shell (SHEL) a hard outer covering for invertebrates such as mollusks

sister chromatids (SIS-tur KROH-muh-tudz) two chromosomes that bind with each other during cellular reproduction

skeletal muscles (SKE-luh-tul MUH-sulz) muscles attached to the skeleton by cartilage

skeleton (SKE-luh-tun) the internal support system of vertebrates, composed of bone or cartilage

skin (SKIN) the external covering of some vertebrates that protects the organism from infection and is an important sensory organ

PRONUNCIATION KEY

CAPITAL LETTERS show the stressed syllables.

ng as in runni**ng**	u as in b**u**t, s**o**me
o as in c**o**t, f**a**ther	uh as in **a**bout, tak**e**n, lem**o**n, penc**i**l
oh as in g**o**, n**o**te	ur as in t**er**m
oo as in t**oo**	y as in l**i**ne, fl**y**
sh as in **sh**y	zh as in vi**si**on, mea**s**ure
th as in **th**in	

smooth muscles (SMOOTH MUH-sulz) muscles in organs and the circulatory system that move mostly through involuntary action such as breathing, digestion, and circulation

solvent (SOL-vunt) any substance that can dissolve another substance, such as water

somatic nervous system (soh-MA-tik NER-vus SIS-tum) the nervous system that controls sensations that an animal is aware of, such as pain, light, and sound, and the voluntary movement of muscles

specialize (SPE-shuh-lyz) the tendency of organisms to evolve toward using specialized food sources, light requirements, and soil nutrients

speciation (spee-shee-AY-shun) a change in populations that occurs when two populations that would normally breed together are isolated

species (SPEE-sheez) any group of organisms that can breed together and produce fertile offspring; in classification, the smallest group of organisms

sperm (SPURM) male sex cell

spermatids (SPUR-muh-tudz) haploid cells resulting from meiosis

spermatocytes (spur-MA-tuh-syts) diploid cells contained within the seminiferous tubules that constantly undergo mitosis

---

PRONUNCIATION KEY

CAPITAL LETTERS show the stressed syllables.

a	as in mat	f	as in fit
ay	as in day, say	g	as in go
ch	as in chew	i	as in sit
e	as in bed	j	as in job, gem
ee	as in even, easy, need	k	as in cool, key

spermatogenesis (spur-ma-tuh-JE-nuh-sus) in the male reproductive system, the point at which the male becomes sexually mature; in humans, this period is called *puberty.*

spermatozoa (spur-ma-tuh-ZOH-uh) male sex cell, or sperm

spinal cord (SPY-nul   KORD) the thick cord of nerve tissue which, in vertebrates, is protected by the backbone

spindle (SPIN-dul) the structure in cells that forms during reproduction; the chromosomes are distributed along the spindle, and they are drawn apart during both meiosis and mitosis.

spirilla (spy-RI-luh) spiral-shaped bacteria; the singular form is *spirillum.*

sponge (SPUNJ) a marine invertebrate that has cells, but no organs or systems

spongy bone (SPUN-jee   BOHN) bone tissue that contains pores, such as exists at the end of long bones

spontaneous generation (spon-TAY-nee-us   je-nuh-RAY-shun) the now-discredited notion that living organisms arose spontaneously from nonliving matter

spores (SPOHRZ) small reproductive bodies in some protists, fungi, and plants

stamen (STAY-mun) in flowers, the male reproductive structure

PRONUNCIATION KEY

CAPITAL LETTERS show the stressed syllables.

ng	as in running	u	as in but, some
o	as in cot, father	uh	as in about, taken, lemon, pencil
oh	as in go, note	ur	as in term
oo	as in too	y	as in line, fly
sh	as in shy	zh	as in vision, measure
th	as in thin		

stapes (STAY-peez) one of the bones in the human inner ear; the smallest bone in the human body

start codon (START KOH-don) the first codon in mRNA, beginning with the sequence AUG

stem (STEM) the part of a plant that provides support for leaves and that carries food and water through the plant

stem cells (STEM SELZ) in the bone marrow, cells that divide constantly, creating red blood cells, white blood cells, and platelets

sternum (STUR-num) the bone over the chest, also called the breastbone

stigma (STIG-muh) part of a flower's female sex organs

stimuli (STIM-yuh-ly) the cause(s) of a response; the singular form is *stimulus.*

stomach (STUH-muk) large digestive organ, where food is partially digested

stomata (STOH-muh-tuh) in plants, small openings on the underside of leaves where gases are taken in and released; the singular form is *stoma.*

stop codon (STOP KOH-don) the last codon in mRNA, ending with one of three sequences

---

PRONUNCIATION KEY

CAPITAL LETTERS show the stressed syllables.

a	as in mat	f	as in fit
ay	as in day, say	g	as in go
ch	as in chew	i	as in sit
e	as in bed	j	as in job, gem
ee	as in even, easy, need	k	as in cool, key

stroke (STROHK) condition in which a major artery near the brain bursts, damaging a part of the brain

style (STYL) in plants, an extension of a flower's ovary, shaped like a stalk; supports the stigma

subcutaneous layer (sub-kyu-TAY-nee-us LAY-ur) the inner layer of skin

substitution (sub-stuh-TOO-shun) a type of genetic mutation in which one nucleotide is substituted for another

succession (suk-SE-shun) the progression from grasses and fast-growing trees to shade-tolerant trees and plants in an ecosystem

succulent (SUH-kyuh-lunt) 1. a fleshy fruit; 2. a plant, such as a cactus, that retains water

sweat (SWET) a secretion performed by some mammals in which water and salts are excreted through glands at the surface of the skin; the water cools the skin and helps maintain the organism's body temperature.

sweat glands (SWET GLANDZ) glands that excrete sweat

swim bladder (SWIM BLA-dur) an organ in some fish used to control depth

symbiosis (sim-bee-OH-sus) a close relationship between two different organisms in which both organisms benefit from the association

---

PRONUNCIATION KEY

CAPITAL LETTERS show the stressed syllables.

ng	as in running	u	as in but, some
o	as in cot, father	uh	as in about, taken, lemon, pencil
oh	as in go, note	ur	as in term
oo	as in too	y	as in line, fly
sh	as in shy	zh	as in vision, measure
th	as in thin		

symbiotic (sim-bee-O-tik) describing a condition of symbiosis

synaptic gap (suh-NAP-tik   GAP) in nerve cells, the space between axons and dendrites

synaptic knobs (suh-NAP-tik   NOBZ) in nerve cells, the structures at the ends of axons

synaptic vesicles (suh-NAP-tik   VE-si-kulz) in nerve cells, membrane-bound sacs found in the synaptic knobs that are filled with neurotransmitters

synovial fluid (suh-NOH-vee-ul   FLOO-ud) a greasy fluid found within membranes located at skeletal joints

synovial membrane (suh-NOH-vee-ul   MEM-brayn) a membrane found at skeletal joints that contains fluid

systolic pressure (sis-TO-lik   PRE-shur) the pressure of blood when the heart contracts

taiga (TY-guh) a zone of cold-weather forests, mostly evergreen

taproot (TAP-root) the large, main root of a plant that grows straight down

taste buds (TAYST   BUDZ) special chemical sensors on the surface of the tongue that can detect sourness, sweetness, saltiness, and bitterness

taxonomy (tak-SO-nuh-mee) the system used to classify living things

---

PRONUNCIATION KEY

CAPITAL LETTERS show the stressed syllables.

a	as in mat	f	as in fit
ay	as in day, say	g	as in go
ch	as in chew	i	as in sit
e	as in bed	j	as in job, gem
ee	as in even, easy, need	k	as in cool, key

T-cells (TEE-SELZ) a special form of lymphocyte manufactured in the thymus that recognizes and destroys certain pathogens

telophase (TE-luh-fayz) the last phase of mitosis during which the chromosomes completely separate and the cell begins to fully divide

temporal lobe (TEM-prul　LOHB) in the human brain, one of two lobes containing the sensory centers responsible for hearing, some vision, and smell

tendons (TEN-dunz) collagen cords that anchor the muscle to the bone

tentacles (TEN-ti-kulz) long, flexible structures in some invertebrates that can grasp, sense, and sting

tertiary consumers (TER-shee-er-ee　kun-SOO-murz) organisms that consume secondary consumers

testes (TES-teez) male sexual organs, where sperm are produced

testosterone (te-STOS-tuh-rohn) the male sex hormone

thalamus (THA-luh-mus) in the human brain, the part of the brain that regulates sensory information

thermoreceptors (thur-moh-ri-SEP-turz) receptors in the skin that detect temperature

---

thoracic cavity (thuh-RA-sik   KA-vuh-tee) the hollow area in the chest where organs such as the lungs can be found

thoracic duct (thuh-RA-sik   DUKT) a large vein that empties out the lymph above the vena cava

thorax (THOHR-aks) the middle segment of an insect; contains the six legs and wings, if any

thymine (THY-meen) a component of nucleic acid that pairs with adenine in DNA

thyroid (THY-roid) a gland that produces hormones that control the metabolism

thyroid stimulating hormone (TSH) (THY-roid   STIM-yuh-lay-ting HOR-mohn) (TEE-ES-AYCH) a hormone produced by the hypothalamus to stimulate the thyroid gland

thyroxin (thy-ROK-sun) the principal thyroid hormone; stimulates metabolism and is essential for growth and development

tongue (TUNG) the sensory organ responsible for discerning taste

toxin (TOK-sun) a poison

trachea (TRAY-kee-uh) a tube that carries air from the nose and mouth to the lungs; also called the windpipe

---

PRONUNCIATION KEY

CAPITAL LETTERS show the stressed syllables.

a	as in mat	f	as in fit
ay	as in day, say	g	as in go
ch	as in chew	i	as in sit
e	as in bed	j	as in job, gem
ee	as in even, easy, need	k	as in cool, key

trait (TRAYT) visible expression of an organism's genetic code; for instance, blue eyes

transcription (tran-SKRIP-shun) the process by which mRNA is produced

transfer RNA (tRNA) (trans-FUR   AR-EN-AY) type of RNA involved in protein synthesis

translation (trans-LAY-shun) the process by which RNA directs the sequence of amino acids assembled by a ribosome during protein synthesis

translocation (trans-loh-KAY-shun) the transfer of part of a chromosome to a new position on the same or a different chromosome, with a resulting rearrangement of the genes

transpiration (trans-puh-RAY-shun) in plants, the release of water through openings on the leaf surface

transport (TRANS-pohrt) the movement of fluids and nutrients around an organism's body

trimester (try-MES-tur) one of three periods of human pregnancy

tropical rain forests (TRO-pi-kul   RAYN   FOR-usts) rich biomes, with a great deal of diversity, that occur where the climate is warm all year round and where it rains almost every day

tropism (TROH-pi-zum) movement in response to a stimulus such as light or heat

---

PRONUNCIATION KEY

CAPITAL LETTERS show the stressed syllables.

ng	as in running	u	as in but, some
o	as in cot, father	uh	as in about, taken, lemon, pencil
oh	as in go, note	ur	as in term
oo	as in too	y	as in line, fly
sh	as in shy	zh	as in vision, measure
th	as in thin		

tumor (TOO-mur) an abnormal mass of tissue

tundra (TUN-druh) a cold, dry biome where few plants grow

tympanum (TIM-puh-num) a cavity in the middle ear also called the
eardrum

unirames (yoo-nuh-RAYMZ) one of three subphyla within the phylum
Arthropoda, which includes all insects, centipedes, and millipedes

uracil (YUR-uh-sil) a nitrogen base found in RNA nucleotides

urea (yu-REE-uh) a compound commonly found in mammal urine and in
the decomposition process

ureters (YUR-uh-turz) tubes that transport urine from the kidneys to the
bladder

urethra (yu-REE-thruh) tube through which urine is eliminated from the
body

urine (UR-in) liquid that is removed from the body, along with impurities

uterus (YOO-tuh-rus) in female mammals, a hollow muscular organ in
which the young develop

vacuoles (VA-kyuh-wohlz) storage chambers in cells that are used to hold
nutrients and wastes

PRONUNCIATION KEY

CAPITAL LETTERS show the stressed syllables.

a	as in m**a**t	f	as in **f**it
ay	as in d**ay**, s**ay**	g	as in **g**o
ch	as in **ch**ew	i	as in s**i**t
e	as in b**e**d	j	as in **j**ob, **g**em
ee	as in **e**ven, **ea**sy, n**ee**d	k	as in **c**ool, **k**ey

vagina (vuh-JY-nuh) in females, the passageway that leads from the uterus to the outside of the body

valves (VALVZ) 1. halves of a shell in a bivalve mollusk such as a clam; 2. flaps of tissue that open and close chambers in the heart

variation (ver-ee-AY-shun) a difference in coloration or other characteristic within the same species

vas deferens (VAS DE-fuh-runz) in males, the passageway through which sperm move from the testicles to the urethra

vascular plants (VAS-kyuh-lur PLANTS) plants with transport systems

vein (VAYN) 1. a vessel in plants that carries food and nutrients from roots to leaves and back; 2. a blood vessel that carries blood to the heart

ventricle (VEN-tri-kul) lower chamber of the human heart

venules (VEEN-yoolz) small veins that carry oxygen-poor blood back to the larger veins, which carry it back to the heart

vertebra (VUR-tuh-bruh) one of seven bones covering the spinal cord; the plural form is *vertebrae.*

vertebral column (vur-TEE-brul KO-lum) the spinal column

vertebrates (VER-te-brayts) animals with backbones

PRONUNCIATION KEY

CAPITAL LETTERS show the stressed syllables.

ng	as in running	u	as in but, some
o	as in cot, father	uh	as in about, taken, lemon, pencil
oh	as in go, note	ur	as in term
oo	as in too	y	as in line, fly
sh	as in shy	zh	as in vision, measure
th	as in thin		

villi (VI-ly) fingerlike projections on the lining of the small intestine that absorb nutrients as food particles pass by; the singular form is *villus.*

virus (VY-rus) small, disease-causing particles that contain RNA or DNA but do not meet the criteria of living organisms

visceral mass (VI-suh-rul   MAS) in mollusks, the area containing the organs

vitreous humor (VI-tree-us   HYOO-mur) the clear gel that fills the eyeballs of mammals

vocal cords (VOH-kul   KORDZ) two ligaments that stretch over the larynx and produce sound when air passes over them

warmblooded (WARM-BLUH-dud) any organism that maintains a stable body temperature

water-soluble (WO-tur   SOL-yuh-bul) capable of being dissolved in water; vitamin C, for instance, is water-soluble.

white blood cells (HWYT   BLUD   SELZ) part of the body's defense system that surround pathogens and consume them

worm (WURM) one of many kinds of long, soft-bodied invertebrates

xylem (ZY-lum) plant tissue that carries water from the roots to the leaves

zygote (ZY-goht) a fertilized egg that will develop into a multicellular organism

INDEX

acid reflux, 199–200
acne, 98
acrosome, 281
actin, 255, 256
active transport, 18, 204
adaptations, 70
    of amphibians, 179
    behavioral, 70
    of birds for flight, 183
    of cheetahs, 73–75
    contributing to success of
      mammals, 185
    desert, 335
    and mutations of pathogens,
      239–240
    physical, 70
    for plants, 145
    predator, 326–327
    prey, 324–326
    of reptiles, 180
    that increase fitness, 76
adenine, 28, 37
adenine diphosphate (ADP), 256
adenosine triphosphate (ATP), 23, 256
    formation of, 25
adrenal glands, 277–278
adrenaline, 277–278
African sleeping sickness, 239
African wild dogs, 75
afterbirth, 289
agar, 105
AIDS, 240
alcohol, chronic drinking of, 208
algae, 14, 84
    cell walls in, 21
    diatoms, 103
    dinoflagellates, 104
    euglenas, 104

    increase of, 315
    kelp, 104, 105
    multicelled, 104–105
    seaweed, 104, 105
    single-celled, 103–104
    sources of energy in, 4
    variation in, 103
algal bloom, 103
alleles, 57, 67
    combinations of, 58
    dominant, 57, 59
    recessive, 57, 59
allergies, 142, 239
alligators, 181
alveoli, 215, 217
amino acids, 11, 27, 197
    leucine, 31
    needed by human body, 206
    proline, 31
amnion, 288
amniotic sac, 288
amoebocytes, 157
amphibians, 178–179
    challenges of early, 179
    metamorphosis of, 179
anaerobic, 96
anaphase (mitosis), 43
anaphase I (meiosis), 47
    nondisjunction in, 53
anaphase II (meiosis), 48
    nondisjunction in, 53
ancestors, 82
animal cells, 350. *See also* cells;
  plant cells
    common features of animal cells
      and, 21
    comparing plant cells and, 89–90
    similarity of plant cells to, 121
    telophase in, 43–44, 45

blood type, 67
  codominance and, 68
blood vessels, 175, 223
  arteries, 223–224
  blockages of, 225
  capillaries, 224
  superior vena cava, 225
  veins, 224
body temperature
  hypothalamus monitoring of, 277
  role of capillaries in regulating,
    242
  role of skin in regulating, 241
bolus, 198
bone marrow, 235, 251
bone marrow transplants, 251
bones, 243, 245–246
  of birds, 183
  common and scientific names for
    some important, 247
  function of, 246
  structure of, 249–251
  tissue of, 250, 251
bony fish, 177
botulism, 230
Bowman's capsule, 209–210
brain
  cerebrum, 271–273
  of chordates, 175
  control of breathing by, 218
  general structure of, 270–274
  hind brain, 274
  in mammals, 185
  parts of, 274
  protection of, by skull, 246
bread mold, 110
  growing: application activity,
    117–118
breast cancer, 69

breathing, 214
  regulating, 218
bronchi, 215
bronchioles, 215
brown algae, 105
bubonic plague, 172, 230
buds, 133
bulbs, 128
B vitamins, 207

cactuses, 334, 335
caimans, 181
calcium, 129, 207
  in dense bone, 250
calcium carbonate, 158
calcium gate, 265
cambium, 133
camels, 335
camouflage, 325
cancer, 50
  breast, 69
  lung, 219–220
  skin, 243
  testicular, 283
  treatments for, 251
canine distemper, 75
canine teeth, 198
cankers, 99
capillaries, 201, 224, 242
  surrounding alveoli, 215
carapace, 171
carbohydrates, 10, 203
  in cells, 13
  in human body, 204
carbon, 8, 309
carbon cycle, 309
carbon dioxide, 309
  conversion into methane gas, by
    archaebacteria, 97

entry into leaves of, 126
exhalation of, 216
increase in air of, 124
and oxygen transport, 217–218
toxicity of, 213
carbonic acid, 217, 218
carbon monoxide, 219, 227
cardiac muscles, 254
cardiovascular diseases, 225–227
carnivores, 305
carrageen, 105
cartilage, 176, 247
cartilaginous fish, 176
cecum, 201
cell membranes, 14, 121
diffusion and, 14–16
impermeability of, 16
osmosis and, 16
permeability of, 15–16, 18
semipermeability of, 16
structure of, 17
cells. *See also* animal cells; plant cells
breaking down of glucose by, 10
cell membranes, 14
chromosomes in human, 28
components of, 13
cytoplasm, 19
diploid, 38, 54
energy production in, 20
eukaryotic, 102
haploid, 46
life cycle of, 36–37
making and using energy, 22–25
manufacturing and transport
in, 20
mutations in, 50–51
nucleus, 19
parts of, 19
parts of plant and animal, 350

production of carbon dioxide
by, 217
prokaryotic, 102
reproduction of, 37
respiration in, 23–24
cellulose, 21
cell walls, 21, 122
functions of, 122
identifying bacteria using, 96
centipedes, 172
central nervous system, 270–274.
See also nervous system
centriole, 43
cephalopods, 167
cephalothorax, 170
cerebellum, 274
cerebral cortex, 271–272
cerebrum, 271–273
cerebral cortex, 271–272
hemispheres of, 272
lobes of, 272–273
characteristics, 39
chelicerates, 170–171
chemical digestion, 199
chemicals
from leeches, medical uses of, 164
needed for life, 7
produced by animals as
protection, 325–326
types of, in living things, 10
chemistry, basic, 7–9
atoms, 8
elements, 8
molecules, 8–9
water, 9
chemoreceptors, 267
chemotherapy, 251
chewing, 197
chitin, 168

corals, 157, 158–159
cornea, 269
coronary arteries, 225
corpus luteum, 286–287
cortex, 209
cortisol, 278
crabs, 171
cranium, 246
crayfish, 171
Creutzfeldt-Jakob disease (CJD), 231
crocodiles, 181
crustaceans, 171
cuttlefish, 167
cyanobacteria, 304
cystic fibrosis, 50, 62, 69
cytoplasm, 19
cytosine, 28, 37
cytoskeleton, 121

dark phase, 25
Darwin, Charles, 76
    Galápagos Islands studies
      of, 79–81
    reaction to Mendel's work by, 66
    theory of natural selection, 73
Darwin finches, 79–81
daughter cells, 37
    after telophase, 44
    mutations passed on to, 50
    resulting from binary fission, 98
DDT, 313
deciduous forests, 338, 339
    animals of, 339–340, 365
    distribution and climate, 364
    plants of, 339, 364
decomposers, 305
dendrites, 261
deoxyribonucleic acid (DNA), 26.
    See also DNA

deoxyribose, 27
depolarization, 264
dermis, 241–242
deserts, 334
    animals of, 335, 362
    in Antarctica, 334
    distribution and climate, 361–362
    plants of, 334–335, 362
diabetes, 277
diaphragm, 214
diastolic pressure, 226
diatoms, 103
    silica in, 139–140
dicots, 143
diet, balanced, 203
diffusion, 14–16. See also osmosis
    of oxygen into cells, 217–218
    through a selective membrane:
      application activity, 88–89
digestion
    chemical, 199
    chewing and, 197
    of fat, 205
    large intestine, 201–202
    liver, 201
    mouth, 197–198
    pancreas, 200
    small intestine, 200
digestive system, 196–202, 354
dinoflagellates, 104
dinosaurs, 136, 181
dioxin, 51
diploid cells, 38, 54
    chromosome pairs in, 40
diploid chromosome number, 38
disease
    carried by ticks, 171
    caused by fungi, 111
    caused by protists, 106

caused by water molds, 108

-causing bacteria, 83–84, 96, 97, 99, 229–230

mosquito-borne, 172, 230

in plants, 99, 314

understanding genetic basis of, 69

viral, 100–101, 229

disk, 247

ruptured, 248

DNA, 26, 27, 121

in cell nucleoid, 95–96

chromosomes in, 37

double helix in strands of, 28

instructions contained in, 71

as key molecule in genetics, discovery of, 54

molecules, 28

resilience of, 51

sequences, comparing, 79

structure of, 27–28

translation of code onto mRNA, 31, 33–35

types of nucleotides in, 27–28, 37

DNA polymerase, 41

dominant alleles, 57, 59

double helix, 28

Down's syndrome, 53

drug use, 208

duodenum, 200

Dutch elm disease, 111, 314

ear canal, 268

eardrum, 268

ear, human, 268, 359

Earth

early, 7

first life-forms on, 95–97

importance of photosynthesis to life on, 124. *See also* photosynthesis

water on, 308

earthworms, 164

and plant growth: application activity, 188–189

ecologists, 302

areas of study for, 302–303

challenges to, 315

ecology, 301–303

ecosystems, 303

changes in, 311

human-caused, 313–315

long-term, 313

natural variations, 311

succession, 312

ocean, 157, 159

protecting, 315

six major types of, 330

ectoderm, 288

effectors, 261

egg, 46, 49, 54

cells, mutations to, 50

ejaculation, 282

elastin, 241–242

electrons, 13

elements, 8

embryos, 50

human, 285

in seed plants, 141, 142

emphysema, 219

enamel, 198

endocrine system, 260, 275–278, 356

control of, 275

endoderm, 288

endometrium, 285

endoplasmic reticulum (ER), 20, 121

energy

definition of, 4

mutagens, 51

needed for chemical reactions, 12

of organisms, 4

production in cells, 20
proteins as source of, 10
regulating body, 276–278
from sun, 7, 304
traveling through food chain,
306–307
energy cycle, 304–307
food chain, 304
environment
as factor in traits, 68
human-caused changes in,
313–315
information provided by skin
about outside, 241
response of living things to, 3, 4
response of plants to, 134–135
role of nonvascular plants in, 138
enzymes, 12
breakdown of food by, 197
formation of, 26–27
involved in photosynthesis, 24
in lysosomes, 20
in pancreas, 200
pepsin, 199, 206
RNA polymerase, 30
in saliva, 197
epidermis, 243–244
epiglottis, 198
epinephrine, 277–278
epiphytes, 331
erosion, prevention of, 138
Escherichia coli, 202
esophagus, 198
essential amino acids, 206
eubacteria, 97–98
most common shapes of, 98
euglenas, 104
eukaryotes, 102
evaporation, 308

evergreens, 127
evolution
compared to tree, 82
definition of, 70
of Galápagos finches, 80
importance of genetic variation
to, 70–72
natural selection and, 73, 75
effect of time on, 77–79
of new species, 78
resource partitioning, 81
speciation, 79–81
exoskeleton, 168–169
experiments
of Gregor Mendel, 55–58
of Louis Pasteur, 6–7
of Francesco Redi, 5–6
use of, to support theories, 5
of August Wiesmann, 55
extinction, 313, 337
eye, human, 269, 358

F_1 **generation,** 56, 57
F_2 **generation,** 57
fallopian tube, 284
families, 83
fats, 10
"good" and "bad," 11
in human body, 205–206
fat-soluble vitamins, 207
feathers, 183
feces, 202
female reproductive system,
284–289, 357
hormonal control and menstrual
cycle, 285–287
journey of sperm, 285
pregnancy, 287–289
femur, 246

Great Potato Famine, 108
greenhouse effect, 309
grizzly bears, 305–306, 342
ground tissue, 242
growth hormone, 276
grubs, 169
guanine, 28, 37
gymnosperms, 142–143

habitats
    birds specializing in different, 320
    loss of, 313
hagfish, 176
hair, 243
haploid cells, 46
Haversian canal, 250
Haversian systems, 250
hay fever, 239
hearing, 268
heart, 175, 220–221
    control of, 222–223
    pathway of blood through, 222
    structure of, 221–222
heart attacks, 225–226
heartburn, 199–200
heart disease, 205, 206
helper T-cells, 236–237
hemispheres, 272
hemocoels, 169
hemoglobin, 217
hemophilia, 50
hepatitis, 229
herbivores, 304, 321
herbivory, 321–323
    grass recovery from, 337
herds, 326, 337
herpes, 229
herring, 177
heterozygous, 58, 68

high density lipoproteins (HDL), 226
hind brain, 274
hinge joints, 248
Hippocrates, 55
histamine, 233
histones, 38
HIV (human immunodeficiency virus), 101, 229, 240
homologous, 39
Homo sapiens, 84
    as relative latecomers in mammal world, 186
homozygous, 58, 68
Hooke, Robert, 14
hookworms, 163
hormones
    definition of, 275
    and glands, matching: application activity, 296–297
    plant, 134, 135
horsetails, 139–140
    life cycle of, 141
host, 161–162, 328
human body, 196, 353
    absorption of nutrients by, 203–204
        carbohydrates, 204
        fats, 205–206
        proteins, 206
        vitamins and minerals, 207–208
    effects of smoking on, 219–220, 226, 227
    physical and chemical defenses against pathogens in, 232–234
    processing of wastes by, 208–211
    skeleton, 246
Human Genome Project, 69

human immundeficiency virus (HIV), 101, 229, 240
humerus, 250
hybridization, 108
hydrochloric acid, 199, 206
hydrogen, 8
hydrotropism, 135
hypertension, 226
hyphae, 109, 110
hypothalamus, 273
    in males, 281–282

ice sheets, 313
ileum, 201
immune response, 243
immune system, 234–235
    allergies and, 239
    blood type and, 67
    mobilization and response of, 236–237
    problems with, 238–239
    production of cells of, 225
    recognition of pathogens by, 235
    recovery and immunity, 238
immunity, 238
impermeability, 16
incisors, 198
incus, 268
inflammation response, 232–234, 242, 243
influenza (flu), 229
inheritance. *See also* alleles
    early theories about, 55
    Mendel's experiments with pea plants, 55–57
inhibin, 281
inhibitors, 256
inner ear, 268

insects, 84, 172
    distinguishing between arachnids and, 170
    importance of, 172
insulin, 204, 275, 277
interferons, 233
interneurons, 261
interphase (mitosis), 41–42
    G_1, 41
    G_2, 42
    M phase, 42
    S stage (synthesis), 41
interspecific competition, 318
intraspecific competition, 318
intravenous (IV) lines, 17
invertebrates, 155–172
    arthropods, 168–172
    cnidarians, 156, 157–159
    mollusks, 165–167
    porfirans, 156–157
    worms, 160–164
involuntary muscles, 253
iodine, 208
ions, 263
iris, 269
iron, 208, 217

jawless fish, 176
jejunum, 201
jellyfish, 157, 158
joints, 248–249
    ball-and-socket, 249
    gliding, 249
    hinge, 248
    pivot, 249
juvenile diabetes, 239

kangaroos, 185
kelp, 104, 105

keratin, 232, 243
kidneys, 209–211
    filtering of urine from blood by,
      210–211
    structure of, 209
killer T-cells, 236
kingdoms, 83, 351
koala bears, 185

lactic acid, 243
lactose, 204
lampreys, 176
large intestine, 201–202
larvae, 158
larynx, 215
leaves, 125–127, 308
    cells in, 124
    color change in, 127
    dropping of tree, 126–127
    needle-shaped, in conifers, 142
    shapes of, 124
    water loss in, 126
leeches, 164
left atrium, 221
left ventricle, 221, 222
legumes, 129, 143, 310
lens, 269
leprosy, 234
leucine, 31
leukemia, 251
lichens, 112, 341
life
    code of, in nucleic acid
      molecules, 26
    -forms, oldest, 95–97
    molecules of, 10–12
    puzzle of origin of, 7
    six basic kingdoms of, 83
    theory of spontaneous generation,
      and idea of origin of, 4

ligaments, 248
light phase, 24–25
lignin, 122
limbic system, 273
lipase, 205
lipids, 10, 197
    in cells, 13
liver, 201
    monitoring of cholesterol by, 206
    substances that can scar, 208
living things, 3. *See also* organisms
    cells in, 14
    classifying, 351–352
    complexity of, 4
    elements most common in, 8
    growth and development of, 4
    importance of water in, 9
    reproduction of, 4
lizards, 181–182
lobsters, 171
loop of Henle, 210
low density lipoproteins (LDL), 226
lung cancer, 219–220
lungs
    in amphibians, 178, 179
    of birds, 183
    bronchioles inside, 215
    disorders of, 218–220
    effect of exercise on: application
      activity, 292–294
luteinizing hormone (LH), 285
lycopods, 136, 139
    life cycle of, 141
Lyme disease, 84, 171
lymph, 225
lymphatic system, 225
lymph nodes, 225, 235
    white blood cells in, 233
lymphocytes, 235
lymph vessels, 205

lysosomes, 20, 233

macrophage, 235
mad cow disease, 230–231
magnesium, 129
malaria, 106, 230, 239
male reproductive system, 280–283, 357
malleus, 268
maltose, 204
Mammalia, 84
mammals, 84, 185–186
   adaptations contributing to success of, 185
   diversity of, 185
   marsupials, 185
   placentals, 186
   reproduction in, 4
mammary glands, 185, 289
mantle, 166, 167
marine worms, 164
marrow, 251
marsupials, 185
mast cells, 242
matter, 213
measles, 229
medulla, 209, 274
medusas, 158
meiosis, 45–46
   anaphase I, 47
   crossing over, 46–47
   formation of four cells from cell undergoing, 60
   meiosis II, 48–49
      anaphase II, 48
      metaphase II, 48
      prophase II, 48
      telophase II, 48–49
   meiotic interphase, 47

metaphase I, 47
   model of: application activity, 91–92
   problems during, 53
   prophase I, 46–47
   telophase I, 47
meiotic interphase, 47
melanin, 243
membranes, 14
memory T-cells, 236–237
Mendel, Gregor, 55
   conclusions of, 57
   early scientific reaction to work of, 66
   experiments with pea plants of, 55–57
   patterns figured out by, 59
   rediscovery of work of, 67
meninges, 271
menstrual cycle, 285
   steps in, 286–287
mesoderm, 288
mesoglea, 158
messenger RNA (mRNA), 29, 33
   manufacture of, 30–31
metabolism, 276–278
metamorphosis, 179
metaphase (mitosis), 43
metaphase I (meiosis), 47
metaphase II (meiosis), 48
meteors, 7
microscopes, 95
   early use of, 6, 14
middle ear, 268
millipedes, 172
mimicry, 326
minerals
   in balanced diets, 203
   needed by human body, 207–208

natural selection, 73
  in action, 73–76
  fitness and, 76
  Galápagos finches and, 80–81
  and pathogens, 234
  prevention of change and, 76
nectar, 144
nephrons, 209–210
nerve cord, 175
nerves. *See also* neurons
  auditory, 268
  sensory, 242
nervous system, 175, 260, 355. *See also*
  central nervous system
    autonomic nervous system, 261
    detection aspects of, 260
    integration of information by, 260
    main tasks of, 260
    response mechanisms of, 260
    somatic nervous system, 261
neurons. *See also* nerves
  in resting state, 264
  structure of, 261–262
  transmission between, 264–265
  transmission within, 263–264
neurotransmitters, 264–265
neutrons, 13
newts, 178
niacin, 207
niche, 318
nicotine, 227
nitrates, 51
nitrogen, 8, 129, 310
nitrogen bases, 37
  in DNA, 27–28
  orderly pairing of, 28
  in RNA, 29
nitrogen-containing base, 27
nitrogen cycle, 310

nodes, 223
nodes of Ranvier, 262
nondisjunction, 53
nonvascular plants, 137
  life cycle of, 137–138
  role of, 138
norepinephrine, 277–278
North Pole, 309
notochords, 174
nuclear envelope, 19
nucleic acids, 26, 197
nucleoid, 95
nucleoli, 19
nucleotides, 27
  added or deleted from a
    sequence, 52
  decoding sequence of, 68
  in DNA, 27–28
  examples of, 27
  mutations involving changes in
    sequence of, 50
  in RNA, 29
nucleus, 19, 121
nuts, 143
nymphs, 169

occipital lobe, 272
octopuses, 167
offspring, 4
oils, 10
olfactory cells, 267
omnivores, 305
oogenesis, 284–285
oogonia, 284
opossums, 185
optic nerve, 269
orders, 83
organelles, 19, 121, 123
organic molecules, 10